Sir Charles Alfred Payton

The Diamond Diggings of South Africa

A personal and practical Account

Sir Charles Alfred Payton

The Diamond Diggings of South Africa
A personal and practical Account

ISBN/EAN: 9783743326859

Manufactured in Europe, USA, Canada, Australia, Japa

Cover: Foto ©ninafisch / pixelio.de

Manufactured and distributed by brebook publishing software (www.brebook.com)

Sir Charles Alfred Payton

The Diamond Diggings of South Africa

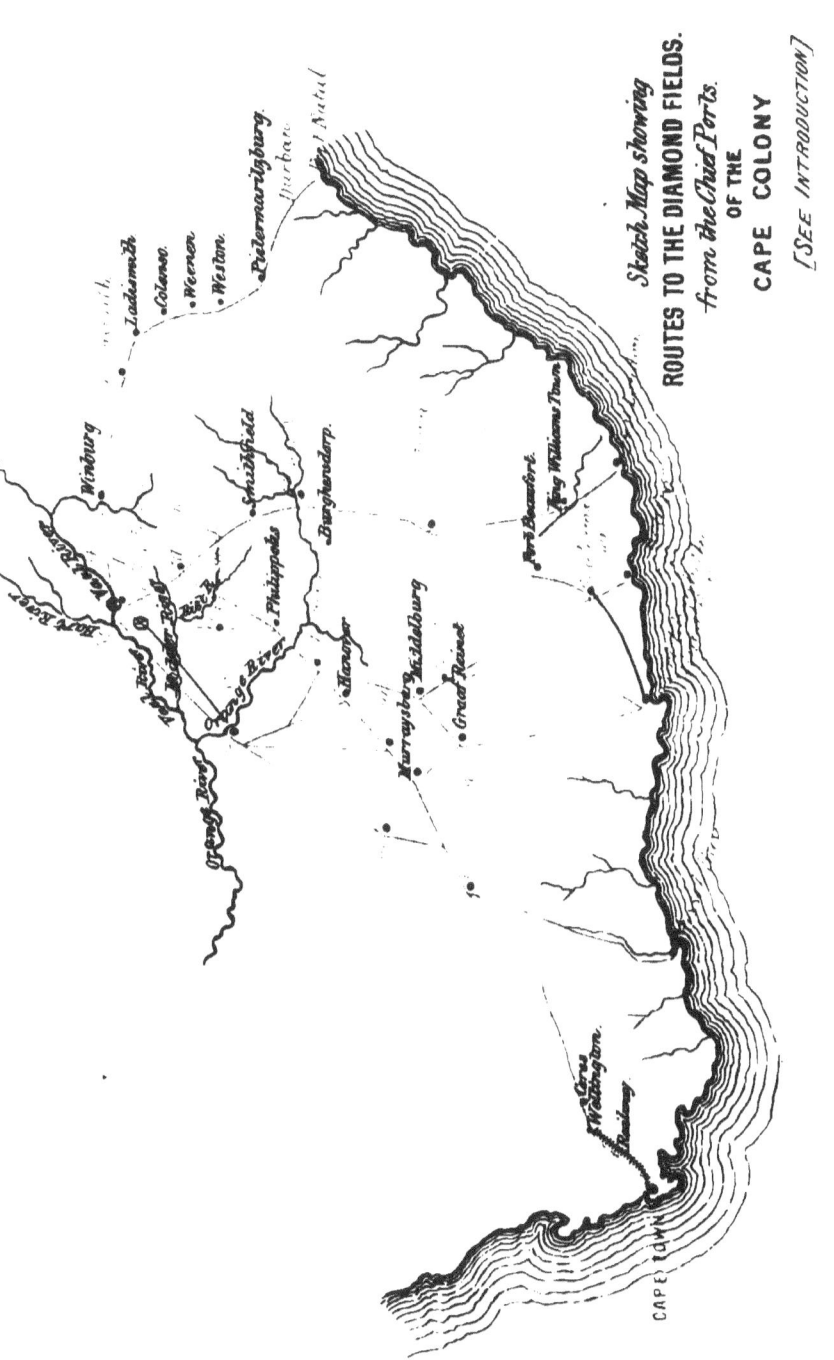

THE DIAMOND DIGGINGS

OF

SOUTH AFRICA.

A PERSONAL AND PRACTICAL ACCOUNT.

BY

CHARLES A. PAYTON,

"SARCELLE" OF "THE FIELD."

WITH A BRIEF NOTICE OF THE NEW GOLDFIELDS.

LONDON:
HORACE COX, 346, STRAND,
1872.

Right of translation and reproduction reserved.

INTRODUCTION.

The wonderful discoveries of the year 1871, far surpassing in richness everything that had gone before, and proving the South African Diggings to be no risky speculation, no exaggerated humbug, but a source of great profit—nay, often of actual wealth, to industrious and persevering diggers—have naturally caused (not only in the Cape Colony, but in Europe, Australia, and America) an all-pervading interest in these Fields, and a constantly increasing demand for reliable information.

To meet this demand, the author has compiled from personal experience a book which will give a detailed and reliable account of the condition of the various digging camps, up to the very latest dates, of routes thither, and of all expenses connected with the enterprise; will enable any who are hesitating at once to decide whether to migrate thither or not; will put faithfully before the friends of men out there the actual advantages and disadvantages, hardships and comforts, cares and pleasures, of a digger's life; and will tell the general public "all about the diggings," and he ventures to hope, amuse them with "Sketches of Life and Character on the Fields."

Before parting from this little book, the writing of which has whiled away so many of the tedious hours of convalescence, the author would now earnestly reiterate—to any for whom the life herein described may have enticing charms—that advice which he gave in the commencement of his diary from the Fields.

Let no one give up a fixed income *at home*, however moderate (so that it be sufficient to live upon) for the vicissitudes and hardships of a digger's life. But let any young, active, strong, "smart," and above all *steady*, man with a few hundreds to spare, start for "West Griqualand" as soon as he likes, following the instructions given in the ensuing pages, and I do not think he will be disappointed.

Note to Map.

This is only a sketch-map, drawn with approximate accuracy, to aid in the comparison of the different routes from the sea-coast to the Fields, and the principal stopping places. The only rivers that are here represented with accuracy are those in the immediate vicinity of the Fields, viz., the Vaal, Orange, Modder, Riet. and Hart. There are numerous rivers in the lower part of the colony which are not shown in this map.

The red lines indicate the postal routes, which are generally also followed by the passenger-waggons.

CONTENTS.

PART I.
GENERAL ACCOUNT OF THE FIELDS.

- CHAP. I. Early History of the Fields ... *page* 1
- II. The Riverside Diggings and How to Work there ... 7
- III. The Dry Diggings ... 13
- IV. Colesberg Kopje ... 22
- V. Climate, Weather, and Health ... 29
- VI. Sport in the Neighbourhood of the Fields ... 38
- VII. Outfit and Working Expenses ... 42
- VIII. Professions, Trades, and other Ways of Making Money on the Fields ... 47
- IX. Annexation of the Fields ... 51
- X. Diamonds and Prospecting ... 57

PART II.
ROUTES TO THE FIELDS.

- CHAP. I. Comparison of the different Routes ... 61
- II. Diary on board SS. "Roman," Southampton to Cape Town ... 66
- III. Port Elizabeth to Du Toit's Pan by Bullock Waggon ... 77
- IV. Pniel to Cape Town by Inland Transport Company's Horse Waggon ... 85
- V. Diary on board SS. "Roman," Cape Town to Southampton ... 95

PART III.

SKETCHES OF LIFE AND CHARACTER ON THE FIELDS.

CHAP. I. Diamond Diggers ... *page* 103
II. Diamond Buyers and Diamond Brokers ... 116
III. Hotel-keepers, Storekeepers, and Auctioneers ... 127
IV. Our Coloured Labourers ... 137
V. Tent Life. ... 147
VI. Food, Water, and Wood ... 152
VII. Our Police ... 156
VIII. Amusements on the Fields ... 161
IX. A Battle Prevented ... 165
X. A Digger's Holiday, and Sport on the Modder ... 169
XI. Fishing in the Vaal ... 178
XII. A Dinner under Difficulties at Mrs. Brown's ... 182
XIII. Churches and Hospitals ... 186

PART IV.

MY DIARY AT THE DRY DIGGINGS ... 188

PART V.

THE GOLD FIELDS.

CHAP. I. The Tatin ... 236
II. The Transvaal or Leydenburg, newly-discovered Gold Fields ... 237
III. Routes to the Gold Fields ... 240

THE DIAMOND DIGGINGS.

PART I.
GENERAL ACCOUNT OF THE FIELDS.

CHAPTER I.
EARLY HISTORY OF THE FIELDS.

THE first diamond discovered in South Africa is said to have been found in the Hope Town Division, Cape Colony (near the Orange River), in the year 1867, by one of the children of a Boer, or Dutch farmer, named Jacobs. For some time it was merely considered as a pretty pebble, and used as a plaything, no one having any idea of its value. Another Boer, named Schalk van Niekerk, calling on Jacobs and seeing the diamond, was struck by its lustre and weight. He offered to purchase it from Mrs. Jacobs, but it is said that the worthy *vrouw* laughed at the idea of selling a stone, and let him have it for nothing. The stone next passed into the hands of a Mr. O'Reilly, and was taken by him to Hope Town, where the idea of its being a diamond met with such ridicule that he was very near throwing it away. He took it, however, on to Colesberg, and from thence it was forwarded for the inspection of a scientific gentleman, Dr. Atherstone, of Graham's Town, who at once pronounced it a veritable diamond. Its weight was 21 carats odd, and I believe it was sold to Sir P. E. Wodehouse, the then Governor, for 500*l*.

Another diamond was soon afterwards found on a farm called "Paarde Kloof," on the Orange River, also in the Hope Town Division. It was a beautiful stone, weighing over 8 carats.

After these discoveries, many people, both natives and Europeans, of course began to search superficially in the Hope Town Division and neighbouring districts, notably along the banks of the now world-famous Vaal River, and a few of the searchers were rewarded with fine gems. The first famous diamond, called the "Star of South Africa," appears to have been found, or at any rate to have first come into the possession of a white man, early in 1869. The first known owner of this gem, which weighed $83\frac{1}{2}$ carats, and will, it is believed, cut into a brilliant of the finest class, was a Kafir witch-doctor, or sorcerer. This savage conjuror was with some difficulty induced to sell it to the same Schalk van Niekerk, who was the quasi-discoverer of the first South African diamond. The "Star of South Africa," in the rough, was of an irregular shape, and about the size of a small walnut. After being exhibited at Port Elizabeth and at Cape Town, and visited by crowds of people, it was finally forwarded to England, where, I believe, it passed into the possession of Messrs. Hunt and Roskell, and was valued at 25,000l.

I will now proceed to quote from an account of the Diamond Fields published in the "Cape of Good Hope Directory and Guide Book," as I am necessarily at a loss for many particulars of proceedings prior to my arrival on the Fields in 1871, and the said account appears to me to be reliable, being corroborated in most material points by what I have heard from older diggers.

News of these discoveries having reached England, Mr. Harry Emanuel, a London dealer in diamonds, despatched a Mr. Gregory to South Africa to make inquiries as to their reality. This gentleman made an examination of the geological features of some parts of the country, and on his return to England reported, at first in private and in speeches, but subsequently in a paper published in the *Geological Magazine* that "the whole diamond discovery in South Africa is an imposture—a bubble scheme." When the news of this reached the colony, several gentlemen exposed Mr. Gregory's erroneous statements, and none more successfully than W. B. Chalmers, Esq., at that time Civil Commissioner and Resident Magistrate of Hope Town, who, in a letter to the *Journal*, gave such particulars of a large number of diamonds that had passed through his own hands as to place the matter beyond all doubt.

In the earlier part of 1870 the number of diamonds found was so considerable that it attracted the attention of the inhabitants of the various colonies and republics in South Africa. Gradually a "rush" set in from all quarters, and the banks of the Vaal in a few months became covered with thousands of busy diggers.

The extent of the diamondiferous region it is at present impossible to say, but, so far back as 1870, it was stated by Dr. Shaw, of Colesberg, the most competent observer that had yet visited the Fields, to be at least one thousand square miles in area. The same gentleman, writing in the *Cape Monthly Magazine* of December, 1870, says that it seems to him that every day the extent of the Diamond Fields enlarges, and that every week a new diamond farm is found in the Free State. The opinion of Dr. Shaw is confirmed by less scientific but in other respects equally trustworthy observers. The general geological features of the Diamond Fields are said by Dr. Shaw to be throughout the whole tract the same. Trap, metamorphic, and conglomerate rocks run through the whole valley of the Vaal. The surface soil consists of water-worn pebbles, and extends from both banks of the river considerably inland; in the narrowest part, he says, two or three miles. The impression made upon his mind is that the whole Vaal region has been subjected to a series of successive disturbances, and that the river has played about in different channels, till now on the top of "kopjes," and in the hollows, we have deposited the diamondiferous alluvial gravel. This gravel consists of nodules of granite, sandstone, basalt, greenstone, agates, garnets, garnet spinel, and peridot, and here and there, of course at rare intervals, the princely gem itself. The alluvial soil lies, in some places, above the calcareous tufa, in other places above the basalt, and in many parts above a clayey shale of various colours. Everywhere, as far as has been investigated, however, the diamonds are in it alone. (Subsequent discoveries have shown diamonds to be found in a wide range of various strata.—Sarcelle.)

What is the real diamond matrix ? has been asked over and over again in the diamondiferous tracts of Brazil and India. They have been found imbedded in a micaceous sandstone in Brazil, and in a conglomerate sandstone in India, but neither of these is believed to be the ultimate matrix. It may be that a region which has undergone no changes since the secondary geological epoch, except those of gradual and uniform denudation, like South Africa, may, by ultimate investigation, solve the problem. At all events, Dr. Shaw does not believe that the diamonds have been carried down by the Vaal. The Vaal region, he feels persuaded, has been the theatre of diamond formation. The component rocks represented in the water-worn pebbles are from the strata and formations of the Vaal—and why not the diamonds? Dr. Shaw states that the geology of the Vaal region is altogether different from the secondary and trappen formations of the colony. When the traveller passes through the Free State by Fauresmith, he has the tabular mountains and "spitz-kops" (sharp-pointed hills and peaks), so common and all-prevailing in South Africa, till he arrives within a few hours' distance of the Vaal. A manifest change sets in, and for miles on miles there is a luxuriant and undulating plain almost undisturbed by any hills. He feels that there is a break in the structure of the country. When he comes to the Vaal, an entirely different landscape appears before him. The perpetual greenstone porphyries of the colony have vanished, and genuine basalt makes its appearance. This basalt he finds protruding through conglomerate and amygdaloid trap. Glittering pebbles of every form and colour glisten at his feet, and he feels indeed that he is in a new region. The Doctor carefully questioned the diggers on the subject of the gravelly mass in which the diamonds are found, and, as a matter of course, got very variable information. Some prefer the summits of the "kopjes" rather than the sides, and this opinion is supported by some show of reason—

as extensive washing by rain and surface water must carry away the accumulation of gravel from the slopes. But surely the "kloofs" (gullies) filled with sand must have under the surface the greater part of the alluvium of the sides. There is no attempt made to penetrate through this sand to the gravel underneath as yet by the diggers, and, indeed, their mining is altogether surface work and mere scraping, to what it ought to be. (*Nous avons changé tout cela.*—Sarcelle.)

In regard to the constituent stones of good diamondiferous gravel, satisfactory information cannot be got. Some diggers prefer a light-coloured and sparkling gravel, others again are greatly in favour of dark pebbly soil. Diggers generally eschew gravel with quartz fragments (not water-worn) in it. Rotten ironstone pebbles (basalt) are considered a favourable sign. Dr. Shaw is inclined to think that the best indications are garnets (what diggers style "rubies") and peridot, a *blue* (qy. green?) transparent crystal. The top of the "kopjes," considerably above the present water level, are mentioned above as having alluvial soil, consisting of thoroughly worn and rounded pebbles. A casual observer will quickly perceive that there have been upheavals, and probably successive, everywhere.

The basalt of the summit has wedge-shaped crevices, wide at the top and narrowing downwards. Forming at one time the bottom of the river, the "kopjes" have been raised and the alluvial gravel has fallen into the interstices to some extent, the greater part remaining as a cover to the "kopjes," or rather appearing now as a sort of matrix, in which the angular blocks of basalt are imbedded.

Those who wish for a more detailed description of the geology of the diamondiferous region, we refer to the series of papers published by Dr. Shaw in the first volume of the *Cape Monthly Magazine* (new series), a portion of which was re-published in *Nature*, a London periodical of great eminence. The discovery of diamonds has naturally drawn considerable attention to the ownership of the diamond-fields. Heretofore this region was in the occupation of various native chiefs, the European population thinking it hardly worth owning.

I have but little to say, in the present chapter, to supplement the above account. The subsequent discoveries of the dry diggings, far inland, twenty-five miles away from the Vaal River, and the finding of diamonds at great and varying depths, and in very varied strata, are rather calculated to upset some of the theories formed above. Equally astonishing and subversive of theory have been the strange finds, for which I can vouch, of ostrich eggs, entire or more often fragmentary, a human skeleton, portions of an ant-hill, and heads and parts of shanks of nails, at considerable depths in claims on the dry diggings. With the establishment of Mr. Campbell as British commissioner for Klip Drift and all the diggings on the Transvaal or further side of the Vaal River, speedily ceased the "Diggers' Mutual Protection Society," and the presidency of Mr. Parker. Offences against "Diggers' Laws and Regulations" were formerly treated with summary justice, *à la Lynch;* parties guilty of theft or other crimes which roused the indignation of the diggers being quickly tried and sentenced. The general sentence was "to be expelled the camp and dragged through the river," an unpleasant operation when we consider the uneven bottom, swift currents, and sharp and rugged stones of the Vaal. Another *amiable* punishment was "making a spread-eagle," wherein the culprit was tied down on the ground to short stakes, arms and legs extended, and left for some time to the heat of the sun and the tender mercies of flies and other insect tormentors. But, long before I reached the Fields, police-courts were established, and diggers had ceased to think of taking the law into their own hands. The "cat" was in full swing: of this terror of garotters in England, and thieves, both white and black, on the diggings, I have more to say anon.

Mr. Parker, the ex-president of the "Diggers' Mutual Protection Society," is now flourishing as an hotel-keeper at Du Toit's Pan and the Colesberg Kopje. With regard to the rival claims of Waterboer and the Free State, and the final adjustment of them by the annexation of the greater portion of the diamondiferous territory to the British Government, and the changes consequent thereupon, the reader is referred to a subsequent chapter entitled "Annexation of the Diamond Fields."

Hard days were those early days for the poor diggers—stores few and far between, only the coarsest of food obtainable, none of the minor luxuries of life, few even of the necessaries, and very inefficient shelter often provided against the inclemency of the weather, the chill blasts of winter, and the terrible heats and nerve-destroying thunderstorms of the summer. But everything is changed now. The diggers form a large, flourishing, civilised, and orderly community. At the stores literally everything can be bought; and are there not hotels and lodging-houses, churches, theatres, concerts, balls, aye, and even schools too? And the flag of old England waves proudly over the busy camps, and the imperturbable British "bobby" is there, too, by this time, reassuring and home-like in aspect, an object of awe to the crowds of strangely-clad or un-clad Kaffirs and Hottentots by whom he is surrounded.

At the early period spoken of above, high prices were paid for diamonds by the great Moritz Unger, and the few other diamond merchants whom the fame of the great discoveries had attracted to the banks of the Vaal. No one appeared to have an inkling then of the great depreciation of "off-coloured" or yellow stones in the European markets, which was to cause some of the early buyers so much loss, and many an apparently lucky finder so much disappointment. Can no market be found for these splendid gems, many of which, though yellow, are of wondrous purity and lustre?

It is a question which often occupies the minds of diggers and of buyers too, and which has received no satisfactory solution as yet. So much for the early discoveries; and now let us carefully review all the principal diggings, both on the riverside and inland, as they were during nearly the whole of 1871.

CHAPTER II.

THE RIVERSIDE DIGGINGS, AND HOW TO WORK THERE.

THE banks of the Vaal River, which for a long time after the first discoveries gave its name to the South African Diamond Fields, have been found to be, in many places, extremely rich in diamonds, and most of the early diggers at Pniel, Klip Drift, and neighbouring places, were well rewarded for their toil. But the "dry diggings," lying about twenty-five miles away from the Vaal River, have been found, during the year 1871, to be so much more *uniformly* remunerative than those on the banks of the river, that the latter have become by this time comparatively deserted. though some of the diggers who have remained at the different waterside camps do still occasionally turn out something good, and the diamonds found by the riverside are, as a rule, of slightly better quality than those from the "dry diggings." During a few days' stay I made at Pniel, in November, 1871, a diamond of $34\frac{1}{2}$ carats was found there by a digger who had been long unsuccessful, and several smaller stones by other parties. But the "finds" are so small on the average, as compared with the wonderful riches daily yielded by the dry diggings, and the instances of long-continued ill-luck are so sadly numerous, that I would not advise our "new chums" to pitch their tents on the banks of the Vaal. True, the temptations to do so are great. The pleasant sight and sound of running water, the facilities for bathing, boating, and fishing, the abundance of splendid trees, affording shade and firewood, and the comparative absence of dust, make a camp on the river seem a perfect elysium, when contrasted with the dry, barren, treeless waste which surrounds the dry diggings. But I think there is little doubt that the latter will continue to prove much the richest, and will, therefore, attract by far the largest proportion of the digging population of the future.

I will, however, endeavour to give some little account of the different riverside camps, premising that I have not worked there myself, and can only speak from the experience of others. Pniel and K lip Drift form the centre of the river diggings, and, some think, the future commercial centre of the Diamond Fields. Pniel is a very straggling little town, or rather village, situated on the brow and slope of a hill overlooking the Vaal River, which is here some two hundred yards broad. The buildings, which are very scattered, are mostly of wood or galvanised iron, with one or two more solid erections of brick. There are stores where literally everything can be bought, a church, and a most comfortable hotel, thoroughly well kept by Mr. James Jardine, the agent of the Inland Transport Company's passenger carts. The number of travellers passing through Pniel is very large, so this hotel is always full, and new arrivals will not only often find that they cannot get a bed, but may be very glad to get a "shake-down" on the floor. Between the town and the river, on the slope of the hill or "kopje," are the "claims." They are big holes, of various sizes and depths, full of large ironstone boulders, the necessary removal of which makes the work here very heavy, slow, and expensive. Among these boulders is the gravel in which the diamonds are found. This gravel is generally washed, to free it from sand and dirt, at the riverside, otherwise water must be brought up from the river to wash it. Generally, the "cradle" is erected close to the edge of the water. In either case, the cost of a cart, with a couple of mules or oxen, must be added to the ordinary expenses of a digger's outfit. When a cartload of gravel or "stuff" has been dug out of the claim, it is carted down to the river, and emptied into a large trough made in the ground, with smooth bottom and sides, or merely on to a smooth floor. A proper quantity of it is put into the "cradle," which is a strong wooden framework, holding two or three sieves of perforated iron or zinc, or wire meshing, one over the other, the top one having large holes, and the bottom one very small ones—the whole framework resting on two strong rockers. While the stuff is being rocked in this cradle, one of the diggers pours bucketfuls of water into it. The gravel being thus thoroughly cleansed by this double process of sifting and washing, the large stones in the top sieve are hastily glanced over, to see if perchance any *big* diamond be amongst them, and the other sieve or sieves are taken out, and the contents emptied on to the "sorting-table," which is an ordinary table of deal, with or without legs, or a smooth sheet of iron or other inexpensive metal.

At this table, the digger either sits or lies, according as it has legs or rests on the ground, and quickly sorts over the stuff with

the aid of an iron or wooden scraper. Nine or ten inches of
ordinary hoop-iron answers very well for this purpose. Diamonds,
especially those of good quality, show out brilliantly, and can
very seldom be missed on a sorting-table; the larger gems,
indeed, are often found in the sieve, or even in the act of digging.
Besides diamonds, one or two valuable rubies and sapphires have
been found on the river-diggings; garnets are very numerous but
almost valueless, and the gravel contains immense quantities of
beautiful agates, also cornelians, jasper, chalcedony, and other
pretty pebbles, which I am sure might be cut and set in large
brooches, bracelets, &c., like the Scotch pebbles which at home
form such an important item in cheap jewellery. Rock crystals
of pretty shapes, clear and shiny, glitter occasionally among the
bright and many coloured pebbles, and woefully deceive the "new
chum." Strong, full-grown Kafirs should be employed for the
river work, as young boys, though they may be hired much more
cheaply, often prove unequal to the heavy work among the
boulders. There are, I think, only between forty and fifty
claims now being worked at Pniel, and about the same number
at Klip Drift, a great contrast to the thousands at the dry
diggings. Klip Drift is just opposite to Pniel, on the slope of a
hill or kopje. It is reached from Pniel by ferry-boats, which are
very numerous, and make a pretty good thing of it, charging 6d.
each way. A little above the ferry is the "pont," an immense
flat-bottomed decked boat, for the conveyance of waggons and
carts, with horses, mules, or oxen, when the river is so high
that the ordinary passage by the "drift," or ford, a few hundred
yards farther up the river, is not practicable. Klip Drift stands
in a very favourable situation as the great depôt for produce of
all kinds from the interior of the Transvaal, a fine fertile
country, growing almost everything, and abounding in large
game. It is the Transvaal which supplies nearly the whole of
the Diamond Fields with meal, maize, tobacco, rheims, or prepared strips of strong hide used as ropes or harness, and many
other necessaries. The merchants at Klip Drift, besides selling
all these things, on a very extensive scale, to storekeepers and
diggers at the different camps, can also often "make a good
thing of it" by purchasing ivory, ostrich feathers, and valuable
skins, all of which frequently arrive in large quantities from the
interior. Here is a slight description of Klip Drift, from the pen
of the correspondent of the *Natal Mercury*:—

Klip-Drift is certainly, in many respects, a most English-looking little town. The situation is pleasant, and the river-scenery extremely pretty. The Vaal here takes a great many turns, and can be seen from all parts of the town. It is here and there hidden by the bends, and then comes into view again some miles off. The original "rich kopje," and the Colesberg Kopje" (which must not be confounded with that wonderful Golconda, the Colesberg Kop or De Beer's New Rush) are rugged-looking hills, and not at all the places where one would naturally think diamonds would be found. The main street (called Campbell-street) is quite smooth, and regularly built upon. There are some very substantial buildings. Mr. James Strong has come out *strong* indeed in his fine stone-built stores. There is nothing this side of Grahamstown to be compared with them. The stone is found in the neighbourhood, and has been well cut and laid. Mr. Unger, the diamond merchant, has an extremely neat office, with prettily-built stone pillars for gates. Mr. Sanger's Masonic Hotel is certainly one of the best constructed and conducted establishments it has been my good fortune to visit. Close to this, on the old market-place, stand Joel Myers' iron store and brick-built stores. Gordon and Co. are in Parker's Music Hall, and Myhill and Co. monopolise both sides of the street. Reid and Co. have a large granary here, for supplying the various diggings with Transvaal produce. The Standard Bank and the Government offices are now under wood, but will shortly be comfortably ensconced in stone and brick. Mr. Strong has let one-half of his store to the former, and Mr. Schultz has hired the other part. Mrs. Schuardt has a very comfortable-looking hotel on the site of the original tent she had the enterprise to put up whilst diamond-digging was in its infancy. An excellent business she does too, and well she deserves it. The shell of the English Church is not badly situated on the hill above Sanger's, but it is very small, and, I am sorry to say, of brick. It is a great pity that a church should be built of indifferent brick when really good building stone is to be obtained in great quantities in the neighbourhood. The Masonic lodge is close to the church, and is a very creditable building considering the number of members of the craft resident here. The Parsonage is also hard by. The less said about this building the better. Mr. F. Thompson is building a house in the style of a bungalow, which will be a very comfortable house if the roof can be kept from blowing off. Altogether, Klip Drift is a very pleasant place, and doubtless it will be a town of great resort for dried-up diggers from Du Toit's Pan. A very large business has been done here of late, but whether merchants will continue to send their goods twenty-five miles beyond the present diggings, and bring them back again, is highly problematical, I think. Still it is the centre of the various river diggings, and the depôt for all Transvaal produce, and will no doubt monopolise the whole of the interior trade, for which it is well situated. The inhabitants live in the hope that diggers will be compelled to come back to the river in the summer, for they say no mortal thing can hold out at the Pan and its vicinity during the warm weather. We shall see.

Klip Drift has always been under English government. Pniel used to be under Orange Free State (Dutch) authorities, but is now, with the whole of the known diamondiferous district under British rule. I shall treat these matters in detail in a chapter on the Annexation.

At Pniel was formerly published the *Diamond News*, the earliest and most important newspaper on the "Fields," but it was removed in September last to Du Toit's Pan. Another newspaper, the *Diamond Field*, is published at Klip Drift. Pniel and Klip Drift have a more settled appearance than most of the other camps, as they are of the earliest date, and contain a much larger proportion of solid structures, and fewer tents; but the quiet streets and absence of noise and dust form a striking contrast to the din, turmoil, and ceaseless activity of the Colesberg Kopje. A company was projected for working Klip Drift and neighbourhood on a large scale, and forms of applications for shares were issued, but I believe it has since fallen to the ground.

About twenty-five miles from Klip Drift up the Vaal River, on the same side as Klip Drift, is Hebron, where there was a busy camp during the greater part of last year, and many very good finds, but also a good deal of unsuccessful work. Hebron has been gradually growing less popular, owing to the wonderful finds at the dry diggings; but a good many still persevere there, some of them being well rewarded, and Hebron has turned out one or two large stones lately. It is a pleasant camp, with pretty scenery, good bathing and fishing, and well supplied with provisions and all necessaries.

For the benefit of my English readers I must explain that if a claim has been left unworked for a certain time, in some camps *three* days, in others *eight*, it may be "jumped," *i.e.*, any person may jump into it, and take possession, on payment of the ordinary 10s. licence, and the original owner has no redress.

Down the river there are several pretty good digging camps. Twelve miles from Klip Drift, on the same side, is Cawood's Hope, an early favourite, but not thought very much of now. Opposite to it is Gong Gong, generally considered to be pretty well worked out. About five miles lower down, are Forlorn Hope and Delport's Hope—neighbouring camps. I hear that the work there is pretty satisfactory. One gentleman, a newspaper proprietor, got, in a fortnight's work at Delport's Hope, diamonds worth at least 300*l.* A stone of $2\frac{3}{4}$ carats he sold on the spot for 27*l.* Of course it was of pure water. This is considered a very good price. About four miles lower down is Sifonell, where some very good finds were made soon after the first "rush" there last spring, but I have not heard much of it lately. On many of these small camps there are hardly any stores, which is a serious drawback to residence there, as the digger must either make frequent journeys to the "town" of Pniel or Klip Drift, or must be satisfied with coarse and monotonous food.

A friend of mine, working at Forlorn Hope, subsisted for months, sometimes, on meat and "mealies" (Indian corn).

I have now enumerated the principal diggings on the river, and will endeavour to sum up their advantages and disadvantages. The former are abundance of water—bathing, a great luxury and very conducive to the preservation of health, plenty of wood, good fishing and consequently an important addition to diet, a slight superiority in the quality of the diamonds, and more interesting sorting, owing to the immense quantity of beautiful pebbles, some of them of slight value. Their disadvantages are less uniformity in success, the diamonds lying a good deal in patches, much harder work owing to the innumerable boulders, far less society, less life and amusement than at the "dry diggings," and, at the smaller camps deficient supplies of food and other necessaries, and total absence of luxuries. Many of our "dried-up" diggers will, of course, make frequent trips to the river for bathing—in fact, we of the dry diggings are beginning to look upon the pleasant little camps by the Vaal River as our Scarborough and Brighton, or, perhaps Harrogate and Matlock would be nearer the mark.

I hear that a rush has lately taken place to a spot called Tsitsikama, three miles from Forlorn Hope, and that fresh ground is being opened up on both sides of the river, so that diggers going out now had better, on arriving at the Fields, make full inquiries as to the state of all the riverside camps, both old and new, though I still hold the conviction that the dry diggings are by far the richest.

Many waggon-loads of goods were, when I left the Fields in November last, still arriving at, and on the way for Pniel, and Klip Drift, taking from a month to six months from Port Elizabeth (Algoa Bay).

I expect, however, that the big markets of Du Toit's Pan, De Beer's, and the Colesberg Kopje will soon attract most of the trade, both from the colony and the interior.

CHAPTER III.

THE DRY DIGGINGS, AND HOW TO WORK THERE.

THE first of the "dry diggings" to attract public attention was Du Toit's Pan, to which a few diggers resorted in 1870. This place derives its name from a large "pan," or shallow depression in the ground, filled with brackish water in the rainy season, and on which no vegetation grows when the "Pan" is dry, it being then simply an expanse of hard mud, fissured in all directions by the heat. Du Toit's Pan is situated twenty-five miles from Pniel, on the road leading from the colony through Fauresmith to the Vaal River township. On the further or Pniel side of the "Pan," which is about a quarter of a mile in length by half that breadth, is a sloping ridge, or long "kopje," towards the top of which the diamonds are found; the main town, called by some enthusiastic journalists the "City of the Pan," lying between the claims and the Pan, while many hundreds of diggers' tents also cover the "veldt" or common, above the claims in the direction of De Beer's and Pniel. The town of Du Toit's Pan is large and picturesque—tents, marquees, and buildings of every possible material being charmingly grouped round the large open market square, from which streets, mostly of canvas, radiate in all directions.

The work here is far more easy than on the river, no water being used: moreover the big boulders are absent, the ground being soft rotten limestone, with green trap, amygdaloid, &c., all of a consistency which is easily worked by pick and shovel, a large rock requiring any trouble in removing being only found at very rare intervals. Here, when the stuff has been loosened by the pick, it is thrown on to the top of the claim with the shovel if the claim is shallow, hauled up in buckets if it is deep, broken up with the shovel, then shaken in a sieve of large mesh to remove all the rough stones which might injure the fine sieve, and then well sifted in the fine sieve, which is generally of very fine but strong wire meshing, sometimes of perforated zinc or iron, in a strong oblong wooden frame, some 3ft. by 2ft., with rounded handles at one end, and two deep notches at the other, by which the sieve rests firmly on a piece of strong *rheim* (hide rope) hanging between two upright posts, called "sieve props." The operator swings the sieve rapidly to and fro till all sand, dust, and dirt has fallen through; then the gravel, which is composed principally of minute pieces of limestone, chalk, green trap, &c., with a slight admixture of garnets, peridot, ilmenite, and talc, is emptied on to the sorting-table, and treated in the ordinary manner. The early diggers, in 1870, only dug to a depth of eighteen inches or two feet, stopping when they got to a stratum of rather hard limestone or green trap, and finding a good many small diamonds, with here and there a big one; but it has since been found that the best and largest stones generally lie deeper, and there seems hardly any limit to the depth at which diamonds may be found.

The natural consequence was that early in the year 1871, there was a rush of diggers to Du Toit's Pan, who commenced to work the whole of the old claims over again, beginning where the former workers had left off. And whereas a man could "work out" a claim (30 square feet) in a week or two when two feet was his limit of depth, now when we go down 30 or 40 feet, or even more, it takes many months to work out a claim properly. It is difficult to say at what depth most diamonds are found. A great many small diamonds lie near the surface, some large ones have been picked up on the surface and very near to it; but, again, I have known diggers find hardly anything till they got to a depth of 20 feet or more, and from that time go on finding regularly one or two stones per day. From general experience I may safely say that by far the greater proportion of large stones are found below five feet, many between that depth and ten feet, and that the quality is often found to improve with the depth. Different diggers, according to their experience and ingenuity, adopt various methods of working the deep claims. One will sink a perpendicular, narrow shaft, that he can easily stride across, and descend and ascend by means of little niches or "toe-holes" picked in each side of the shaft. Another will have a knotted rope or rheim hanging down the side, fixed to a strong post above. Where trees are plentiful, which is *not* at Du Toit's Pan, I have seen a big tree with convenient branches lowered into a claim and used as a staircase. Others, again, work their claims in regular stages, with a little kind of flight of steps to each, if the ground be hard. Many make tunnels or shafts, horizontally or slanting, when they arrive at a certain stratum which seems to be particularly good. But this is dangerous; first, because the ground at Du Toit's Pan is hardly of sufficiently firm consistency for this purpose, and small "landslips" are frequent, especially after heavy rains; and secondly, because a man is working, as it were, in the dark, and may unwittingly burrow under his neighbour's claim, for all the claims touch one another. Many disputes as to ownership of diamonds have occurred from this and similar causes. One great drawback to the work at our dry diggings, which would otherwise be exceedingly easy and comfortable, is the dust. This is of two kinds—red dust from the open *veldt* beyond the claims, and white limestone dust from the claims themselves. The supply of both seems unlimited; they are both equally fine and penetrating, so much so as to stop a hunting watch; this is a fact—very few watches can be kept in order on the Fields, the works get clogged up in "no time." As it is nearly always windy, our camps are generally enveloped in clouds of this irritating element, of which the editor of the *Diamond News* eloquently says, doubtless with eyes smarting and lungs oppressed by it: "The dust of the dry diggings is to be classed with plague, pestilence, and famine, and, if there is anything worse, with that also."

Du Toit's Pan is certainly *the* camp which has yielded, up to the present time, the largest stones, a considerable number of stones weighing *over one hundred* carats having been found since I went there in May, 1871. The largest that I *know of* was 175 carats, a very fair size, and would have been of immense value if it had only been a pure white stone. I have heard, it is true, of a wonderful stone of, some say 314 carats, others 318; and there is certainly no reason why even larger gems should not be found, especially as I have seen a stone weighing 124 carats, which was evidently only a fragment of a much larger gem. I will speak more fully of some of the principal large stones found on our South African Fields, in a special chapter on diamonds and other precious stones.

There is an immense area of ground being worked at Du Toit's Pan, I should think not less than half a square mile, entirely full of claims, all joining—at first sight, a chaotic mass of irregularly shaped holes of various depths, and endless whitish mounds of various sizes. Claims, last year, in good positions, sold from 1*l*. to 50*l*. per claim (30ft. square). License 10*s*. per month. In consequence of the immense exodus to the new rush, many claims at Du Toit's Pan are now for sale pretty cheap, and although there are very few where a man can be *certain* of daily or even weekly finds, yet it is a tempting place to work at, owing to the frequent finds of *very large stones*, and the sanguine digger, especially if a "new chum," feels a constant nervous excitement, or half expectation, hoping to see something shining, about the size of a pigeon's egg, in the floor or wall of his claim, as he is picking. I think Du Toit's Pan is not a bad place for a man with small capital to begin ; living is comparatively cheap and comfortable, there being an active and salutary competition of numerous large storekeepers, who are well supplied with everything, and an immense market every morning at seven, where cattle, sheep, food, and produce of every kind is brought in by Dutch farmers, and sold by auction.

Du Toit's Pan boasts many large hotels, immense stores, two churches, several billiard-rooms, an hospital and a theatre, which latter is also a "canteen" or liquor-bar, performances being only held there occasionally. The scenery immediately around the Pan is flat, a broad expanse of "veldt" or prairie, with stunted growth of scrub, and here and there a mimosa or thornbush, but at a distance, varying from five to twelve miles, run ranges of picturesque hills, many of them well wooded.

The claims, during working hours, present a most animated and striking appearance, each claim employing on the average, I should say, two "white folks" and three or four Kafirs, all ceaselessly busy at the various occupations above and below ground, picking "stuff," throwing it up, breaking, sifting, and sorting, the whole accompanied with much barbaric singing and shouting on the part of the half-naked Kafirs.

Joining Du Toit's Pan is another large camp called Bultfontein, presenting similar characteristics.

I must mention here that each of these camps possesses a large dam, where water collects during the rainy season, and supplies the cattle of the camp, and many of the human beings too, with drinking water, while a smaller dam is set apart for washing, and is constantly surrounded by a chattering crowd of washerwomen of every possible shade of colour, and clad in every variety of dress, the brighter colours being naturally prevalent.

Bultfontein was originally a cattle-breeding farm, and when it got bruited about, early in 1871, that diamonds had been found on the surface, the proprietors refused to allow diggers to come on their ground. A number of miners of the rougher sort "jumped," or took forcible possession of the farm; but, after too short a stay to do much good there, were driven away by some of the Free State police. Towards the end of May, however, the proprietors, fearing that the farm would again be "jumped" by so large a force of determined diggers that a handful of police could do nothing against them, wisely threw it open to the public on payment of the ordinary monthly licence of 10s. per claim. This gave general satisfaction. The day I arrived on the Fields, 29th May, 1871, over a thousand diggers were busy marking out claims on the "kopje," all round the old farm-house, and in a few days the Bultfontein diggings were at full work.

From this time all the available ground there kept thousands at work, with average satisfactory results, till the news of Colesberg Kopje drew many of them away. The Bultfontein diggings have been found to yield an immense number of small stones, a few good-sized ones, but hardly any very large ones. So great is the number of small diamonds, most of which are here of very good quality, that the holder of any claim in a moderately good position is almost sure of finding *something* every week,—and a great many diggers regularly kept a claim at work at Bultfontein, on which they relied for the payment of their expenses at least, while they would work a claim at Du Toit's Pan on alternate days in the hopes of big stones. Owing to the number of large stones found at Colesberg Kopje and elsewhere, many good claims at Bultfontein are abandoned, and it would, I think, be an excellent place for a beginner to work, while looking out for a chance of getting a share in one of the rich claims elsewhere. He will only have to go to the registration office in the old farm-house on the top of the "kopje," where he can peruse the list of licenses, and take down a few of the numbers of claims on which the license has not been renewed. Armed with this list, he can go amongst the claims, and look at those on which the license is unpaid, and which are consequently "jumpable." He can inquire of the diggers working in the neighbourhood of such vacant claims—they are generally pretty communicative—and if diamonds are being found *all round* any claim, it is a pretty sure criterion that that claim is good. Having looked at a few such, and made all needful inquiries, the intending digger can make his choice, return to the office, take out a license in his own name for the claim he has chosen, and set to work as soon as he likes.

Another digging camp, Alexandersfontein, joins Bultfontein, and precisely similar remarks apply to the diggings there.

About two miles from Du Toit's Pan, to the left of the Pniel Road, lies the large, scattered, and very picturesque camp of De Beer's (Old Rush). The "business" part of this camp—*i. e.*, the stores and hotels—lies all close together, along the roadside, while the tents of the diggers are scattered in all directions over the "veldt," and are generally pitched near one of the numerous *kameeldorn* (camel-thorn) trees. (See Chapter on "Tent Life.") The old De Beer's Kopje contains many exceedingly good claims, the diamonds are generally of good quality, and there are plenty of large stones. I know many diggers who have done exceedingly well there. It was first regularly worked about May, 1871, and soon attracted a very large digging population and became a town. Here is an advertisement relative to De Beer's, which appeared in a Cape paper of 30th September, 1871.

NEW TOWNSHIP AT DE BEER'S.

THE Proprietors of the Farm "VOORUITZIGT," commonly known as "DE BEER'S," beg to intimate to the Public that they have laid out a

TOWN ON THE ABOVE FARM,

THE ERVEN OF WHICH WILL BE OFFERED AT

PUBLIC AUCTION ON THE SPOT,

ON

SATURDAY, THE 21st OCTOBER NEXT,

At 11 o'clock in the Forenoon.

The site selected is eligibly situated on a gentle slope contiguous to the Two RUSHES which are now yielding such LARGE FORTUNES to the Diggers, and the Erven will be sold with all the PROPRIETOR'S RIGHTS TO THE DIAMONDS which may be found on them.

The Pniel Road will pass through the Town, which is situated within easy walking distance of "DU TOIT'S PAN," "BULTFONTEIN," and "ALEXANDERSFONTEIN" Diggings.

In selecting the spot for this Township, the Proprietors have specially regarded the HEALTHINESS of the situation; the fact of GOOD WATER being found at moderate depth and the proximity to the several digging Camps.

Ample space has been provided for a MARKET, and eligible allotments reserved for CHURCHES and SCHOOLS.

It is scarcely necessary for the Proprietors to point out the advantages that will accrue to possessors of Erven in this Township, so conveniently situated in close proximity to all the successful Diamond Diggings, either as a centre of Business or Healthy Residence.

Plans of the Town may be seen on application at the office of "The Friend of the Free State," Bloemfontein; The office of the Proprietors, De Beer's; Messrs. Dunnell, Ebden, & Co., Port Elizabeth.

Vooruitzigt, 18th September, 1871.

Claims at De Beer's have always commanded a pretty good price —50*l*. and 100*l*. being an ordinary figure in the early days. Soon after the great rush to the Colesberg Kopje the old De Beer's claims fell very much in price; but as many of the new arrivals found that the purchase of claims at the "New Rush" was far beyond their means, they began to turn their attention to old De Beer's, and claims there soon rose again in price. Active work is now going on there, and with generally satisfactory results. De Beer's is rather an aristocratic camp, many gentlemen blessed with wives and families have encamped here, and made themselves comparatively comfortable, and the English element predominates pleasingly over the Dutch or Boer.

Well-dressed gentlemen, and well-dressed ladies too, may be seen cantering over the "veldt" on well-groomed horses; the tents are more like marquees, covered generally with a wide awning as an additional protection against the hot rays of the sun. Kafir servants are numerous, horses, mules, and oxen plentiful, and the whole place has a thoroughly "well-to-do" air.

The soil is pretty much the same as at Du Toit's Pan. The excavations in the claims are generally larger and deeper, owing to many of the diggers here being men of capital, employing much more labour, and, consequently, getting through the ground much more quickly than at Du Toit's Pan and Bultfontein.

Colesberg Kopje is scarcely a mile from De Beer's, farther to the left of the Pniel road, but Colesberg Kopje requires a chapter to itself.

I subjoin the rules and regulations issued by the Digger's Committee for the Du Toit's Pan camp in 1871. They are not likely to be very materially changed, and will be similar on other diggings:—

Rules and Regulations of the Dorstfontein (Dutoitspan) Diggings.

THE following are the Rules and Regulations framed and agreed upon between Martin Lilienfield and Henry Webb, acting on behalf of the proprietors of Dorstfontein, and the following gentlemen, deputed by a General Public Meeting of diggers at Dorstfontein, on the 15th day of May, 1871, for that purpose, viz.:—James Buchanan Finlayson, Barend Woest, Joachim J. Rothman, William Devine, William Stratford Wright, as representing such general public:—

1. The Committee shall consist of five members.
2. That from and after the 15th May, 1871, a fee of ten shillings and sixpence sterling per month for claims shall be payable by each digger, in advance, to the proprietors or their agents, at their office, Dorstfontein, save and excepting those who hold briefes or permits prior to the 15th

April, 1871, who can satisfy the proprietors and Committee that such are *bonâ fide* permits, to be exhibited within one week.

3. All claims shall be surveyed and measured off by the proprietors, and the Committee shall be entitled to impose a fine, not exceeding five pounds sterling, upon anyone removing or altering any beacon after the same has been finally measured and adjusted.

4. No one shall be allowed to throw any ground, dirt, or filth on his neighbour's claim. All loose ground shall be kept by the owner on his own claim. The Committee shall have the power of imposing a fine, not exceeding two pounds sterling, in case of any infringement of this rule.

5. Any person or persons, with or without a licence, found working any claim other than his own, or without consent of the owner, shall be subjected to a fine not exceeding five pounds sterling.

6. Any person or digger finding a diamond on the claim of another person, and not returning the same to the owner of the claim, shall be considered as a thief, and be expelled the diggings.

7. The spot or locality for burial of carcases and other filth shall be selected and pointed out by the Committee.

8. No person or persons shall be entitled to select or work any claim without having first signed and submitted to the Diggers' Rules and Regulations, which the Committee shall at all times have the power of enforcing and making operative.

9. The Committee and proprietors shall have the right conjointly to amend or add to these Regulations, and such amendments or additions shall at all times be taken to be as effectual as if inserted herein.

10. Any member of the Committee absenting himself for fourteen days or more, without intimation or notice to the other members, shall, *ipso facto*, cease to be a member of the Committee.

11. Every digger shall be compelled to assist the Committee in giving effect to, and support in, the execution of their judgments, subject to a penalty of one pound sterling in case of non-compliance.

12. Every digger shall pay the sum of one shilling to the Committee on the signing of these Rules.

13. No person shall be entitled, under the new licence, to have more than two claims at one time.

14. Any claim or claims having been abandoned for eight or more successive days, shall be liable to be selected and taken possession of by any person or persons taking out a licence for the same—the claims of members of Committee being specially exempt from such a rule.

15. Each licensed digger shall be entitled to pasturage on the farm Dorstfontein for six sheep and one span of oxen, at the following rate, viz.:—For six sheep, the sum of threepence sterling per month; and for each ox the sum of threepence sterling per month. Such sheep and oxen to be the *bonâ fide* property of the licence-holder, and such privilege being in no way transferable.

16. The proprietors shall, as soon as the same becomes practicable, sink six wells, which they will, on completion, place at the disposal of the Committee for the benefit of the diggers, who shall pay the proprietors the sum of one shilling sterling each per month, from the 15th day of May, 1871.

17. The Committee and proprietors shall select a person or persons competent thereto, to regulate the formation of streets and squares, and

the former are empowered to enforce rules necessary for the accomplishment of such purposes.

18. All disputes and differences between the diggers and proprietors under these Rules shall be submitted to the arbitration of the Committee, whose decision will be binding and final.

19. Any person signing these Rules and Regulations, and having been fined by the Committee for any misdemeanour or infringement, or having been ordered to comply with any order or judgment, shall be bound to pay such fine or fulfil such order or judgment; and in case of failure so to do, submits, by signing these Rules, to such process as shall be by the said Committee directed, for the carrying out of their judgment.

20. The proprietors engage at the end of each month to pay over to the Committee as custodians for the diggers—to enable the latter to carry out sanitary measures, pay a permanent secretary, and uphold the Committee—ten pounds sterling upon every one hundred pounds sterling, of all revenue collected by them from "Dorstfontein Diggings."

21. Monthly permits of occupation for establishing places of business other than those already established under permission, will be granted by the proprietors on terms which can be ascertained on application at their office. Parties holding licences or permission prior to the 15th of May, 1871, shall continue to hold such licences upon the same terms as hitherto, and all persons holding shop licences shall be subject to the following rules, viz.:—1. No servant to have drink unless he have a written permission from his master. 2. No gambling to be permitted on the premises. 3. No drink to be sold on Sundays, or during the hours between 10 p.m. and 5 a.m. on week days.

22. Any infringement of the above rules shall subject the party so infringing to a penalty or fine of not less than 1*l.* (one pound sterling), and not more than 5*l.* (five pounds sterling).

23. It is strictly forbidden to anyone to purchase a diamond or diamonds from any servant, black or white, without a certificate from such servant's master or mistress, under a penalty of five pounds sterling, and expulsion from the Camp at the discretion of the Committee.

24. All transfers of claims or portions thereof shall be registered in the proprietors' books, for which the person applying for such transfer shall pay a fee of sixpence sterling.

CHAPTER IV.

THE COLESBERG KOPJE.*

EARLY in July, 1871, a "new rush" was prospected about a mile beyond De Beer's, and many diamonds being found on or near the surface, a great many claims were at once taken out. It is only a small "kopje" or hill, about 250 acres in area, surrounded by a reef of hard rock. In about a fortnight after the first discovery claims were selling there at from 20*l*. to 100*l*., and lucky indeed were those who bought any at those prices, luckier still those who originally marked out claims, and paid only the 10*s*. license, for little more than three months after the opening of this "kopje" a whole claim in a good position there would not be sold for less than 2000*l*. to 4000*l*., and half or quarter claims in proportion.

The daily finds there are something marvellous, fortunes having already been realised by single individuals between July and the end of October, when I left the Colesberg Kopje. A friend of mine having taken out a claim there, sold half of it to a Mr. Arie Smuts, a Dutchman, for, I think, 50*l*. In two months time Smuts found diamonds the value of which is estimated at from 15,000*l*. to 20,000*l*. The other half of the same claim has also turned out very well. The daily increasing riches of this wonderful place soon attracted crowds of diggers, diamond buyers, store and hotel keepers; and, within three months from the first discovery, the De Beer's New Rush, subsequently christened "Colesberg Kopje," has become a busy, thriving town, with regular streets, handsome buildings of every material except stone, and an immense encampment of tents and wagons all round the "kopje." As to the appearance of the "kopje" itself during

---

* " Kopje," pronounced *koppie*, is a Dutch word, meaning literally " little head," but generally used in the sense of " hillock " or small (generally circular) elevation of ground. It is a diminutive of "kop" or "head," which is used for a larger hill. The De Beer's New Rush is often also called " Colesberg *Kop*," but I do not think it is quite large enough to merit that designation. The diamonds are generally found in rather elevated ground (ridges or hills), so that plenty of " kopjes " will be noticed on the different diggings.

working hours, no words of mine can give an adequate idea of the immense activity which is here displayed.

In consequence of the high price of claims and richness of the ground, most of the claims have been divided into halves and quarters, the latter being the most general; and every digger being anxious to get through the ground as quickly as possible, puts on as many Kafirs as he can get hold of, so that such a number of men, white and black, are congregated on this little space, all working with ceaseless energy, that the place is like a magnified ant-hill, with a combination of beehive. Each claim has to allow 7ft. for the road. Roads runs parallel through the whole of the kopje; the refuse stuff, rock, &c., being rapidly removed by mule-carts, the drivers of which are at work all day long, and make a fair thing of it at ninepence or one shilling per load, which does not take long, as the stuff is shot out on to the "veldt," just outside the kopje. This refuse stuff consists of large pieces of hard limestone and other kinds of rock. too hard to be easily broken either by the shovel or in the rough sieve. but diggers are *now* careful to break as much of it as they possibly can, using mallets and sledge-hammers, for many diamonds have been found embedded in this hard stuff; and some people who could not afford claims were, and probably still are, in the habit of making a living, and sometimes a very good one too. by going about and breaking the refuse stuff carted away from the claims. In one instance, a piece of limestone fell out of the front of a cart, the hinder wheel passed over it and crushed it. when out came a 20-carat diamond. A 33-carat stone has lately been found embedded in solid quartz.

The noise, dust, and heat at the Colesberg Kopje are intense and most trying. Thirst is keenly felt, and the canteens drive a roaring trade. In consequence of the small portion of ground each digger has to work on, there is no room on the claims for most of the sorting-tables, and they are generally placed on the "veldt" outside the kopje; and here, under awnings of various kinds, rugs, blankets, &c., &c., placed on four props round the table, sit men, and many ladies too, with the "scraper" in one hand, and sometimes a horse's, cow's, or wildebeest's tail in the other, for flicking the flies away, while their partners, or the more than half naked black labourers, bring down the precious stuff from the claims in carts, wheelbarrows, or very commonly in a bullock's hide sewn to two poles, and sift it there—the sieve props being also erected near the sorting-table, so as to leave the bit of

claim clear for working. Diamonds are found here at all depths: in some claims they find every day from the surface downwards; in others a man will find hardly anything till he has got down to 20ft. or more, and will from that time be richly rewarded for his perseverance. As a fine diamond of 10 carats was lately found at a depth of 96ft. in sinking a well, it is difficult to say to what limit the diggers of the future will go. But already the working of these claims, with the holes so close together in the crumbling white limestone, red sand, and green trap, is becoming dangerous. Portions or sides of claims frequently slip in, and some lives have already been lost by diggers being buried under such landslips. Moreover, the heavily-laden mule and ox-carts, going along the very edge of numerous claims, tend very much to loosen the earth. Often will the side of a claim give way, and the cart and quadrupeds topple over into the hole. The curious visitor to the Colesberg Kopje will be frequently startled by a loud and gathering "hurrah" or confused shout. He will see many diggers running from their claims to a certain spot, on reaching which he will probably find that a large diamond has just been "turned up;" but even more frequently it will be a cart with a couple of mules or oxen which has tumbled into some claim, and has to be extricated, for which purpose volunteers, with plenty of ropes and rheims, are speedily forthcoming. I saw a cart with two oxen topple over into a claim 40ft. deep; a nigger was working at the bottom, and he yelled out lustily, but, fortunately for him, about 10ft. down was a large rock jutting out, which narrowed the claim considerably in that part, and prevented the further descent of the cart and oxen, which were firmly jammed in the narrow shaft, and took much time and trouble to extricate.

It is difficult to form an estimate of the number of stones daily found here, for a very great number of the diggers never report their finds, and it is, I know, only a small proportion of the diamonds actually found which appears in the weekly list published by the *Diamond News*. But even this small proportion is sufficiently exciting. Here is, for instance. the summary of one week's list of diamonds found at the Colesberg Kopje:—657 stones, from one. 103 carats, found by one Piet Otto, downwards, including stones of 102, 84, 83, 82, &c., &c. The uniformity in size of many of the stones found in one week is often very curious:— Another week's list contains 477 diamonds, including stones of 81 carats, 42, 35, 31, 30, 20, &c. At the time I left the Fields, viz., in the middle of November, 1871, it was estimated roughly, but I think with no exaggeration, that from £40,000 *to* £50,000 *worth of diamonds were weekly taken* from this small kopje, only about 250 yards square, and containing about 1000 claims, I have been told, on good authority, that one dealer in diamonds had then in his possession *more than one pound weight of first-class stones!* The amount of money at this kopje, the lavish way in which it is spent, and the carelessness with which it is risked, surpass all belief. The following I can vouch for as a fact, knowing the parties concerned. A party of three, possessing a claim valued at about £1500, out of which they had taken a goodly amount of diamonds, tossed up, "odd man out," who should keep the whole, as they were desirous of leaving the Fields. The partner who won, and consequently had to stay some time longer in the heat and dust of the hottest and driest place of the dry diggings, will probably yet make a fortune out of the claim he won on a toss !

Diggers at Du Toit's Pan, De Beer's, and other camps, meeting one another, immediately ask, "Have you found anything lately?" and only too often the answer may be in the negative. But at the Colesberg Kopje, the question is always, " How many have you found to-day?" And, generally, the answer will not be less than two or three, while even a dozen or fifteen is not looked upon as anything very astonishing. Parties who have bought a half or quarter of a claim for £500 or £1000, have frequently got their purchase-money back in a few days or a week or two.

But I must not forget to say that a great many of the diamonds found here are of such bad colour and shape as to be worth simply the price of boart, *i.e.*, 15s. to 1*l.* per carat, on the Fields, and perhaps about double that in Europe. And most of the larger ones, in fact, a very great majority of those over 10 carats, are off colour. But then there are so many of them that working there *must* pay, but there is already (Dec. 1871) hardly room for the "new chums" who are flocking to the "rich kopje" from all parts of the colony, and it is sincerely to be hoped that some equally rich spots may soon be discovered. I fully believe that this *will* be the case, if the surrounding country is thoroughly "prospected," and just before I left Cape Town, I heard that very rich new diggings had been discovered about four miles from the Colesburg Kopje.

I am also glad to hear that claims are going up in price at the old De Beer's diggings, especially those alongside of and near the "reef." (There is a reef of rock and shale running round nearly all the rich tracts of ground which constitute the different dry diggings, and the claims close to this reef often produce the most numerous and largest gems. Many of the claims at the Colesberg Kopje are "on the reef;" so much so that only half the claim is workable stuff, but in this case, though the digger gets virtually only a half-claim, he may probably find it as good as a whole one elsewhere.) Many of those reef claims at De Beer's are turning out remarkably well, and some of them are equal to the good claims on Colesberg Kopje. Most of the diamonds found there are perfect stones. A little before I left, two young men from Natal found in one week, out of a claim at De Beer's, fifteen diamonds, the largest being 13 carats.

Such an immense number of hands are now at work at the Colesberg Kopje, that many people say it will be entirely worked out it in from six to twelve months' time. And I think this quite likely, if diggers stop at the present usual depth, viz., thirty to fifty feet. A correspondent of the *Natal Mercury* writes as follows:—

Although Du Toit's Pan is still a large place, its proportions are not now nearly so great as the enormous encampment around the Colesberg, which increases in size daily. It would be extremely difficult to form an estimate of the population, as the tents are so scattered, but it is really a wonderful place; and just as we have read with surprise the accounts of African travellers of large towns in the interior of 40,000 or 50,000 black inhabitants (*sic*), so may the black regard with astonishment the sudden rise of so large a town by the white people. Indeed, I know of nothing so calculated to cause astonishment—supposing one to be in ignorance of what had already occurred at the Diamond Fields—as, after travelling through the barren sandy track (tract?) which surrounds these inland diggings, to come into view, instantaneously, as it were, of the neighbourhood of Du Toit's Pan, a large city springing out of the desert. At night, the scene is even more surprising—the encampment seems larger still, the lights appearing to extend for miles. Standing between De Beer's and the Colesberg, at night, with lights on either side, the scene is exactly like that observed at a certain point in Hyde Park, where the long line of lights on the Bayswater road can be seen at the same time as those at Knightsbridge. The delusion, however, only exists at night time. We are curious to know where claims can be found for all the parties who are likely to arrive soon on the Fields. There is no room at the Colesberg.

This writer does not appear to have had much experience of the Fields, or he would know that even in the most improbable event of no new diggings being prospected, there is plenty of room, and probability of doing moderately well, at Du Toit's Pan, Bultfontein, and old De Beer's. People who would not be satisfied without finding six to a dozen diamonds per day, must be prepared to pay down their thousands for the luxury of that sensation (and it *is* a luxury), but for the more modest crowd, I would not say, "odi profanum vulgus, et arceo," but would tell them that there is plenty of room for hardworking men to make a good living.

I subjoin a description of the business part of the Colesberg Kopje, written early in October, and I have reason to know that the said business part had nearly doubled itself a month later:—

Half-way between De Beer's and Colesberg Kopje the Committee Tent is pitched. Alongside it stands its placard board, which is literally covered with notices, &c. This tent is pitched between the two camps for the convenience of the diggers, as the Committee, I believe, act for the two fields—De Beer's and Colesberg. In the neighbourhood of this point the tents are pitched far from each other, but nearer the kopje they are denser. The kopje, like De Beer's, is surrounded by hundreds of tents of various descriptions and sizes (many of them very large and luxurious). From the west side of the kopje the tents stretch away until they reach the ridge beyond. The business places are very numerous. They are the following:— In Lower-street—Moss's general store, a billiard room, Crowder's general store, a butchery, Squire's shoemaking shop, Harmsworth's Hotel, Brown's retail store and refreshment rooms, a general store, three hotels and stores, Norris's Odd Fellows' Arms, and store. Upper-street—Bromwich's Dispensary, Muirhead and Co.'s store, Robinson, diamond merchant, Parker's club and billiard rooms, Eldorado bar, a store, Royal Oak Hotel, Jessup's Hotel and billiard room, a canteen, London bakery and confectionery shop, an eating house, a store, Webb and Posno's diamond buying establishment, Royal Hotel and billiard room, a store, a billiard room and bar, London Hotel, a canteen, a butchery, McWilliams' wholesale spirit and provision store, a restaurant and boarding house, a general store, The Diggers' Arms, Honiball's butchery, &c. Round the kopje—Spring's canteen, Von Kraut and Co., general agents, auctioneers, &c., two canteens, Holm's general store, a hotel, &c., &c., besides many business places just completed, and many more in course of erection."

Many diggers at the "rich kopje" live at Du Toit's Pan or De Beer's still on account of less crowding of tents, and greater convenience, and cheapness of wood, water, &c. So there is ample employment for the different omnibuses, carts, and other vehicles, which run between De Beer's, Colesberg Kopje, and Du Toit's Pan. The roads, at sundown especially, are crowded with vehicles of every description, and drawn by all kinds of cattle, while innumerable diggers and buyers, the latter always on horseback, many of the former on foot, in every variety of costume, and niggers in no costume at all, add to the animation of the scene.

Two gentlemen holding good positions in Australia came over to the South African Diamond Fields in the middle of 1871.

They were working on the Colesberg Kopje when I left, and had for some time been pocketing £300 per week. What will folks say in Australia?

A correspondent, dating from Du Toit's Pan, 20th October, 1871, says:—

Several accidents have happened on Colesberg Kopje. The other day a white man fell down a deep shaft upon a nigger, whom he seriously injured besides hurting himself severely. Landslips are of frequent occurrence. Lately a portion of a claim gave way, falling upon a white man and a nigger, completely burying both. When extricated, it was found they had received little or no injury. Accidents to carts, oxen, mules, &c., are of daily occurrence. A fatal accident occurred on Wednesday last. A loaded cart, drawn by mules, fell into a claim. The driver (a black boy) and one of the mules were killed. The other mule escaped uninjured.

The following extract from the *Standard and Mail* (a very good Cape Town paper) of 5th December, 1871, the day on which I sailed for England, will not be devoid of interest:—

The Diamond Fields.—The finds are something enormous, and not surpassed by any fortnight's work that has gone before. The news from home with respect to the value of diamonds above ten carats are anything but satisfactory; but we are confident that well-shaped, faultless stones, of good water, will still find their price, and not a few such come with the large quantities that find their way to our market. Sickness at the Fields is terribly on the increase, and it is alleged to be attributable principally to the bad water, of which even there is a scarcity. Of the value of claims at the New Rush (Colesberg Kopje) we can give the following instance; Mr. Jacobus Swanepoel, of Wipener, in the Conquered Territory, has recently given two good farms in that territory, valued at £1000 each, for half a claim in the New Rush, and disposed of the same the next day for £1600 cash, on condition that when the latter amount (£1600) shall have been realised by the purchaser, he (Swanepoel) shall get a half share of the finds. The other day £450 was paid cash down for a small portion of a claim 7 feet by 10 feet only, and £1000 was, we understand, given for half a claim by Messrs. Adler, Escombe, and Co., of Natal. These claims will eventually be sunk to the depth of 60 feet from the surface. One party has already reached that depth. About seventeen feet of red sand has, in some cases, to be removed before the diamondiferous soil is reached. The best diamonds are, it is said, turned out at twenty or twenty-five feet. People are very curious to know whether another equally rich kopje will shortly be hit upon. There is no reason why it should not. A few months ago nothing was known of the Colesberg Kopje.

CHAPTER V.

CLIMATE, WEATHER, AND HEALTH.

THE climate of the district in which the Diamond Fields are situate is, though not absolutely unhealthy, in many respects extremely trying to newly-arrived Europeans. For the purpose of becoming gradually acclimatised, it is best to reach the fields, if possible, in autumn, or beginning of winter. The seasons may be put down as follows : Spring—August, September, October; Summer—November, December, January ; Autumn—February, March, April ; Winter—May, June, July. The spring weather is bearable enough—pretty hot during the day, but not oppressively so, with a good many cold nights and mornings, now and then a slight frost, but very little rain or storms. The summer at the Fields is excessively hot—I think more so than in most other parts of South Africa. While I was at Pniel, early in last November, the thermometer frequently registered 100° Fahrenheit in the shade ; while the heat and glare of the sun acting upon the white limestone and uniform light colour of soil, tents, and almost everything at the dry diggings, try the head and eyes most severely. In the summer time there is almost always a strong wind blowing—this is very often a *hot wind*—in addition to which it keeps the whole of the camp enveloped in a cloud of the horrible dust mentioned in a previous chapter. And when the wind does *not* blow, the stifling, oppressive, sultry heat renders breathing difficult, and the slightest exercise almost impossible. Moreover, from the middle or end of November to the end of January thunderstorms are of frequent, in fact almost daily, occurrence, generally bursting over the camps about sundown. They are terribly violent, and many strong men grow nervous when they see the lurid, coppery clouds gathering up to windward. Lightning so vivid and thunder so painfully loud I have hardly ever experienced elsewhere, but I am happy to say that fatal accidents are comparatively rare. Most of the diggers place glass bottles on the iron spikes of their tent-poles as a security against the lightning. These thunderstorms are sometimes accompanied by a descent of huge hailstones, sometimes by a deluge of rain.

which causes considerable hindrance to work. The storms are perhaps a little more violent at the river-side diggings, owing to the high hills, the trees, and the masses of ironstone which abound there. Two most terrific thunderstorms burst over the Vaal River on the 12th and 28th of November, 1870; during the latter the lightning struck and shattered the tent-pole of a bell-tent, in which five Kafirs, belonging to Mr. Jardine, were sleeping, all with their heads towards the pole; three of the unfortunate natives were killed instantaneously, and the other two seriously injured. Apart from the hindrance to work caused by the very frequent rains, these constant thunderstorms have a very weakening effect on the nervous system, except in men of very strong constitutions.

True, they cool the air considerably. I took an observation in this respect of a storm which occurred in the daytime. At 11 a.m., previous to the gathering of the storm, the thermometer stood at 100° in my shady room at Jardine's; after the storm, at 2 p.m., the temperature was 70°.

It will easily be understood that, during the summer, very few Europeans feel inclined to engage in the more active operations of picking, shovelling, hauling, breaking, or sifting. It is quite sufficient for them to sit under an awning and sort, leaving the Kaffirs to perform all the other stages of the work. During the worst part of the summer, say December and January, even existence in the camps becomes almost intolerable, and many diggers, especially those who reside in the Cape Colony, leave the diggings and visit their homes for a month or two, whereby unless they leave a partner or other representative to work for them, they lose much money probably, but are infallibly great gainers in health. In autumn the weather begins to be tolerable again, and all hands are back at the Fields resuming work with activity. Of course the great proportion of diggers, impelled by that all-powerful "auri sacra fames," remain through the whole summer at the diggings; but many a strong man has found a grave on the barren "veldt" beneath the solitary black flag that marks our cemetery, or at least had his constitution radically injured thereby. Many again, escape scot-free, and laugh at their more timid or prudent comrades.

After the tempered heats of autumn, comes the really delightful weather of a South African winter. Truly the frosts are frequent and sharp. I have found *thick ice* in my water-buckets outside the tent, and even half the cold tea frozen in my kettle inside, and have looked out to see the whole of the surrounding "veldt" white and glistening with thick hoar frost; but all this only reminds a man of Old England, and bids him take a stiff "night-cap" before he "turns in," and put on plenty of warm blankets. And, soon after the mighty South African sun rises, all is changed—the frost disappears as swiftly as if by magic, and about two hours after sunrise the air is as warm as that of a fair English June day. This is the time when diggers work "with a will," and enjoy their work too—when we gaily handle pick, shovel, or sieve, with light hearts in our breasts and merry songs on our lips. Now and then during the winter there will occur rainstorms, and perhaps two, or at most three, raw, cold, cloudy days in succession; and it can be *very cold* at the diggings, a kind of cold which I have felt more keenly than the hardest frosts in England, and at such times the claims are deserted, and the hotels and canteens crowded. But storms and cold wet weather are rare and not of long duration. and even on such occasions the hardy digger may spend the day profitably if he puts on thick clothing, takes his gun, and wanders over the "veldt," where he is pretty sure of finding game in abundance, and *may* chance upon indications of some new diamondiferous spot. Accounts of one or two of these winter-storms will be found in my diary. Apart from these rare occasions, the sky is almost always cloudless, and the sun powerful; so that even in winter it behoves the digger to wear light head-gear, broad brimmed straw hats, with light muslin "puggerees" being the best wear, and "pith helmets" the next.

As to health, it is generally good at the camps, except in summer. During this summer fever, diarrhœa, and dysentery have been alarmingly prevalent, and I have had my share of them, but I believe they are to be attributed not so much to the heat, or natural atmosphere of the district, as to the scarcity of good water, and the abominable deficiency of all sanitary arrangements. If cleanliness is neglected, amid so large a congregation of people, in a crowded camp, the public health must suffer; but I believe that now, under British rule, both these fertile causes of disease will be removed, and the summer of 1872, will, I trust, be less fatal than that of 1871. The principal ailments of this summer have been a very trying low fever, acute diarrhœa and dysentery, colic, inflammation of the lungs, and a very mild form of scurvy. Some deaths have resulted from intemperance—of which, as may be expected, there is a good deal. Owing to the heat and dryness causing incessant thirst, the temptations held out by the innumerable canteen keepers, and the total absence of all restraint, a young man who drinks is totally lost on the Fields; many a man of good connections, who might have gone home in a year or two in health, and with wealth too, to gladden the hearts of his friends, now lies in a nameless grave, beneath the black flag, having killed himself by hard drinking, which is totally incompatible with this climate. I will here give a few extracts from different papers bearing on the subject of this chapter.

Diamond News, 11*th Nov.* 1871.

DUST STORM.

On Sunday evening week the Du Toit's Pan, De Beer's, and New Rush Camps were maddened by a dust storm from the north-west, which lasted nearly a couple of hours. We have been asked to write an article descriptive of the event, but as we had to shut ourselves up within our small cabin to prevent ourselves from being blown away and to ballast the cabin itself; and, as during the said two hours our eyes, in common with the eyes of all the camps, were blinded with dust, and our ears deafened with the flapping of canvas, and the rush of the wind and the roar of thunder, description is impossible. All we can say from personal observation and experience is, that the dust was the finest, the most searching, the densest, the most pervading, and the most irritating we ever had the bad fortune to see, smell, taste, or feel. It was not only moving about in the air, on the plain, and in the Pan, but it entered into tent, shanty, and store; and, penetrating broadcloth, flannel, and linen, plugged up the pores of the skin, and dried up the very source of life. The dust of the dry diggings is to be classed with plague, pestilence, and famine, and if there is anything worse, with that also.

The wind was very wilful, and did a deal of damage. Half the population in the Fields had to hold on by poles and ropes like grim death during the time the storm lasted. In some cases holding on was of no use. Bell tents went after bell tents by the score, especially at the New Rush and Du Beer's. The Central Hospital tent came miserably to grief, and a canvas house put up for Mr Stockdale, of Du Toit's, was knocked over and smashed. This last-mentioned result of the storm might have been fatal to life, as Mr and Mrs Stockdale were both in the house at the time, and narrowly escaped the falling of wood-work. It was some time before they could extricate themselves from the canvas.

A little rain followed the dust, scarcely enough to make the ground damp.

A correspondent of the above paper, dating "Klip Drift, 3rd Nov., 1871," says:

"We had the first hint on Sunday that we must look out for squalls. At about four o'clock in the afternoon there was a streak of gold over the Colesberg Kopje (an old kopje near Klip-Drift, not the famous New Rush) that the weather-wise of Klip-Drift understood. The streak soon widened, and before the hour hand of the clock had made "five," the sky had changed from blue to orange. The special magistrate said, "It is going to thunder, by Jove, sir!" The chaplain of the Fields, who had arranged for an evening service, put away his sermon-book and surplice with an air of thankfulness that he was as secure from the weather (*not* the service) as the vicarage can make him. Those who watch the thunder of these latitudes with about the same enjoyment as little boys do rockets, must have enjoyed themselves amazingly, for the lightning on this occasion was to ordinary lightning just as "Home, Sweet Home," with variations, is to the original melody. It commenced, as some printers do, with "broadsheets," and ended with "fizzers," and then it recommenced with fizzers, and ended with a fizzer and a crack, which looked like anything but keeping the Sabbath, and sounded like the crack of doom. There was very little rain. The only damage which occurred amongst my acquaintance from this outbreak happened to Mr. Webster (Wm. Hume and Co.) One stroke of the electric fluid knocked off the chimney of Mr. Webster's residence, entered the bedroom, knocked off the plaster, and took a turn round the iron bedstead, leaving its trail behind it everywhere it travelled. Happily nobody was killed and nobody hurt. Mrs. Webster, who has recently arrived on the Fields, was stunned for some little time; but having rushed out of the house into the store, and finding that the whole place was *not* "coming down by the run," she speedily recovered. It is an exceedingly gratifying thing that at Klip Drift comparatively little damage has been done to either person or property by these frightful "squalls." The squall lasted about an hour and a quarter. We must now look out, not for squalls merely, but for storms.

This appears to have been identical with the dust-storm described by the editor of the *Diamond News* at Du Toit's Pan, and of which I have given my impressions in "A Dinner under Difficulties at Mrs. Brown's."

November 8th, the same correspondent writes again:

We had a *storm* on Monday; I presume the first of the season. It was a beauty in every respect. It came and went precisely as all our summer storms do. There was first the leaden hue over the whole firmament; then thick heavy clouds chased each other in every direction, as if the clerk of the weather had lost his register, and was puzzled about what orders to give. After a while there seemed to be some sort of drift in the air, and the wind puffed the clouds round the camp of Campbell towards the hotel of Jardine. Then there is a glare over the hills on the right (Pniel side from our point of view), and down comes a rattling hail, the stones about the size of hazel nuts. That little game played out, we have thunder and lightning, and rain—a good deal too much of the two former; not one half enough of rain.

Cape Argus, November 25th, 1871:

A good deal of fever, colic, and other diseases, is said to be just now very prevalent at the Fields, especially at Du Toit's Pan and De Beer's. Mr. W. Miller, waggonmaker, of Bloemfontein, has returned home, looking exceedingly unwell from the effects of fever. He has, moreover, lost one child, two years old, on the road, at the farm of Mr J. Wessels, and has brought back another very ill. Three strong men died at Du Toit's Pan, within one hundred yards of each other, on Monday morning week. Mr. J. A. Hayselden, of Bloemfontein, likewise returned home quite prostrated with fever, but is now gradually recovering. The doctors at the Fields are, it is said, ordering the sick (especially women and children) to leave without delay. declaring that nothing can be done for them while they remain there. The Rev. Mr. Doxat (Church of England) has had a touch of the fever, but is now, we are glad to say, getting over it. Several who have recently arrived at Bloemfontein from Du Toit's Pan and De Beer's, assert that they left because they latterly felt far from well, and were getting afraid to remain during the summer months.

A letter in the *Natal Mercury*, dated 23rd October, 1871, speaks on sanitary arrangements (*or rather a very minor detail compared with some I could mention*), and speaks mildly of flies, as follows:

A stop should be put to slaughtering in the camps. Sheep and goats are slaughtered alongside the tents, especially by the Boer portion of the community, who seem to have very little regard for cleanliness in the vicinity of their encampments. The offal is allowed either to fester in the sun, or dragged about the camps by packs of half starved cur-dogs. The committees should look into the matter, and impose a heavy penalty on all who persist in slaughtering in the camps. Flies are beginning to become troublesome. It will be remembered that they were a great nuisance about this time last year on the river fields, especially at Pniel, where we poor diggers were so troubled by these abominable little insects that it became necessary to carry a handkerchief to brush them off the exposed parts of the body. I hope we shall not have them in such numbers as they were on the river. I believe the filthy state of the camps will tend to increase them by myriads. Perhaps the next nuisance will be fleas.

The practice of slaughtering small animals close to the tents is certainly objectionable on many grounds, but I cannot corroborate the writer as to the "half-starved curs dragging the offal about the camp." I hardly know any part of a sheep which the Kafirs will not eat. having frequently seen them consume the foulest offal, so that if the *curs* depend on that kind of food, they run a risk of becoming *totally* starved. But as to the flies—they had become. by the time I left the fields, a fearful plague, for they filled the air both outside and inside the tents, and they are far more aggressive and irritating than the European insect. They come at you with a loud threatening buzz, and their contact is excessively irritating. producing almost the sensation of an actual sting. Moreover, they are particularly fond of plunging into the corners of your eyes, and sticking there if you will let them, or into your ears, nose, &c.

It is thought by many that they communicate opthalmia, which is prevalent in many parts of the colony in a mild form, though excessively painful, generally lasting a month. I suffered terribly from this affection of the eyes, which came on after I had pretty nearly got rid of fever and diarrhœa, and had left the dry diggings.

A solution of sulphate of zinc and rose water makes a good lotion for this painful ailment. To return to the flies. During the summer they swarm in the tents, rendering the afternoon *siesta* impracticable, and spoiling every article of food or drink that is left uncovered. I found it almost impossible to keep meat from them, for even if I adopted the precaution of putting it into a large close-lidded tin box directly I bought it, I generally found that one or two of the horrible insects had managed to slip in with it, and the next day the meat would be found fly blown. The flies are of two kinds: a little black fellow, like the common house fly of Europe, and a rather large bright green fellow; the latter the more endurable insect of the two, because he very seldom settles on the person or attacks the face, in which the little black beast is most pertinacious. It is common on summer days to see a large number of diggers going about armed with long tails of different animals, which they constantly flick before their faces. Different kinds of fly traps are in use in the tents, but they are of little avail. You see a number of disgusting corpses it is true, but no apparent decrease in the number of your tormentors. But there is a certain wild satisfaction felt at the death of even a few—indeed, even now, on board the good steamer *Roman*, in mid-ocean, I have such a vivid recollection of the constant misery I suffered from these winged pests, that I am at great pains to kill a fly, if I possibly can, whenever and wherever I see him. The same writer also alludes, interrogatively, to fleas. I can answer him. There are thousands of them by this time (December, 1871). But though they certainly do bite, I esteem them as nothing compared to the filthy flies. When one reflects that there are, outside the camps, hundreds of carcases of cattle which have died of different diseases, in different stages of putrefaction, and that when I left, the public *latrines* were huge open trenches, lying in many cases in the midst of the tents—the horror felt at the contact of a fly can be easily imagined. A writer from Du Toit's Pan, 9th October, says:—

I am sorry to say that the sanitary measures of the camps are as far from completion to-day as they were some time back It is time something was done, for in certain parts of the camps the stench is dreadful—almost sufficient to knock one down. Surely, if this continue, we will be visited by some pestilential disease. Is it not time that the diggers acted for themselves, instead of leaving it to a Free State Government official, who makes all sorts of excuses.

Well, let us hope that long ere this is in print the British

Sanitary Inspectors will have taken vigorous measures to put all these matters to rights, for in truth it was sadly needed.

Here is another writer, a Natalian, who had just arrived on the Fields early in October. He writes from the Colesberg Kopje:—

As regards sanitary matters, but very little indeed has been done; the consequence is, that with a population of so many thousands, all congregated on a small space of ground, the atmosphere is completely polluted, and unless some steps are taken to remedy this evil, I much fear that the summer will bring a great deal of sickness. Already the weather is getting very warm at mid-day, and the flies are very troublesome; this, I take it, arises from the number of dead cattle, and the filth that surrounds the camp, and should sound a warning note. The work is very laborious, and trying to white men, and now that the hot season is setting in, I have no doubt many will be obliged to give in. The dust from thousands of sieves, combined with the heat and glare of the white soil, is extremely trying, and brings on with persons inflammation of the lungs; indeed, the larger number of deaths that have taken place—if we leave out of the question those who have died from the effects of intemperance—have been caused by inflammation of the lungs.

I am not at all sure that this writer is correct on this last point. During my six months' residence there I heard very little of inflammation of the lungs, but much of fever, diarrhœa, and dysentery. Quinine and Collis Browne's Chlorodyne are good medicines to take up. It is an unfortunate thing with regard to the camp fever, that even when the fever appears to have left the patient, he does not regain the least strength as long as he remains in the vicinity of the camp. It seems to be a kind of malaria. Nothing but removal to a distance, and thorough change of air, can promote restoration to health. There are plenty of doctors on the Fields. I cannot lay down better rules for general health than that a man should live soberly, have abundance of good food, plenty of good vegetables, no matter what he pays for them, and good water at any price; and choose a clean, healthy, open spot, far from any latrine or slaughtering-ground, for pitching his tent.

Re weather. Here is another extract from my favourite *Natal Mercury:*—

The weather continues dry, hot, and uncomfortable. Rain has occurred on two occasions during the week. A constant gale of wind is blowing, and this, with the sun, is most trying to the eyes. Clouds of dust extend, occasionally, for miles, and the incessant whirlwinds cause a great deal of annoyance.

Ah, by the way, I forgot to mention the whirlwinds, which used to cause me more amusement than annoyance. I never saw one on a very large scale, but was constantly gratified by the sight of a tall revolving column of dust, pursuing a most erratic course through the claims or through the camp, growing bigger as it advanced, and snatching up every moderately light article that came in its way. Thus hats, papers, sheepskins, &c., &c., would be seized, and would go comically gyrating to the top of a column, while the owners had to run a long way before they recovered them, to the great amusement of all the diggers near. But if the open door (?) of a tent stood in the way of one of these "young whirlwinds," and it got in, it would play "old gooseberry" with the tent and contents, with a vengeance.

A chapter treating of health at the diggings would be incomplete without some notice of the very unpleasant sores to which we diggers are liable. We frequently find that the slightest scratch, on the hand especially, will fester, and become an open, discharging sore, which often prevents a man from using his hand, and takes several weeks to heal. I have heard these sores attributed to lime dust getting into any scratch or cut; but this is not an adequate explanation, for I have frequently known —even in my own case—these sores to come spontaneously in places where the skin was perfectly sound. I have had them often, and sometimes many at a time, always on the hands, and have known innumerable other diggers who suffered in the same manner. They can be treated either with carbolic ointment, after the discharge has ceased, or with frequent applications of cold water, or even left entirely alone, and I found that they got well just as quickly if I took no notice of them whatever. But I think they must be attributed to an impure state of the blood, being in fact, a mild form of scurvy; and I think a good course of sarsaparilla or some similar blood-purifying agent, might either prevent their occurrence, if taken in time, or at any rate expedite their healing. Not having visited the colony of Natal, I am not aware if these are the same as "Natal sores," which appear to be very frequent there, and for which certain infallible specifics are advertised in the Natal papers. It might be worth while to give the famous Holloway's Ointment a trial on these diggers' sores. I have heard of some cures being effected by it. There is a certain large bulb found on the Fields, the thin skin of which is considered very efficacious in healing all kinds of cuts, wounds, and sores, and it is certainly a useful thing to have by one, and costs nothing. Any old digger will describe the bulb or root to a "new chum," or give him a piece.

CHAPTER VI.

SPORT IN THE NEIGHBOURHOOD OF THE FIELDS.

VERY fair sport, both with shot-gun and rifle, may be had in the immediate neighbourhood of the different camps. About two and a half miles from Du Toit's Pan, to the left of the Boshof road, lies a large tract of scrub, with here and there a stunted thornbush, which abounds with game, especially the "knorhaan" (*Otis afra*) a small species of bustard. This bird, which generally rises at a longish range, is best brought down by a shot from directly behind him, *i.e.*, when flying straight away from the sportsman, being less easily killed when crossing. The harsh cry of this bird soon becomes familiar, and the practised eye will often detect the black and white head of the cock, or the smaller grey head of the hen, raised a little above the thick scrub. In this case, it is well worth while to try a little careful stalking, if the ground affords any cover at all, by which means the birds, hens especially, may often be approached within quite short ranges. The birds will frequently lie very close, especially in stormy weather, and will not rise unless the sportsman come within a few yards of them, but they unquestionably afford the best sport to him who sees them at a distance, and goes in for a persevering stalk. They afford excellent eating, when kept for a few days. I think they slightly resemble in size and plumage our black cocks and grey hens.

On this same tract of ground there are a good many grey partridges, very like our English bird, and a good sprinkling of hares, rather small, long-legged, and wonderful runners; but as they seldom get up until you almost walk over them their agility rarely suffices to save their lives. Besides these there are numerous red-legged plovers, handsome birds of black, white, and grey plumage—small bodies, but very fair eating.

In numerous parts of the "veldt" may be seen a lot of little holes in the limy, sandy soil, a little larger than rat holes. These are generally found twenty to forty together, and are the entrances to the abodes of the "meerkat," a small feline animal, something like a weasel, with a nice furry coat—which makes very pretty tobacco-pouches—and fine bushy tails. The meerkat may often be seen scampering over the "veldt" at a great pace, and, if followed, will be traced to one of these colonies. and will dart into one of the holes before you can get within range ; but if you lie down at about twenty-five yards from the colony, and wait patiently, perfectly still, in a quarter of an hour or so you will see first a knowing little head, then a pretty furry breast, and lastly perhaps the whole animal, emerge from one after another of the holes. At the slightest movement you make, they are in again ; and though by waiting some time you may get a shot, your victim, even if killed outright, will probably tumble back into its hole again. Still, by dint of great patience, and only shooting such animals as are seen to have come well away from their holes, a couple of skins may be secured in a morning. It is lazy work, and reminds one of angling, as it may be called " a contemplative man's recreation." So much for meerkat shooting.

Larger holes are frequently found, which are the dwellings of the porcupine, and still larger ones of the jackal. and the great Cape ant-eater, but these animals are rarely seen, except at night-time. It is not uncommon, indeed. in walking over the "veldt," to come upon the carcase of a porcupine which has been killed by the camp-dogs, and quills of all sizes are very frequently to be found.

The slaughtering-grounds in the neighbourhood of the camps naturally attract large numbers of the different species of vultures, some of them very large. and some possessing handsome plumage ; it may amuse the digger who has not time to go far, to try a long shot at some of these ravenous birds with his rifle, or to try to stalk them to within buck-shot range. Carrion crows are numerous, with a broad white ring round their necks. I must not forget to mention the "paanw," or Cape bustard, a fine large bird, the size of a turkey, with very strong wings, handsome plumage, and excellent eating. Though frequently seen flying high over our camps, they are not often found on the "veldt" in the immediate neighbourhood ; but there are great numbers of these magnificent birds near the banks of the Modder River, and doubtless of the Vaal also. They can be approached without difficulty to easy rifle range, and sometimes, by careful stalking, or by riding round them on horseback, in gradually narrowing circles, within shot range. Hawks, and other large birds of prey, also abound. By going farther from the camp, past the hills on the Boshof Road, the hunter. if he has a good horse to carry him, or if he can spare time to get away for a few days with a waggon or cart, may get good sport with the rifle among those graceful antelopes, the springbok and the larger blesbok, individuals of both which, with occasional flocks, I have sometimes seen close to Du Toit's Pan. One or two "vleis," *i.e.*, water-holes, or "pans" filled with water in the winter-time, may be found in the neighbourhood of the camps, and near these, especially towards evening, you will frequently get shots at Kafir cranes; singly or in flocks. These are magnificent large birds, of most graceful proportions, and beautiful bluish-grey plumage; they are also fair eating. I think the scientific name of this beautiful bird is *Anthropoides Stanleyana*. Within two days' journey of the camps (by bullock waggon, *i.e.*, thirty to forty miles) may be found abundance of different antelopes, and even the big, diabolical-looking wildebeest, some of which we saw down by the Modder River.

Immense quantities of "bucks," as all the antelopes are called, are daily, during the winter especially, which is the proper shooting season, brought on the Du Toit's Pan market, and sold at very moderate prices, owing to their abundance. I have seen a large waggon loaded with springbok and blesbok, with a couple of wildebeest; I should think five or six dozen animals altogether, all of which had been killed in one day by two guns, only two days' waggon journey from the camp. From De Beer's and the Colesberg Kopje, very pleasant and successful shooting excursions may also be made; and some of the aristocratic diggers of those camps see no harm (nor do I) in turning out with horses and dogs on Sunday, and organising a "chasse" on a large scale, the result of which is that many a buck, hare, bustard and partridge may next day be seen hanging among the legs of mutton and pieces of beef, on the big *mimosas* outside their tents, which form their winter larders. Along the wooded banks of the beautiful Vaal may be found abundance of guinea-fowl, wild ducks, occasionally wild geese, and plenty of smaller game. The sport to be obtained on the Modder River, about the same distance from the "dry diggings" as the Vaal, I have described in a chapter entitled "A Diamond Digger's Holiday." Leopards are occasionally seen on the banks of both these rivers. Anyone really fond of hunting should not think of leaving South Africa without getting a few months' thorough enjoyment in the shape of big game shooting in the interior, which can be easily managed by arranging to accompany one of the regular hunters and traders, who go up with blankets, powder, and other commodities much prized by the native tribes, and return with skins. ostrich feathers. and ivory, frequently realising several thousands of pounds by one trip. Some of these traders, who are very well known men. and can easily be heard of. pass through the Diamond Fields on their way; others go by a different route, starting from Natal.

The "new chum" must beware of letting his love for sport draw him away too long or too often from attending to his claim or other business at the fields ; but a little change of air and good healthy exercise occasionally, is highly beneficial. especially when it involves facilities of bathing in cool. running water. With regard to weapons, it is not absolutely necessary to bring out any, as plenty can be bought at fair prices on the Fields. But for anyone who intends to shoot much. I would recommend a Henry Express Rifle, and a good strong 12-bore muzzle loading smooth bore. In the event of wishing to realise money on weapons, I may mention that I have seen a great many sold by auction ; and that while a rifle, or double-barrel rifle and smoothbore will always fetch a fair price, yet a smooth-bore *only* is not much esteemed, because the sportsmen "up country" only go in for large game, and hold "small deer," either furred or feathered, in contempt. About 5*l.* or 6*l.* is the price a double-barrel smooth-bore will fetch by auction, apparently almost irrespective of quality or maker's name.

There is plenty of good fishing to be obtained on both Vaal and Modder, of which I treat fully elsewhere. I have heard of wild ostriches being found only a few days' journey from the Vaal, on authority, however, of which I will not vouch for the veracity. On my way down from Pniel to Cape Town, I saw a large number of tame ones on the farm of a gentleman named Devenish, not far from Victoria West.

CHAPTER VII.

OUTFIT AND WORKING EXPENSES.

With regard to outfit for the Diamond Fields, under which heading we may comprise tent, bedding, cooking utensils, digging tools, weapons, and clothing, it appears to be by no means certain that any great advantage is gained, or any great saving of money effected, by bringing these things out from England. Owing to the increasing competition among storekeepers on the fields, and the frequency of persons leaving, and consequent large bi-weekly auction sales of these and all other necessaries, everything may be obtained at fairly moderate prices. Moreover, if the intending digger studies my account of the different routes, he will probably decide in favour of the quickest and cheapest, *i.e.*, by Inland Transport Company's waggon from Cape Town, in which case he will only be allowed 40lb. of luggage, and can consequently hardly bring out more than a change of clothing.

Any who may decide upon travelling up the country by bullock waggon for the sake of the sport to be obtained on the road, may judge for themselves of the advantage to be gained by bringing their outfit from England, and see if it is worth the extra trouble, by reading the following statement of average prices on the Fields in October, 1871.

A "square" tent (this is really oblong, but is the regular term in opposition to bell tents, which are not advisable) suitable for one or two persons, say 10ft. long by 7ft. wide, will cost new 8*l.* or 9*l.*; larger sizes rather cheaper in proportion. This price should include tentpoles, pegs, and lines. I got a good straw mattress made for 1*l.*; woollen blankets are about 15*s.*; cotton ditto about 5*s.* each. Cooking utensils may be bought pretty cheaply at the diggings, but for anyone going up by waggon I can confidently recommend, from experience, one of Silver and Co.'s *canteens*, costing about two guineas, and containing in a very portable form every requisite for plain cooking and eating for two persons, suitable both for the road and for the tent. With regard to diggers' tools, they had better be bought on the

Fields, as otherwise the novice might waste his money on unsuitable articles. They are, first, the fine sieve, fine but strong wire meshing, in a strong frame, costing 1*l*. 10*s*. to 2*l*. 5*s*. new; second, the coarse sieve, large mesh in a small square frame, costing 10*s*. to 15*s*.; third, pick and shovel, about 7*s*. 6*d*. to 9*s*. each; fourth, a crowbar, about 2*s*. 6*d*.; fifth, two or three galvanised iron buckets, indeed half a dozen is not too many, they being so useful not only in hauling up stuff out of the claims, and drawing water, but also in fetching home small lots of vegetables, &c., from market and many other purposes, including the collecting of dry bullock dung for fuel. These buckets cost on the Fields about 6*s*. 6*d*. each. Some rope or one or two good strong rheims will also be required. Rope is very dear just now. Rheims about 2*s*. 6*d*. each in stores, but can be bought much cheaper in the market. Clothing, made expressly for the diggings, canvas and corduroy suits, &c., can be bought at moderate prices in the stores, and still more cheaply at the auction sales. The hire of Kaffirs will probably cost 30*s*. per man per month, their food (mealie meal) about 15*s*. to 20*s*. per month more, with a bit of coarse meat once a week, some Boer tobacco, and a Saturday night's "tot" of "Cape smoke," which may be put down altogether at 1*s*. 6*d*. per head per week.

The digger, if he wishes to live economically, must do all his own cooking, marketing, and washing. A plain cookery book will be of much assistance to him in the former department. With regard to marketing, he should attend the morning market (7 a.m.) pretty often, taking a Kafir with him with a wheelbarrow or a sack; he will soon get *au fait* at the prices, and will only buy when he can buy cheaply. As to washing, hear what those who are too proud or too lazy to do their own say about the expense of having their washing "put out":—"Since I have been here I have only been able to get one sack of clothes washed, the Koranna and half-caste women are too lazy to work, and get their money more easily. They ask 10*s*. to wash a small sack, and it costs about 10*s*. more for water in addition to soap, so that cleanliness is a most expensive luxury."

I always found that, with care, I could wash all I had dirtied during the week with half a bucketful of hot water and a little soap. I did not, perhaps, produce results which would have satisfied the critical eye of a British housekeeper, but it was sufficient for purposes of cleanliness. The "freshman" will also, as

I had to do, soon learn the art of taking a thorough bath—or, at any rate, total ablution—on Sundays in half a bucketful of water. With regard to the price of this great essential to health and comfort, I paid, at Du Toit's Pan, at Clarke's or the Royal Engineer's Well, which contains the best water in the place. 4s. per month water-rate, for which I was entitled to draw four buckets of water daily. But at Colesberg Kopje I never paid less than 3d. per bucket, there being no monthly rate, though I believe wholesale buyers, as hotel keepers, &c., could get water at 10s. per hogshead—in their own casks, of course.

I need not here enumerate the prices of food of various kinds, which will be given in another chapter, but I will look over the housekeeping accounts which I kept for myself and partner, and shall thus be able to give a very fair approximate estimate of monthly expenditure. Details of expenses on the voyage and journey out will be found elsewhere, but I will put down first-class expenses from London to Du Toit's Pan at 65l., which is ample. I will then give the following reliable statement, showing on what capital two men may be able to work for six months, by the end of which time it is hard lines indeed if they have not found something to keep expenses going for some time longer :—

Preliminary Expenses.

Voyage out (first-class) and journey to diggings by Inland Transport Company (9 days), including everything, with a moderate allowance of drinkables, 65l. each	£130	0	0
Tent	9	0	0
Bedding, say 1 mattress, 1 woollen blanket, and 2 cotton ones, each person	5	0	0
Tools, say 1 fine sieve, 1 coarse ditto, 1 pick, 2 shovels, 1 crowbar, 6 buckets	6	9	0
Cooking and eating utensils, including an iron cooking pot for the Kafirs, at outside	3	0	0
Planks, to make sorting-table, skirting-board for tent, &c.	2	0	0
Light clothing, and sundries	5	0	0
Total	£160	9	0

Monthly Expenses.

Claim licence	0	10	0
Four Kafirs at 30s. per month	6	0	0
Food for Kafirs	4	4	0
Food and general expenses of partners, at 3l. 3s. per month each	6	6	0
Water, say 3 buckets per day at 3d. per bucket	1	2	6
Total	£18	2	6

Six months at the above rate £108 15 0
Add preliminary expenses 160 9 0

                                  Total..................... £269 4 0

Thus we arrive at, say 270*l*., as the sum necessary to enable two persons to make a very fair start at the diamond diggings, or 135*l*. each. One man alone will spend rather more in proportion. To arrive at the above estimate correctly and at the same time liberally, I have taken the average of three months' total expenses of myself and partner, including hotel expenses on many occasions when we were washed out of our tents for a day or two by heavy rains (which will not happen to my readers if they follow my directions), and including also Cape brandy, occasional beers and other liquors, candles, firewood, and small incidental expenses. I have not included purchase money for a claim; if the new comers commence at Bultfontein they may "jump" a claim for nothing, as before explained. At Du Toit's Pan a good claim should not cost more than 10*l*. or 20*l*., at De Beer's (Old Rush) 20*l*. to 100*l*. according to position, at the Colesberg Kopje (De Beer's New Rush) a quarter of a claim in first-rate position, 250*l*. to 1000*l*.: but all these prices may be very much modified by the time any of the readers of this book reach the diggings, and it may fairly be expected that by that time, many good new camps will be opened. I need hardly say that it will certainly be advantageous to a man of energy and "cuteness" to take out much more money than the sum above mentioned, there being, besides the certain investments in a claim known to be good, many other ways of making money at the fields, which I shall point out in a special chapter. Should the emigrant decide on trying his luck first at the river diggings, to which he may be influenced either by good new diggings which may have been discovered on the Vaal or elsewhere, by the time he arrives, or by the consideration of greater security to health if he arrives during the hot season; then he should add to the above mentioned preliminary expenses that of a strong Scotch cart and four oxen, or two good mules would do:

Scotch cart (second-hand), say £15
Two mules, or four oxen, about 30

                              Total................ .... £45

and the food of the animals will form a considerable monthly item, varying so much according to the part of the diggings to be worked at, that I will not attempt to put it down. But it must be borne in mind that either on the riverside or at the dry diggings, considerable profit may be derived from letting out cart and mules, or oxen, for carting off stuff, transport of goods from one camp to another, and many other purposes; moreover there is a constant demand for carts and cattle, and if kept in good condition they are sure to sell at good prices, and may be considered, on the whole, as a profitable investment. I have spoken elsewhere on the prices of firearms on the fields, but should anyone decide on going in for a good deal of sport, and have a predilection for breech-loading weapons, which have unquestionably many great advantages, let him by no means forget to bring out an abundant supply of ammunition or cartridge cases, which he will hardly be likely to obtain on the fields. A pair of good diamond-scales will be a useful article to bring up, also a good test-case, especially for anyone who thinks of going after gold, of which it is likely that many new discoveries may shortly be made. Some specks of gold-dust have been discovered on the Vaal River, but it does not as yet appear to exist there in paying quantities.

CHAPTER VIII.

PROFESSIONS, TRADES, AND OTHER WAYS OF MAKING MONEY AT THE FIELDS.

WITH regard to the different professions and callings, the exercise of which will be found profitable on the Fields: I will now proceed to enumerate the principal of such avocations, leaving aside diamond-diggers, buyers, and brokers, hotel-keepers, storekeepers, and auctioneers, all of whom find full mention elsewhere.

And first let me treat of the medical profession, whose services we poor diggers so often stand in need of, during the summer especially. There are at present on the Fields many *soi-disant* "doctors," few of whom, I fear, could show a diploma, and I do not know of many in whom I should place confidence if attacked by a serious illness. Therefore, there is certainly a good opening for energetic and talented young members of the medical profession, and diggers would be very willing to pay a high fee for consultations, and a high price for medicines to a man in whom they could have confidence. There are certainly one or two such, but there is plenty of room for more. The medical man on the Fields need not confine himself to the exercise of his profession. He can, and probably will, take out a claim, and spend a good deal of his time at the sorting-table. He can either have the sorting-table close to his tent, or if he sorts on his claim, his tent should be pitched not very far from the latter, and he can have a particular flag flying on his claim with a notice to patients as follows : "Apply at claim No. 10, marked by a red flag."

A doctor, too, may often get a good berth as sanitary inspector of one of the camps, with fair pay and light duties. A pleasant change truly, for a young doctor, from his gloomy consulting-room in the neighbourhood of Cavendish-square, to a seat by a shaded sorting-table, close to a well-pitched tent on the banks of the Vaal, where, whilst waiting for the patients who will be sure to come, he may sort a variegated, glittering heap of fresh-washed pebbles, and turn out a diamond now and then. At the dry diggings our practitioner will probably make more money in both ways, but will not find life so comfortable there. When he gets into good practice, however, the monotony of existence will often be necessarily varied by a ride on a good horse from one camp to another, for the fame of a good doctor will soon spread amongst the digging population.

Next in order I will take the lawyers. We diggers are a peaceable set of men as a rule, and by no means litigious, yet awkward disputes, beyond the power of a digger's committee to decide, *will* occur sometimes, and "gentlemen of the long robe" will find occasional profitable employment. There are several magistrate's courts at the different camps, and though I hardly think that a man would make enough by law alone to enable him to witness, with equanimity and without envy, the daily finds of lucky diggers; yet, by getting all the legal practice that comes in his way, he may make a very desirable addition to his income, and should, in fact, more than pay his *working expenses*, if, as is almost certain, he, like everybody else, works a claim, or has one worked for him.

I don't know whether it will be necessary for the barrister to bring out his wig and gown with him. During my residence at the Fields, the practitioners in the Free State courts did not wear them; but perhaps the British authorities may be greater sticklers for these imposing adjuncts.

Engineers and land-surveyors will find frequent employment, at good remuneration; the latter especially, if qualified, standing a good chance of securing lucrative appointments as surveyors to the different camps.

Carpenters are particularly well paid, and realise large sums of money, both by erecting wooden houses, doing different kinds of woodwork in hotels and stores, and by making sieves, for which there is a constant demand at high prices, so that a good carpenter can easily realise from £1 to £3 per day, if he is active. He can both make sieves to order, charging his own price, and can put two or three sieves, if he finds time to make them, on the public auction sales, where a new well-made article in this line never goes very cheap.

Tent-makers also, of whom there are but few on the Fields at present, do an excellent trade.

Blacksmiths, too, will find constant employment in repairing waggons and carts, and in many other ways.

One or two butchers are already making fortunes by that trade alone, the amount of meat daily consumed being enormous. A butcher with a little capital has frequent opportunities of buying flocks of sheep and cattle very cheap, so that they realise a splendid profit. selling at the uniform rate of 4*d*. per lb., 5*d*. for the prime cuts.

Bakers and confectioners are in great demand. At one little tent in Du Toit's Pan may constantly be seen a crowd of diggers, demolishing small mutton-pies, fruit tarts, buns, and various small articles of indigestible pastry by the dozen, undeterred by the enormous prices, washing them down with repeated draughts of home-made ginger-beer. This same baker also makes a very good thing of it by sending a boy with cakes, tarts, and ginger-beer amongst the crowds which attend the Saturday afternoon auctions; and it is amusing to see the avidity with which rough-bearded diggers, perhaps with thousands of pounds' worth of diamonds in their belts, and stolid old Dutch Boers, consume these juvenile dainties. The wives of many of the poorer diggers, especially of the Dutchmen, industriously keep the expenses going by making bread, cakes, pies, and dubious-looking sweetmeats, baskets and trays of which are carried round the claims. Many a digger pauses in his sorting to buy a shilling's-worth of cakes or sweetmeats, brought round by some small nigger, or still more tiny Dutch boy or girl, or to take a bottle of home-brewed ginger-beer from a basket carried by a grinning Kafir.

Men—and women too—who can turn their hands to a little of everything, are sure to do well at the Fields. I have known amateurs do very well at making sieves and wheelbarrows, the latter being also in great demand, and selling at four guineas each. Then there is the sinking of wells, for which the committee can afford to pay very handsomely indeed—all diamonds found in sinking to be the property of the man who does the job.

Some diggers, after working a part of their claim to a good depth, have persevered till they came to good water, then turned that part of the claim into a well, boarded it over, and either sold the water by the bucketful or let it out to subscribers. A private well, with a good supply of water, will easily find a hundred or two hundred subscribers at four or five shillings each per month, or perhaps double that amount. Then there is the making of dams and other work connected with the sanitary arrangements of the camp, simple, easy pick and shovel work, and all *well* paid, for no one will work cheap at the diggings.

Again, one or two men with good voices and a little wit and humour, may easily get up some kind of entertainment, or amateur theatricals; and our diggers are always ready to throng to anything in the nature of amusement. I have seen what would be in England something like the programme of an ordinary "Penny Reading," one or two songs, a reading from Dickens, and a half-impromptu stump-speech, fill a large room with a well-pleased audience at 2s. 6d. and 4s. These sort of things are easily got up, and will always pay.

Many of these ways of making money may be looked upon with distaste by many of my readers, but I am simply endeavouring to show that what the Yankees term "a smart man" with some "notions" about him, even if not successful in digging, will have no difficulty in "keeping the pot boiling." And I can affirm, too, that there is no false pride at the diggings, no man is thought the worse for *any* honest avocation he may pursue, and that, as long as he *is* honest and steady, "one man is just as good as another, and very likely better."

There are a couple of photographers on the Fields, but there is room for more. Dentists, watchmakers, jewellers, two hairdressers, and a somewhat strange item for the last—Du Toit's Pan is fortunate in the possession of a matrimonial agent!

CHAPTER IX.

ANNEXATION OF THE FIELDS.

HERE is good news for the British digger. The diamond fields are annexed, have become British territory, and the reign of the Boer is over. This has been foreseen for some time past, and charitable people have said that the lamentably inefficient state of postal, sanitary, and other arrangements under Free State rule was mainly attributable to the fact that President Brand and his subordinates knew that the day was at hand when the long-pending territorial dispute between the Free State authorities and the Griqua Chief, Nicholas Waterboer, should be definitely settled by the British Government nominally pronouncing in favour of Waterboer's claim to the territory in which the diamond fields are situated, but virtually annexing that valuable territory to the British possessions in South Africa, already so large and important. So the poor Free State officials, knowing their tenure of office to be short, naturally took but little pains to "keep things square," and much grumbling was heard amongst British diggers. But now what do we expect? Increased taxation, which every right-thinking digger will be most willing to submit to, for it will bring a corresponding increase in the efficiency of police, postal and sanitary regulations in the different camps, the latter being of the most vital importance.

A number of proclamations were issued from Cape Town by Sir Henry Barkly, Governor of the Cape Colony, on the 27th October last, and came into force on the Diamond Fields about a week afterwards.

The first proclamation declares Captain Nicholas Waterboer, chief of the Griquas, and his people, to be British subjects; and that his territory shall be considered British territory, and become part of the Cape Colony. This document also takes the award of his Excellency, R. W. Keate, Esq., Lieutenant-Governor of Natal, as the basis of the boundaries of the newly acquired territory, to be called West Griqualand. The annexation is based on the continued refusal of the Orange Free State to submit the territorial disputes between it and the Chief Waterboer "to any reasonable settlement."

The second of Sir Henry Barkly's proclamations appoints Courts of Justice for the Diamond Fields, and gives full regulations for the conduct of such Courts, and qualifications necessary for advocates, barristers, or attorneys to practice therein.

The third proclamation issues the different regulations under which the control and working of the Diamond Fields is in future to be conducted, stating the necessary officials, system of registering and transferring claims, and discretionary powers given to Government Inspectors. It goes on to make an alteration in the old rate of licensing, which I conceive to be of sufficient importance to be given *in extenso*. "The license money, royalty, or rent, payable in respect of such claim (the old measurement of thirty square feet) shall be, where the same shall not be worked by more than three persons, five shillings per month. Where the same shall not be worked by more than six persons, ten shillings per month. For every additional hand or person employed two shillings per month. Hands or persons shall be deemed to be employed in working a claim who shall be engaged in digging, picking, or shovelling with any implement, or drawing or carrying on any vehicle and by any means the soil, gravel, or rock raised from the claim."

A fourth proclamation declares that the laws and usages of the Cape Colony shall be deemed to be the laws of the new territory, so far as they are not inapplicable thereto; the laws relating to the sale of wines, &c., shall be the same as the laws of the Colony relating to the same matters; and all stamp and license duties payable in the Colony shall be payable likewise in the new territory; and all stamps of the Colony shall be deemed to be stamps for the said territory, and to be valid therein.

A fifth proclamation divides the Diamond Fields into three magistracies—Klip Drift, Pniel, and Griqua-town, establishes Courts of Magistracy within each district, and declares the said districts to be subject to the said courts from the 27th day of October.

A sixth proclamation assures all holders of land titles in the annexed district that their titles will be respected and their rights secured. Landholders are instructed to send in particulars of their claims to the Civil Commissioner of their district.

Then follows Mr Keate's award, which lays down the boundaries of the new territory of West Griqualand, and takes in nearly all the existing Diamond Fields. The following is the plan of the three above-named districts;

District of Klip Drift.

A line commencing at the junction of the Vaal and Steinkopf Rivers, following the course of the Vaal River to where it meets the boundary line defined by Proclamation No. 67 of this date, as running "from the summit of the Platberg in a straight line in a north-westerly direction, along the north-east of Roeloff's Fontein and cutting the Vaal and Hart Rivers to a point north of Boetsap; from the point where it meets the last-mentioned boundary line, along that boundary line to the said point north of Boetsap; thence along the straight line defined by said Proclamation as running in a westerly direction between Nelsonsfontein and Koning, and further in a south-westerly direction along a line passing south of Marimani and north of Klipfontein to a point in it where the shortest line from the principal or north-western source of the Steinkopf River meets it; thence to the said north-western source of the Steinkopf River, following its course to its junction with the Vaal River.

District of Pniel.

A line commencing at the junction of the Vaal River and Modder or Riet River, and following the course of the Vaal River to where it meets the boundary line defined by Proclamation No. 67 of this date as running "from the summit of the Platberg, in a straight line in a north-westerly direction along the north-east of Roeloff's Fontein, and cutting the Vaal and Hart Rivers, to a point North of Boetsap;" from the point where it meets the last-mentioned boundary in a straight line in a north-easterly direction to the summit of the Platberg; thence in a southerly direction in a straight line cutting the northern branch of the Modder or Riet River to David's Graf: thence to a point in the southern branch of the Riet or Modder River intersected by the boundary line from David's Graf to Ramah, from the said point in the southern branch of the Modder or Riet River, following the said river's course to its junction with the Vaal River.

District of Griqua Town.

A line commencing at the junction of the Vaal River and Modder or Riet River, and following the course of the Vaal River to its junction with the Steinkopf River; along the Steinkopf River to its point where such line meets the line mentioned above as the boundary of the district of Klip Drift, viz.: that running in a south-westerly direction along a line passing south of Marimani and north of Klipfontein, thence along the said line last mentioned to the northerly point of the Langeberg; thence in a straight line in a southerly direction to Kheis, near the Orange River; thence by the shortest line to the said Orange River, thence along the course of the said Orange River to the point on the same nearest to Ramah, thence to Ramah, and thence in a northerly direction to the point on the southern branch of the Modder or Riet River, mentioned in the definition of the district of Pniel, thence following the course of the said Modder or Riet River to its junction with the Vaal aforesaid.

President Brand, of the Orange Free State, issued, on the 7th Nov., a counter-proclamation, or rather a protest against the British annexation. It is not very long, and is worthy of attention. Here it is:

Whereas I, Johannes Hendricus Brand, President of the Orange Free

State, have received a copy of a Proclamation from his Excellency the Governor of the Cape Colony, dated —— day of ———, 1871, by which Captain Waterboer and his people are proclaimed British subjects, and a large portion of the territory, which has for many years been under the jurisdiction of the government and law courts of this state, and in the quiet and peaceful possession of its burghers, British territory, against which the government of the Orange Free State protested to his Excellency the Governor of the Cape Colony; and

Whereas I, this morning, received information from the Landdrost of Pniel, Mr. O. J. Truter, that Inspector Gilfillan, with fifteen men of the Colonial Frontier Armed Mounted Police, have moved on to Du Toit's Pan, and with twenty men of the said Frontier Force of the Cape Colony on to Vooruitzigt, within the territory of the Orange Free State, and are stationed there now, against which the Landdrost of Pniel beforementioned formally and solemnly protested to the said Inspector Gilfillan, as also against the exercise of any authority by him, or any person in the name of the Government of the Cape Colony; and

Whereas I, on the receipt of the letter of his Excellency the Governor, dated the 23rd October, protested on the 2nd inst., on behalf of this Government, as a violation of Art. 2 of the Convention of the 23rd February, 1854, and an encroachment upon the rights and territory of the Orange Free State,

I therefore herewith protest against the entrance of the above mentioned armed force of the Government of the Cape Colony on the territory of the Orange Free State as a violation of its territory, and as an hostile invasion in time of perfect peace which has hitherto existed between the Cape Colony and the Orange Free State, and against the exercise of any authority by or on behalf of the Government of the Cape Colony, on or over the before mentioned farms, or on any diggings or places situated within the territory of the Orange Free State; and

Whereas I am desirous of preventing any collision between the Governments and peoples of the Cape Colony and this State, who are allied to each other by the strongest ties of blood and friendship, therefore I hereby order and enjoin all officers, burghers, and residents of this state, to guard against any action which may lead to such collision, in the fullest confidence that the informations and explanations which will be given to Her Britannic Majesty's Government in England by our plenipotentiary, will secure the acknowledgment and recognition of our just rights.

Given under my hand and the Great Seal of the Orange Free State, this seventh day of November, 1871.

An Englishman, lately arrived on the Fields, asked a colonist why this proclamation resembled the month of March. The colonist "gave it up." "Because it comes in like a lion and goes out like a lamb," was the reply; but still the colonial gentleman "did not see it." His apparent obtuseness is easily accounted for by the fact that the March to which men are accustomed in the colony is a mild, quiet, autumn month

The following appointments were gazetted, and notified in the *Diamond News* of 4th Nov.: John Campbell, J. H. Bowker, and J. C. Thompson, Commissioners; J. D. Barry, Recorder; J. C.

Thompson, Public Prosecutor; A. Tweed, Registrar and Master;
P. J. Buyskes, Sheriff; J. Campbell, Civil Commissioner and
Resident Magistrate at Klip Drift; Francis Orpen, Civil Commissioner and Resident Magistrate at Griqua Town. Many other
appointments have been made since that date.

There was naturally a good deal of grumbling and muttering
among our friends the Boers when it became generally known
that annexation was decided upon, but the proclamations were
received at the different camps most peacefully, and not the
slightest resistance is expected from the burghers of the Free
State.

The only overt protest against British rule on the Fields is
said to have been made by a certain American digger, residing at
Du Toit's Pan, who deliberately, and in broad daylight, hauled
down the British flag hoisted in that camp. I only just received
news of this prior to my departure from the country, but I have
every reason for believing that the " flag which braved a thousand
years" still waves there. I subjoin a slight account of the
ceremonies at Du Toit's Pan.

Hoisting the British Flag at the Fields.

This ceremony has been performed at the various camps with much *éclat*
and great rejoicing. There was not an obstacle raised, nor the slightest
opposition shown; but, on the contrary, the diggers, as a body, seemed
delighted with the change. Du Toit's Pan, which we have been led to
believe all along had such strong Free State proclivities, was the most
enthusiastic in its reception of the commissioners. There were Chinese
crackers, cheers, and a dinner, and a ball. In the address of welcome the
following paragraph occurs:—" That under that flag we shall prosper, that
our lives and liberties will be protected, and that a wide and rich country
will now be opened up to the surplus population of the United Kingdom,
under the protection of the majority, we doubt not, and so long as British
subjects know that the English flag is that under which they work and live, so
long will there be no lack of energy and determination to help you, gentlemen,
or your successors, in the arduous duties your high position now demands of
you for the protection of all British subjects. And as we have every reason to
confidently expect, the functions and duties devolved on you, gentlemen,
conjointly, will be carried out in the same honest, straightforward and impartial manner as they have been by John Campbell, Esq., during the time
he has been on the Fields; we state then, indeed, we have cause to hail with
double satisfaction the planting of the English flag."

At the dinner, Mr Commissioner Thompson made a speech which has
given great satisfaction. He said "he would take the opportunity of saying
a word or two upon a matter which had been to him a subject of careful
thought, as it was to the company one of deep interest. Gentlemen present
were aware that the Proclamation stated broadly, that the laws of the Cape
colony were to be administered here. That taken literally had given rise
to some apprehensions. It had been felt, and quite reasonably, that the

colonial law in its entirety was hardly suited to the state of things here. But he would remind them of the reservation in the Proclamation, whereby that law is only to be made use of in the new territory, so far as the same is not inapplicable to the circumstances there existing. Therefore he would counsel all to put away from their minds the unfounded dread of such things. For example, a strict and literal application of the Masters and Servants Act, and the sudden and immediate appearance in their midst of a crowd of independent native diggers. In conclusion, he expressed his earnest confidence that the labours of the Commissioners and of all the officials would tend to the welfare and advantage of the vast population here assembled."

The *Diamond Field* sums up the action of the Government in the following way:—" The new Government is acting most judiciously at Du Toit's Pan and De Beer's (old and new rushes) under the discreet and able management of Mr Thompson. Licences for claims were commenced to be issued on Monday, and a most liberal construction was put upon the first readings of the Proclamations. New regulations are to be made in reference to the working of claims at the New Rush, in regard to cartage, &c. Carts will enter at one side and file out at the other so that they will not be passing one another, which is leading to daily accidents. The old committee is to be allowed to work as before, save with the exception of assessing the amount of damages where a claim has been invaded. The roads are all to be levelled a foot or more per day by the diggers, and Government, at its own expense, will scarf the reef at the outside, so as to facilitate the exit and entry from and to the claims. Mr Thompson is fully justifying the favourable impression created by his known antecedents as a man of tact and business talent, and we feel sure Mr Barry will be found to make an excellent judge."

The name of Duffy is apparently destined to take a place in the annals of South Africa. A man bearing that name was arrested on a charge of theft by the Free State Police, but while being marched to the presence of Mr. Truter, the Free State Landdrost or chief magistrate at Du Toit's Pan, Duffy saw some British officials, and claimed their protection as a British subject. Messrs. Campbell, Thompson, and Gilfillan deliberated over this case, and determined to interfere. The Colonial Police rescued Mr. Duffy from the emissaries of the Free State. This was the beginning of the last act in the drama of annexation. As Duffy walked away with Commissioner Bowker's police, Mr. Truter rose, closed his Court, and thus terminated the jurisdiction of the Free State over that part of the Diamond Fields.

Should any of my readers wish to study the whole of the political questions and negociations concerning the ownership of this long-disputed territory, I would refer them to a very lengthy article on "South Africa and her Diamond Fields," in the *Edinburgh Review* for October, 1871, in which these questions are most exhaustively treated.

CHAPTER X.

DIAMONDS AND PROSPECTING.

THE reader who expects a scientific chapter will be very much disappointed here. I am not a scientific man, and never shall be. Harry Emanuel, and many other authorities, have written fully on the subject of diamonds and other precious stones, and I have no desire either to pirate from them or to emulate their example without a chance of success. With regard to Cape diamonds, as compared with Brazilian, it is an undisputed fact that in South Africa a very much larger proportion of large stones is found than in Brazil. Stones over 10 carats are comparatively rare in the latter country, while in "West Griqualand" (as I suppose we must now call the diamondiferous territory) those over 10 carats are exceedingly numerous, and generally several stones within a few carats of 100 are among the weekly finds.

Marvellous would be the riches, and immense the fortunes made in South Africa, but for the lamentable fact that the vast majority of our large diamonds, *i.e.*, of stones over 10 carats, are "off-colour," being, instead of pure "white"—or rather transparent—tinged, apparently throughout, with a yellowish tint, varying from the palest straw-colour to that of the topaz, or pale sherry colour. Already, when I left the Fields, "off-coloured" stones would barely command one-third the price of pure "white" gems, and it is to be feared that by this time, owing to the news of the unsaleableness of these stones, they will be still further depreciated. Consolation for the digger is, however, to be found in the fact that a great number of the *smaller* gems are of perfect shape and colour, and such stones will command high prices for many years to come. I saw a $12\frac{1}{2}$ carat *white* stone, found in the next claim to mine at Du Toit's Pan, which should have been worth at least 200*l.* on the fields, but, alas! there was a horrid black spot nearly in the centre of it, so it was only worth 60*l.* or 70*l.* Many off-coloured or yellow stones are of perfect shape and of great lustre, still they are not the fashion, so *que faire?* Accept the low prices and be thankful.

Du Toit's Pan is famous for large stones, and they vary very much in shape, colour, and brilliancy. Bultfontein has held from the first a great reputation for numbers of small stones, most of them white, and of good quality. Tiny little gems of from $\frac{1}{4}$ to 1-16th of a carat are very numerous there, especially near the surface.

Most diggers used to pay their expenses at Bultfontein, but a great many did not do much more, so it has never been a very favourite camp after the first few days, when the numerous small surface diamonds gave it a temporary good name.

At De Beer's the stones are generally very good, many of them being white.

At the Colesberg Kopje there is an immense abundance of all sorts, from the pure white lustrous octahedron, or dodecahedron, to the irregular fragment or chip of faint lustre and inky dulness, called *boart*. The river stones are generally good, but apparently not so numerous as on the dry diggings.

For prices of diamonds I would refer the intending digger to Emanuel and other authorities, also to my chapter on "Diamond Buyers and Diamond Brokers.

A few sapphires have been found at the river diggings, but they are scarce, and not apparently of the very best quality. I have been told, at different times, of the finding of real rubies at the dry diggings, but I will not vouch for their genuineness, having seen myself nothing but garnets and *spinel* rubies, generally small, fragmentary, and comparatively valueless. I saw one small stone which I pronounced to be an emerald, but I have not heard yet whether my opinion was correct ; and some of the fragments of bright transparent green *peridot*, called by some diggers "green garnets," are of such fine colour as easily to deceive a novice.

Here is a description from a colonial paper, of a strange stone, which I should very much like to have found :

EXTRAORDINARY STONE.—Mr. Thornbury, who has just returned from the Diamond Fields, has shown us an extraordinary stone which he has brought down with him for the purpose of sending it to England. At first sight it looks like a large ruby of a peculiarly beautiful colour. Looked at from two different points it presents two different colours—one the light amethyst and the other the deep, lovely pigeon-blood. The stone is of $17\frac{3}{8}$ carats, and has been found at Hebron. Mr. Thoms, the lapidary, has stated it is a most unique stone, that he has never seen the like of it before, and that he would sooner have it than two diamonds of 72 carats each. He says it is a combination of crystals of the Oriental amethyst and the pigeon-blood ruby. The stone is supposed to be of great value.

It certainly must be a beautiful stone, but I cannot quite agree with Mr. Thoms, and I think I would *very much* prefer two diamonds of 72 carats each. If they were pure stones, their price would make a handsome fortune.

One or two clusters of diamonds of different sizes, apparently partly fused together, have been found, and have excited much speculation among the *savans* who have pet theories as to the *matrix* or origin of diamonds.

With regard to prospecting, I shall only speak of the dry diggings, the gravel and surface indications on the river being different, and having already been alluded to under the heading " Early History of the Fields." What prospectors like on the dry diggings is as follows :—A small hillock, large mound, or ridge, is the favourite conformation of ground for prospecting. Grass does not, as a rule, grow much over the known diamondiferous patches, they are more generally covered with a low, stunted, rough scrub, slightly resembling heather. Rotten white limestone cropping up through the surface is considered a good sign, though in many places, and notably the Colesberg Kopje, the surface stratum is composed of red sand, varying in thickness from one to sixteen feet. If a minute examination of the surface soil reveals the presence of small fragments of garnets, transparent green stone or *peridot*, and of the shiny metallic black substance known as " carbon," but which is really ilmenite, these signs are considered to denote " promising stuff," and the digger will do well to dig down a few feet and sift and sort the stuff. A pick and shovel, small fine hand-sieve, and smooth board or sheepskin for sorting, will suffice for ordinary surface prospecting, and may be easily carried. But, if prospecting be done at all it is worth doing well ; and it has often been found that at a new place no diamonds have been seen till a considerable depth was reached, sometimes even 16 feet, so here the surface-prospector might have missed a " good thing." Under old regulations the prospector of a new digging was allowed two extra claims free, and could mark out others for his friends.

A good deal of time is often wasted in fruitless prospecting, and it is better to let others do this, and wait till something genuine is found and the place surveyed, when good claims can be marked out, or bought cheap. I have seen hundreds of diggers at work prospecting on one small hill ; little sticks with papers on them marking the position of claims ; white men and black men, all working with intense eagerness with pick and shovel ; a few sieves and sorting-tables put up, and people poring most anxiously over their contents. This was some four miles from Du Toit's Pan. It was a likely looking kopje, but I believe nothing was ever found there.

Trees are much favoured, and their immediate vicinity, in likely-looking ground, is always most carefully examined. Some of the claims close to trees, at De Beer's for instance, are very rich, and "tree-claims" on a new camp, always command rather higher prices.

I prospected a kopje myself once, found a good deal of peridot. plenty of limestone, but no garnets or "carbon." Still, a lot of diggers who came over pronounced it a very promising looking place, and many marked out claims, and worked for a day or two, but nothing came of it.

Frequently may be seen on the "veldt" the white or grey heaps of stuff, and neatly-dug holes, signifying that a prospecting party has been there; but generally they appear to leave off too soon, for it is quite possible that just on that spot there may be no diamonds at less than sixteen feet deep, and then plenty. In some parts of the Colesberg Kopje, for instance, nearly that depth of red sand has to be laboriously got through before the real diamondiferous stuff is reached. A great many diamonds are there found just at the junction of this red sand with the first stratum of white limestone, then again much deeper in rotten green trap, soft and easy to work.

Prospectors going out for a proper exploration should take with them niggers, a cart and oxen if possible, a small tent, or at any rate plenty of blankets, cooking utensils, provisions, a gun for getting game, and plenty of water, unless they are *quite* certain of finding it.

PART II.
ROUTES TO THE FIELDS.

CHAPTER I.
COMPARISON OF THE DIFFERENT ROUTES.

In treating here of the several routes by which the Diamond Fields may be reached from England, I will assume it to be the object of the intending digger to reach the scene of his new labours as cheaply and quickly as possible. In the case of the Diamond Field Routes, these two important elements—cheapness and quickness—are combined. The first step is to take a passage from England by a mail steamer—it is a very false economy to go by a sailing ship, which will probably take from two to four months in reaching the Cape, while the mail steamer does it in thirty to thirty-eight days, the latter being an exceptionally long passage, and the limit of time allowed by the postal contract. Dismissing, then, all idea of sailing ships, we come to the consideration of the two mail companies now running steamers to the Cape of Good Hope, Algoa Bay, and Natal. The mail steamers of the Union Steam-Ship Company leave Southampton on the 10th and 25th of each month, the fares by which are, to Cape Town, 30 guineas first class, 20 guineas second class; to Algoa Bay, 33 guineas and 22 guineas, and to Natal, 37 guineas and 25 guineas; while the steamers of Messrs. Donald Currie, and Co.'s London Mail Line, sail direct from the Thames on the 4th and 20th of each month, calling at Dartmouth for the mails on the 7th and 23rd; the fares by this line being, to Cape Town and Algoa Bay, 30 guineas first class, 20 guineas second class, and 5 guineas extra to Natal.

The advertisements of both these steam companies will be found at the end of this work. The accommodation by both lines is first-rate in every respect, a very liberal table being kept for passengers, both first and second class, and the voyages are made with punctuality and despatch.

There is a slight pecuniary advantage to persons going to Algoa Bay or Natal by the latter line, but I do not recommend any one to go further than Cape Town by sea. On arriving at Cape Town, the traveller, if his baggage be light, as it should be (I have explained elsewhere that no outfit is necessary), can at once get his portmanteau passed by the Customs officials, jump into a *Hansom*, and drive to the Royal Hotel in Plein-street, where he will meet with every possible comfort and attention. But he should lose no time in securing a seat in one of the comfortable passenger waggons of either the Inland Transport Company or the lately established Diamond Fields Transport Company. The fare by each of these companies is 12*l.*, from Cape Town to the Diamond Fields, which journey, about seven hundred miles, is accomplished in seven to nine days. The Inland Transport Company's waggon passes through the towns of Wellington. Ceres, Beaufort West, Victoria West, and Hope Town, and its terminus is Pniel, on the Vaal River, the centre of the river-diggings. That of the Diamond Fields Company passes through Wellington, Ceres. Beaufort West, Murraysburg, Richmond, Colesberg, Philippolis, Fauresmith, and Jacobsdal, arriving at Du Toit's Pan, the metropolis of the dry diggings (if not superseded by the neighbouring Colesberg Kopje). As the dry diggings are at present far more generally flourishing and remunerative than the river-side diggings, the latter route would seem to be preferable, as the journey from Pniel to Du Toit's Pan or the Colesberg Kopje would otherwise have to be accomplished by a separate conveyance—fare. ten or fifteen shillings. Each of these companies allows 40lb. of luggage per passenger, and charges one shilling or one shilling and three pence per pound for all in excess of that weight.

Should the traveller elect to go up from Port Elizabeth (Algoa Bay), he has the choice of either Cobb and Co.'s American coaches, going up in about five days, with light baggage, or mule waggons taking passengers and heavier goods in about fifteen days. The fare will, of course, be proportionately less than that from Cape Town. but as the steamer waits two or three days at Cape Town before proceeding to Port Elizabeth, and the voyage thither takes three days more, it is perfectly evident that both time and money will be saved by adopting the direct Cape Town route.

A line of quick passenger waggons is, I believe, by this time established from Natal; but here again the objections to the Algoa Bay route apply still more strongly, in consequence of the length of the sea voyage from Cape Town to Natal. Bullock-waggons are continually starting from Port Elizabeth, Natal. and other ports, to the Fields, but these slow, old-fashioned colonial conveyances will, I hope, soon be things of the past, except for the transport of heavy goods, for stores, &c. Thirty days is considered a quick journey from Port Elizabeth to Du Toit's Pan, by bullock-waggon. I, in my inexperience, went up that way, and was *fifty* days on the road. In addition to this great loss of time, which may be very detrimental to the digger—arriving just too late for a good "new rush," for instance—there is no money saving effected by the slow route, but quite the contrary. as, although only about five pounds is charged for each passenger. and two hundred pounds or more of luggage carried free, the traveller has to purchase food all the way, and stoppages of a day or two at little towns are frequent; when, after the jolting of the waggon, the want of comfortable sleep, and the very rough dietary, the temptations of hotels, good meals, soft beds, and other luxuries, are almost irresistible, and it is no uncommon thing for twenty or thirty pounds to be spent *en route*.

To any one desirous of seeing much of the country, or passionately fond of sport, the bullock-waggon route certainly offers some inducements. It is a rough kind of pic-nic the whole way, travelling ten to fifteen miles a day, camping out, cooking your own food, procuring your own wood and water, wandering through wild regions with gun or rifle among plenty of game, and it is certainly a very jolly life for a month or so; but, after all, the great object should be to get direct to the fields as quickly as possible. I have shown elsewhere that the digger can obtain plenty of sport by an occasional short holiday in the immediate neighbourhood of the Fields; moveover, if successful in digging. he can afterwards combine pleasure with profit by a hunting and trading trip into the "big game country." Having given a general comparison of the principal routes to the Fields, and I hope, established the superiority of the *direct route*, viz.: mail steamer to Cape Town, passenger-waggon thence to the Fields in nine days or less, I will now proceed to give my own experience of these routes, in which I trust some amusing and interesting details may be found, and the "new chum" may know exactly what he has to look forward to.

NOTE TO CHAPTER I.

New Algoa Bay Routes.

Since writing this chapter I have received from Port Elizabeth (Algoa Bay) full information as to two transport and passenger companies which have just been started to facilitate trade and travelling from that port, and I cannot, in justice to the enterprising promoters, withhold this information from the public.

"Cobb and Co. (Limited)," a company with a capital of 10,000*l.*, was to start the first through coach for the Diamond Fields early this month (Jan. 1871), after which two coaches would run each week, doing the journey in five days each way. The carriages are American-built, exceedingly strong and comfortable. Arrangements were being made along the route for a reasonable and uniform scale of charges at the various hotels; also to allow reasonable time for rest, and generally to secure in every way possible the comfort and convenience of passengers.

"Port Elizabeth and Diamond Fields Conveyance Company (Limited)." This company has been formed to meet the increased demand for the transport of *goods* to the Fields from Algoa Bay. The carrying trade from this port (the growth of thirty years) has hitherto been done by bullocks; but, although vast numbers are engaged in the business, the demand for transport, in consequence of the unparalleled success of the diggings generally, has increased much more rapidly than the means. The promoters of the Conveyance Company are certainly deserving of every encouragement, having introduced the system of *quick* conveyance of goods to the Fields, so important to our merchants and storekeepers. Their waggons, drawn by good *mules*, will reach the Fields in fifteen days. Each waggon will carry from four to five thousand pounds weight of goods; and six of these waggons will start every fifth day. By this "mule train" passengers who are unable to avail themselves of the coaches of Cobb and Co. may obtain cheap passage, with the loss of only ten days. The rates of carriage and passage will depend on the current rates for transport. The prospectus of the company estimates the rate at 20s. per 100lb. This is a good deal less than the present bullock-waggon rate, and as much as 60s. per 100lb. has lately been given by mule waggon. The charge for parcels will be higher; about 1s. per pound. No parcel will be sent under 5s. The distance is 436 miles. This is very creditable to Port Elizabeth, and I have no doubt both the new companies will have the success they deserve. For goods traffic this route is, I think, the best, but for passengers I keep to my original recommendation of the Cape Town route. Mr G. Leslie, Port Elizabeth, acts as secretary for the two companies here mentioned.

CHAPTER II.

DIARY ON BOARD S.S. "ROMAN," SOUTHAMPTON TO CAPE TOWN.

23RD FEB., 1871.—At 2 p.m. steamed away from Southampton, with about fifty first-class passengers (a few more to join at Plymouth) and a heavy cargo. Lunch at 12.30. Dinner five. Dead calm.

24th Feb.—Arrived off Plymouth about 7 a.m. (N.B. The steamer no longer calls there.) Went ashore with M.; walked all over Plymouth, also up to one of the forts, from which there was a magnificent view of the town and sea, and of that lovely spot Mount Edgecombe. Dead calm, sea unrippled, brilliant sunshine, quite warm—happy omen for our voyage. Came on board in time for dinner. Quiet evening, game at écarté, good night's rest.

25th Feb.—Sailed from Plymouth about 11 a.m. Dead calm. Got rather breezy in a few hours. In the afternoon, when out of sight of land, a wagtail flew on board to rest. Good dinner, cards, pipes in smoking-room. bed.

26th Feb.—Sunday. In the Bay of Biscay; oh! Very much oh! and worse noises than that. Nearly everybody sick. At 10.15, after smoking a pipe, presented my undigested breakfast to the unpleasantly heaving Bay; after which, went to prayers in saloon; during service one of the saloon lamps fell and was smashed. Beastly uncomfortable. Heaving, rolling, pitching all combined. Managed to eat a pretty good lunch, and was quite recovered by dinner, to which I did full justice. Quiet evening, reading in saloon.

27th Feb.—More Bay of Biscay. Not quite so much heaving. Some getting convalescent. Smoked many pipes, ate tremendous meals, played much écarté, turned in at eleven, in the dark (saloon lights always put out at ten, smoking-room and bedroom lights at 10.30). A little before ten a tremendous lurch had sent all the cards and a fellow-passenger's bottle of brandy off the saloon table. There was a vocal concert in the smoking-cabin from 6 to 8 p.m. Some capital singing.

28th Feb.—Up at 5.30 a.m. Am told ship has been rolling

tremendously all night. People ill again. Not I. Sighted large steamer in the morning, and brig after lunch. Breeze freshening now (3.15 p.m.), glass low, and every prospect of dirty weather. I object, but it's no use protesting. Overhauled firearms, found them hardly at all rusty. *Fiddles* (wooden frameworks placed all along table for holding plates, &c.) and other precautions necessary at meals. A very good muster at lunch to-day; one young man turned up who had not been seen since we left Plymouth. In the evening stiff breeze again, but every one got "sea-legs" now. Lots of card-playing going on, also a little music—instruments, cornet-à-piston and penny whistle.

1st March.—Ship been very "lively" all night. A quiet day. Lots of écarté. Just before dinner a tired swallow came on board, and was caught. Sighted two ships. Turned in at 11.30, in the dark. Ship rolling tremendously.

2nd March.—Found everybody this morning talking about row in the night—ship had taken in a tremendous sea, fore part been under water five minutes; sea carried away part of fore-hatch; knocked pots and pans about in cook's galley, and slightly damaged the cook. Also, a passenger fell down this morning, and put his shoulder out. Many passengers had bad falls yesterday. To-day it is blowing very stiff, and interesting anecdotes about shipwrecks are going round rather suggestively. At ten we sight a barque and a brig, homeward bound; also, first shoal of porpoises—lively animals. Ship tremendously on one side. Turned out a wet day; stiff breeze in the evening. Some rather high card-playing. 175 miles run by noon to-day.

3rd March.—A charming day—bright, warm sunshine, and strong favourable breeze, especially in the afternoon. 167 miles run. At twelve saw a small turtle paddling along on the rough surface of the water. After lunch, drawing up of the "Grand Madeira Sweepstakes," 50 members, 2s. 6d. each; 48 quarter hours marked on little tickets. Member holding quarter hour during which we fire gun on arriving in Funchal Roads to receive 5 guineas, next quarter before and after 10s. each. Winner to stand three bottles of champagne to committee. One or two bets made on same event. Ecarté playing, and betting still rather high.

4th March.—Calm; porpoises, numerous and playful, right under our bows in the clear water. Over-hauling of luggage; stoppage of the "pirate's" liquor (nickname of a fellow-passenger addicted to liquor, and inclined to D. T. Since dead). 191 miles run. First-class passengers "pay their footing" to sailors on passing limits of the forecastle. I and M. being the first caught, proceeded in our turn to decoy a lot of the other passengers beyond the chalk line, on various pretexts of whales, sharks, &c.

5th March.—On awaking at six, had a fine view of the Madeira Islands, and by the time breakfast was served we were anchored off Funchal; and little Madeira youngsters, of whom there were many little cockle-shell boat-loads alongside, were diving in the clear water for sixpences; utterly refusing copper. After breakfast, went ashore; rambled about the town and up the hills, admiring the glorious scenery, magnificent flowers, quaint curtained carriages on wooden runners, drawn by oxen, snug hammocks slung on poles and borne on men's shoulders, strange fish in the market, including huge albicores, &c., bananas, plantains, guavas, other fruits, and sugar-canes. Didn't much admire the samples of the fair sex. Tasted some wine of the country and approved of it. Had good lunch—fish, bread and cheese, and wine. Then went on board again, and sailed about 3 p.m. After dinner, although Sunday evening, had lots of jolly songs, with rollicking choruses, in the smoking room, scandalising one or two Scotch passengers. Query, effect of the Madeira wine?

6th March.—Fine weather, and a good run made. Two ships sighted, also one or two birds seen. Cards and singing as usual.

7th March.—A pleasant day, with hot sunshine and light favourable breeze. No incidents, except a hoopoe hovering round the ship. Also a little revolver practice, at a bottle trailed astern on a long line. I smashed him first. A very strong breeze in the evening.

8th March.—Ship has been rolling awfully all night. I woke to find luggage, clothes, brushes, books, cards, &c., &c., all mixed up together in horrible chaos on the floor of my cabin. Made my way to the bath-room. Bathers not very numerous this morning. Saw a good-sized flying-fish. Very rough weather all day, and a good many absentees both from breakfast and lunch. M.'s knee hurt, "sky-larking" last night. 2.45 p.m. Ship rolling worse than ever. Got a little calmer towards evening. Trade wind.

9th March.—Trade wind still blowing, but much calmer. Calm, hot day. In the evening sighted a ship; threw up a rocket and burnt a blue-light, to which she replied. The piano was got up on to the poop, and a very jolly evening spent in dancing and singing, it being perfectly calm and bright moonlight. Two ship's lamps were hung over the piano, and a couple of large Chinese lanterns swung gaily from the boom.

10th March.—Before breakfast saw nine smallish sea-gulls, with dark-brown wings and white breasts; also, a stormy petrel, or "Mother Carey's chicken." After breakfast another petrel. Lots of masses of floating yellowish weed all the time. 10 a.m., breeze freshening; many stormy petrels seen at different times to-day, also quantities of nautilus. or "Portuguese men-of-war." One flying-fish, the size of a smallish herring, came on board, I fished in the afternoon with Hearder's spinner, No. 6, on 2lb. lead, and 80 yards line; lost two baits, the first on single stout gimp, second on double ditto; going too fast. In the evening, more harmony. Several passengers slept on the poop-deck, because of the heat in the little cabins, I amongst the number.

11th March.—Awoke at 4.20 a.m. by the deck washers. Lay down again at 5.15 on deck, and slept till 6.15, then bathed. We spoke a large steamer, and saw a vessel supposed to be a man-of-war. Lots of nautilus, two or three shoals of flying-fish, and two unknown birds. Took soundings just before breakfast, during which halt I tried in vain to catch a fish. In the afternoon got amongst sharks; whereupon I and a great many more of the passengers produced rifles and revolvers, and amused ourselves shooting the "varmint," many of which we severely wounded. The scene in the bows was most picturesque—three of us sat astride on the bowsprit, and the rest clustered thickly all along the bows, dressed in every variety of free-and-easy light costume, with a wondrous diversity of head-gear—pith helmets, "puggerees," and hats of all nations—I with a head-cover I had manufactured out of a Madeira grass mat—all most piratical in aspect, each looking eagerly out, weapon in hand. This excitement lasted until dinner-time, after which we had cards, music, and, finally, a long vocal concert on the poop. Slept on deck.

12th March.—Sunday. Up at 6.30; bathed, lounged, and breakfasted. Flying-fish very numerous. Saw a big shark just now (9.45 a.m.) Prayers on the poop, picturesquely adorned with flags; Mrs. D. at piano, and Mrs. G. leading the choir; all the sailors in full rig, captain all in white, officers in smart uniform, man at the wheel attentive in background, white awning above, blue sea and blue sky all around. The whole of this day was intensely hot, and everybody in a state of languid, perspiring *ennui*. Turned in at 10.30 in smoking-room,

13th March.—Fine warm morning, after a stifling hot night.

Not quite so bad to-day as yesterday; light refreshing breeze. One of the second-class passengers practising with his revolver at flying-fish and "men of war"—ridiculous waste of ammunition. Like yesterday, the consumption of liquids most alarming, that of solids proportionately on the decrease. Still nearly a dead calm. Iced drinks procurable at 11 a.m. and 4.30 p.m., A 1. Card-playing in full force again to-day. Day passed pleasantly and uneventfully; music in the evening as usual. Several passengers slightly tipsy, owing to large number of "big drinks" consumed during the day. A slight shower in the evening.

14th March.—Up at 6 a.m. Went forward, and had the hose played on me—most delightful, much more refreshing than ordinary bath, or even shower-bath. Found there had been a slight tornado in the night. Captain says. if we had had canvas up might have come to grief. A quiet day; tolerably cool in the bows; reading, cards, and drinks all day. After dinner, very extensive sky-larking—assault and storming of the bridge. I got hauled off twice, and M. came down on his face, hurting his mouth and cutting a deep gash under his chin, which had to be sewn up by the "experienced surgeon." A great deal of loud singing in several parts of the ship. At 8 p.m. Neptune and his "suite" came on board, and obtained captain's permission for the usual games.

15th March.—After a pleasant night in the smoking-room, not being awoke by a heavy squall and rain, got up and had hose and another bath. Great preparations going on for the shaving, &c. A huge canvas bath prepared, also three razors, and other formidable items. Soon after breakfast Neptune, his wife, secretary, doctor, and barber, all splendidly rigged in most comical costumes, came aft in procession. and invited the company to the fore part of the ship. After the novices of the crew had been "shaved," ducked, and otherwise tormented, one or two of the second-class passengers volunteered to go through the ordeal in order to get a lot of their comrades into the same mess, and there was great fun—a dozen at a time, with all their clothes on, splashing, struggling, and tumbling about in the big bath. The proceedings terminated at about 11.30, though we did not really cross the line till seven at night, when rockets were sent up. This day was also marked by the appearance of a magnificent and abundant claret-cup at the captain's end of the table, ten members. The iced "cup" was delicious. After dinner we had some capital "cock-fighting," then card-playing, and music and harmony reigned fore and aft, only marred by one of the first cabin stewards getting beastly drunk, for which he received a good pummelling, was put in irons on the bridge for a short time, and then banished to the fore cabin.

16th March.—Up at six; hose and other bath, and quiet lounge till breakfast-time. Double-barrelled gun raffled in smoking-room. A quiet, warm day; claret-cup very accceptable. Plenty of music in the evening.

17th March.—St. Patrick's-day. Grand procession and promenade concert of Irish passengers, headed by Captain C. in shirt and trousers, green ribbon in hat, bottle of whiskey under his arm, shillelah, and penny whistle; other instruments being a piccolo, tambourine, cornet, drum, and triangle. In the evening, concert both fore and aft. In the fore part the sailors got up an excellent band; played, sung, and danced famously. Good but quieter music aft.

18th March.—After a good night's rest in smoking-room, learn that said room is to be converted into a "sick bay" for Mrs. G. and the little H.'s; the latter have scarlet fever; don't know what is the matter with Mrs. G. A fresh breeze ahead, and sea rising rather fast. Immense shoals of flying-fish and a stray bird or two. Rather an uncomfortable evening, there being no smoking-room. Slept on saloon deck.

19th March.—Fine breezy morning, and heat quite bearable. Service in saloon. Flying-fish very numerous. No particular incidents.

20th March.—Strong favourable breeze. Ship tremendously on one side. Sales by auction in fore-cabin in the afternoon, grass hammock, pipes, cigars, pistols, books, &c. Fair prices realised, The auctioneer lively and facetious. Quiet evening, mild card-playing and smoking. Slept in berth again.

21st March.—Fine cool morning. Quiet day. In the evening, "jubilee" in fore-cabin, in honour of Princess Louise's marriage. One shilling admittance, entitling to refreshments—rum-punch, claret-cup, and Scotch whiskey. Plenty of jolly good songs, speeches, toasts, &c., and nobody very drunk.

22nd March.—On getting up, found we were quite close to St. Helena, a grand rugged island. Numerous pretty sea-birds, some pure white, others brown. We anchored off the pretty little town, nestling in a snug valley, between two high sloping mountains. Stopped two hours, but not allowed to go ashore, quarantined because of scarlet fever. Boats came off, manned mostly by negroes, with bananas, apples, pears, peaches, cabbages, and water-cresses, which found a ready sale at moderate prices. Small fish and horse-mackerel were numerous round the stern, and several of us tried hard for them with every kind of tackle and bait available. At last a small gar-fish was brought on board, and I hooked and lost a great many. Sailed at 10 a.m. Soon afterwards spoke the barque *Hastings*, of and for London. She passed quite close to us. In the evening the band of the crew came aft, and sang and danced in capital style on the poop, being very much applauded.

23rd March.—A pleasant day, with light breeze. At 7 p.m. ceremony of "dead horse," symbolical of completion of a month of the voyage, the animal, made of a couple of casks, artfully covered with canvas, &c., was carried in procession by the crew, singing, then hung to the yard arm, and cut adrift, and went floating astern—having been previously set fire to—amid cheers, to the light of a huge "Roman candle." At eight performance of the farce "Mad as a Hatter," in the saloon, to a large and appreciative audience, by our captain and third officer, "The General," "The Admiral," and Mr. and Mrs. G. A most creditable performance, every one highly pleased.

24th March.—Mock court-martial held on the poop. "The General" tried for drunkenness. Great fun. Found guilty, but recommended to mercy, and sentenced to "stand a liquor" to the judge. Strong breeze, sea rising rapidly.

25th March.—Second court-martial—on me, for abstracting two bottles of beer from "The Admiral's" bunk. After a protracted, but somewhat slovenly conducted trial, found "not guilty." People getting excited and speculative as to time of arrival at Cape Town ; I opine for Saturday next.

26th March.—A very quiet Sunday, without a single incident. Pleasant weather, light breeze, and ship very steady.

27th March.—Usual bathing business. Discovery and capture outside a port-hole, of a lady's false ringlets, red in colour, which, amid much laughter, was run up on the signal halyards.

28th March.—A few "Cape hens" seen. Strong breeze, and heavy rain in the afternoon. Considerable amount of "tightness." Slight row between two passengers, terminating peacefully, with ample apologies.

29th March.—Cape hens about, and two lesser albatrosses continually crossing our wake. They refused biscuit. Strong breeze and huge rolling waves. Ship getting very lively.

30th March.—At 10.15 a.m., great sale by auction in fore

saloon, advertised by the big dog, "Lion," perambulating the ship with his usual solemnity, with a big bill on his back. In the afternoon half a dozen guns out practising at Cape hens. Three killed, and a few wounded. I rigged up a line to try to catch one, but being badly fastened on winder, the whole line jumped overboard. First large albatross seen. In the evening the usual whist, &c., followed by a good bit of music, concertina and vocal. Head wind all day.

31st March.—Head wind, heavy sea, and occasional rain. "Cape Arrival Sweepstakes" got up.

1st April.—Many good "sells." Birds numerous. Wind dead ahead, but not so much sea as during the night. Drawing of the "Cape Arrival Sweepstakes." Bets made freely. At twelve 173 miles to run. Wind still dead ahead. Sea getting calmer. Drawing of lots to find who is the "Jonah," to whom the adverse weather may be attributed, the lot falls to R., the invalid, who is brought before the captain, and finally "remanded for a fortnight." In the afternoon a little desultory shooting at Cape hens. In the evening much conviviality. I promoted the brewing and circulation amongst eight members, of a bowl of hot rum-punch, the partakers of which afterwards formed a concert party on the poop. We had some jolly good songs up to 12.30, followed by much noisy sky-larking, finally put a stop to by a middle-aged married passenger rushing on deck in his shirt, and abusing us all roundly. Retired to rest in smoking-room at 1.15 a.m.

2nd April.—Glorious sunshine, cloudless sky, only a light wind ahead, and comparatively little sea, so we hope to arrive this afternoon. Soon after breakfast, M. and I. making up our minds to be partners, and discussing business matters near the bows, get a very thorough ducking from a stray wave, but are not "put out" by this trifle, though my pipe is. 10.30. Every one on the look out for land. Church time. At twelve o'clock we were surprised and disgusted to find that we were still seventy miles from Cape Town. The afternoon passed slowly, though there were a great many strange birds and fish to be seen, besides the bold outline of Table Mountain visible in the distance, with other mountains and headlands of the South African coast. All the evening we were very convivial, several bowls of punch were drunk, a lemon being found for the first, and some lime-juice as flavouring for the second. We arrived in Table Bay about 10.30 p.m., and boats came off for the mails, also relatives of some of the passengers.

3rd April.—Got up early and went ashore. The scenery grand in the extreme, and aspect of the town exceedingly foreign. Had some Cape beer at 3*d*. the quart bottle, which I found very refreshing, bought some fruit and tobacco, and returned on board to breakfast. Afterwards, strolling along the beach, observed a negro fishing off a jetty. Found he was catching lots of small mullet, with bits of the flesh of cray-fish, which are very numerous and cheap here. Sent a coolie to get me a cray-fish, went on board to get rod and line, the latter a fine Thames roach line, which I never dreamt last year of using in South African waters. Caught in about two hours, fifty-one small mullet, 6in. to 8in., and a couple of brown gurnards. A small species of cormorant, termed by the natives " duiker," extremely numerous. Saw some little niggers knock one over with a stone, and one of them swam out and got it. In the afternoon went down to a breakwater close to the *Roman's* berth. Here the deep water was perfectly clear, the bottom thickly covered with bright red *echini* or sea-urchins, in astonishing masses, anemones and beautiful weeds. Spider-crabs and cray-fish were creeping about here and there, and a bluish-coloured water-snake crawled about the lovely natural flooring, while shoals of mullet and other fish frequently darkened the water so that none of the beautiful objects at the bottom could be seen. Fishing with same bait and tackle as in the morning, I caught a good many of the so-called Hottentot fish, a fat little fellow, somewhat like a black bream, with very sharp prominent teeth. I found that these little rascals, if allowed time to *swallow* the hook, invariably bit through the gut, therefore they should be fished for with a fine wire or gimp snooding. A Dutch clergyman standing near me was fishing for these fat little darkies, which are very good eating, with a large leaded triangle of hooks, a little above which a goodly lump of cray-fish bait was tied on the line. The "Hottentots" came by dozens, swimming round the bait and tugging at it, so he easily caught a good many of them " foul " by jerking up the triangle. He also hooked and injured a snake, which emitted from the wounded part a vast quantity of thick glutinous slime, exceedingly disgusting in appearance, and said to be poisonous to other fish. A native fisherman told me that, when a water-snake is taken in a net, all the other fish in the net turn yellow. My afternoon's bag was forty-six Hottentot fish, and two pretty little striped wrasse.

4th April.—Got up early and caught eleven Hottentots before

breakfast. Afterwards went to see the snook-boats coming in. The snook is a fish shaped something like a pike, only rather longer, and in skin and colour something like a dusky mackerel. It has a huge mouth and terrible teeth, the bite of which is said to be poisonous. The fish itself is excellent eating, and smoked is said to equal kippered salmon. Large quantities are exported dried to the Mauritius, and elsewhere. The ordinary weight is from 5lb. to 15lb., and price from $1\frac{1}{2}d.$ to $2d.$ per fish, according to the season's supply. Dozens of boats were coming in, containing immense quantities of fresh snook, caught with a red rag or other showy bait, on a very large hook, towed astern of a sailing boat. In the afternoon I and three others went by train to a village close to Cape Town, called Salt River, having been told we should find some fish which would rise to a fly in the river there. The little railway trip was very enjoyable, the carriages far more roomy and comfortable than ours at home. Some amusement was created at the first station, by a difference of opinion as to the name which the guard shouted out, one *Roman* saying it was "Uppatuptup" and the other vowing it was "Long Tom." I have forgotten what the real name was, but I know each of my comrades was equally far from the mark. We saw only a few very small fish in Salt River, and could not induce any to take fly, minnow, or fish bait, though a young Africander managed to "jigger" two or three little mites. Passing a lot of native washerwomen, one of whom, though as black as my boots—used to be in London—was very good-looking and exceedingly well-made. We went farther up the river and found a splendid deep pool, wherein we had a delightful bathe, and then chased one another about in the sun to dry. We observed several snipe by the banks of this little stream, also a large kite, a "secretary-bird," a bird like a hooded crow, and many others. Having refreshed ourselves at a funny Dutch inn, we returned to Cape Town with a good appetite for dinner, at which we had a very excellent fish called "red stump-nose."

5th April.—Went down to the fishing quarter to charter a boat for snook-fishing. The whole atmosphere down here was of the snook, snooky—all the fishing population busy opening, gutting, and hanging them up to dry. We got a very large, roomy, clean sailing-boat for 15s. for the day, and were soon outside the breakwater with tackle and guns. There is a fine, 20l., I believe, for firing a gun inside the breakwater. We soon had lines out, but we had yet some distance to go before we reached the regular fishing ground, clearly shown by the number of sailing boats cruising over it in close company. Birds were wonderfully numerous, thousands of cormorants, Solan geese, penguins, and two large birds, termed by our natives "mollimauks" and "malagasses." So. soon lines were disregarded, guns out, and the magnificent birds, the biggest we had ever shot, began to cumber the decks. We only caught three snook. but one of them was a fine fellow, over 15lb. I lost a spoon-bait in a big fellow. As to birds, we shot twenty-eight, my share being one lesser albatross (*Diomedea metamophrys*), one Solan goose, four penguins (*Speniscus demersa*) and three "malagasses," a large speckled grey bird which I had never before seen. It was astonishing to see the thousands of these birds, Solan geese especially, hovering high over the parts of the sea where fish were thickest, many of them darting down from a great height with a bewildering and dazzling velocity, as if shot from some powerful aerial weapon, and evidently entering deep into the water. Several of the birds, the penguins especially, had fish in their mouths when brought on board, most of which appeared to be small grey mullet. A thick damp mist came on in the afternoon—they seem to be frequent both morning and evening at this season—and I wondered how our niggers would manage to get in; but we were soon alongside the breakwater, and half an hour afterwards I was smoking my pipe with a stem taken from the wing of a "malagasse." We handed over the rest of the birds to a coolie, who volunteered to skin them for us for the sake of the carcases, many of them being eatable. My albatross measured 8ft. 6in. from tip to tip of wings. I believe the wandering albatross (*Diomedea exulans*) is a much larger bird.

7th April.—In the morning had an interview at the Masonic Hotel with a successful diamond digger, just returned from the Fields, and going up again in a fortnight. He gave us much valuable information, and showed us a diamond of $37\frac{1}{2}$ carats, which he says will cut to pure water, though it is at present straw-coloured. He does not think there is any likelihood of a war with the Boers, in spite of what the Cape papers say.

Left for Algoa Bay at 9 p.m. this (Thursday) evening.

We arrived there about 6 p.m. on Sunday the 9th April, after a totally uneventful voyage along the coast. Some further account of Cape Town will be found in a subsequent chapter.

CHAPTER III.

PORT ELIZABETH TO DU TOIT'S PAN BY BULLOCK WAGGON.

PORT ELIZABETH, as the town in Algoa Bay is called, occupies the important position of chief sea-port to the Eastern districts of the Cape Colony. And yet it seems to me a misnomer to call it a port, for it is really nothing but an open roadstead, only very partially protected by a large breakwater, now in course of erection. And it is a dangerous roadstead, too, very rough, with a terrible surf, during the prevalence of certain gales. Steamers and ships lie well out in the offing, and passengers are landed at a small jetty. It is a long town, with plenty of churches, large warehouses, and handsome public buildings. It has one long main street, with a few short little streets radiating from it. At the back of this main street rises "The Hill," a slight and gentle elevation whereon are situated the cosy villas and fair gardens of the enterprising merchants of Port Elizabeth.

In front of the town is the sea-beach, with its ever-sounding treacherous surf, and some half-dozen big black skeletons of ships which have been wrecked there are scattered over the beach, adding a gloomy picturesqueness to the scene. It is a very busy town, doing an immense trade in wool, hides, and other colonial produce, and also importing a very large quantity of European manufactures for the interior and the Diamond Fields. Graham's Town, the principal inland town of this part of the colony, is about eighty-five miles from Port Elizabeth. We arrived here as I said in my last chapter, on Sunday evening, 9th April, and were not able to get a waggon to start till the ensuing Saturday, 15th April. We put up at Dreyer's Phœnix Hotel, but it is a rough, uncomfortable place; the other hotel, on the hill, is much better. There was no quick line of horse or mule waggons from Algoa Bay then, so we were obliged to look out for a "transport rider," and charter a bullock waggon.

Thirteen of us joined together for the journey up, and succeeded in getting a good waggon, driven by J. W., of King William's Town, to take us up for 70*l*. That expense was to be divided amongst the thirteen of us, and we were entitled to load the whole of our waggon with our own goods, not to exceed however a total weight of 7000lb., including weight of our own persons. The passage up was to be performed in "usual time," which we considered to mean about thirty days. On Saturday, about noon, there was much cracking of whips and shouting in front of our hotel. A black waiter came rushing frantically into the room where M. and I were finishing our packing, shouting "Baas, here de waggon for de Diamond Field!" We hurried down stairs, and there stood the waggon. It was a long, rather low-hung concern, some 20ft. long by 5ft. 6in. broad, with a high arched framework, on which would shortly be stretched a strong waterproof canvas covering, with a curtain at each end to be let down at night or for bad weather. Into this novel conveyance, which was drawn by a long team of sixteen sturdy, patient oxen, with big wooden yokes on their necks—driven by a white man with an ostrich feather in his hat—we hastily deposited our portmanteaus, boxes, guns, blankets, and sundry stores we had bought for the road, such as tea, coffee, pickles, pepper, flour, rice, curry powder, dried sausage, dried herbs, sugar, &c. We had also a keg of "pickled fish," which the Malays at Port Elizabeth are very skilful in preparing. Then we went along the town, the "admired of all observers"—for the diamond fever was getting very strong in Port Elizabeth—and picked up by degrees the other eleven passengers and their luggage. So soon the waggon was loaded half way up to the roof with the miscellaneous property and provisions of thirteen men—boxes, portmanteaus, carpet bags, little bags, big casks, sacks of biscuits, potatoes, and onions, and hosts of other articles, while, outside the waggon, buckets, cooking-pots, and kettles swung gracefully, and jangled noisily as we jolted slowly over the road.

Guns and fishing rods were tied up to the frame work of the roof. Great was the excitement we all felt at fairly starting for the Diamond Fields, and many were the farewell glasses drained with hospitable acquaintances; so that when at last about 4 p.m., the long whip cracked, and we fairly "trekked" out of the town, marching gaily beside the waggon, some were rather "unsteady on their pins," and nearly all were shouting and singing, to the great gratification of the nigger population of the outskirts of the town. We trekked on slowly till nightfall, then one of the wheels got into a deep rut, and we stuck there for the present; so a fire was lighted by the driver and his nigger assistant with a few miserable little bits of wood that were to be found on the scrubby plain by which we were surrounded, coffee was made, a slight supper eaten, and pipes smoked round the wretched little camp-fire. We then rolled in our blankets and lay down to sleep, but it was very cold and there was a very heavy dew, so we got little good rest. We stopped there the greater part of the next day, Sunday. By the time the sun had warmed us we were quite happy, some wandering over the veldt to secure wood for the cooking-fire, others roaming about with guns in search of game, of which we only saw one or two curlews, some sandpipers, and a big black and white kingfisher, by the banks of a creek, about two miles from our camping-place. In the afternoon some friends from the town, hearing we had not gone far, came out to see us, and we made merry with them; gave them coffee and biscuits, and then went and dined with them on oysters, eggs, sardines, bread and butter, and bottled beer, at an hotel on the banks of the creek above mentioned. The same evening we trekked on, and then began our pleasant wanderings through the interior, travelling by easy stages, averaging ten or fifteen miles a day, getting plenty of shooting, stopping a day or two at each of the towns on the way, viz., Graham's Town, Fort Beaufort, Queen's Town, Burghersdorp, and Fauresmith. Sometimes we would lose our oxen for a day or two, moreover one or two of the cattle died on the road, so delays were numerous. But it was a wild and jovial life, it did us good, and we enjoyed it much. It was good practice for the "roughing" at the Fields, too, for we had to draw our own water, cut or collect our own firewood (often very heavy work), cook our own meals, and wash up our own plates and dishes. Some extracts from a letter of mine, written from Queen's Town, 6th May, 1871, may give a somewhat more vivid idea of the life than I can now draw from my recollection.

We have had a very pleasant journey so far. Left Algoa Bay on 15th April, and expect twenty-one days from here will land us at Pniel, where we shall see people we have letters to, and get information about latest "new rushes," &c., &c. The weather has been simply delightful, just like English summer, with rather chilly nights. At night rugs and blankets are arranged so as to diminish as far as possible the painful irregularities, sharp angles, and utterly impracticable differences of height of our boxes, portmanteaus, casks, &c. A space of 17in. wide is nominally allowed to each man as sleeping accommodation, and each person's berth is denoted by a pencil mark on the wooden framework of the waggon; but, when *all* sleep in the waggon, owing to the peculiar differences of size and shape in the luggage, some get more than their allowance, others not nearly enough. For instance, one man will be lying on a big box, and have an inch or two to spare, while the other, on a portmanteau very much lower than the box, cannot level them by any number of blankets, so can't take any advantage of the two inches of the top of the box, which ought to belong to him, but is wedged into fifteen inches or so between the side of the box and a neighbouring cask. Generally, though, many sleep out on the veldt when the waggon "outspans" for the night. M. and I never sleep both in the waggon together, so whichever of us happens to be in has plenty of room. But sleeping in the waggon has many disadvantages. Two or three lively spirits, who will *not* go to bed (?) early, even in the bush, are sure to come in late, and walk calmly over other people's stomachs in the dark to their place in the middle or at the other end of the waggon. Then, when we are moving on, or "trekking," which is the proper expression, the jolting is frequently something fearful, not only for the shaking and noise, but because it frequently loosens and shakes down sundry small but heavy articles hung to the top of the framework to be out of the way. For instance, one night, going along a very rough road, a fishing-rod of mine jumped down, and hit a man on the cheek with its butt-end. A double-barrelled gun came down and nearly broke a fellow's rib; shortly after which a concertina bounced on to a man's face, the squeak of the astonished sleeper mingling ludicrously with a faint strain of music from the offending instrument. The same night, waking up with uncomfortable sensations, I found the toe of a dirty boot in my mouth, while another was trying to gently insinuate itself into my left ear. This sort of thing was only during the first few days, really; we "arrange matters differently" now, never all sleep in the waggon together, and tie up our things securely. For the first fortnight from leaving Algoa Bay we used to "trek" chiefly by night, seldom travelling after 8 a.m. till about 4 p.m., then perhaps moving on till 9, "tying up" oxen till 12 or 1 a.m. and then going on again till daylight. Each waggon has eight yoke, or sixteen oxen. Mr. W., our transport rider, drives one waggon, which contains his family, Mrs. W., two girls, and three boys, who, though very young, already know how to crack a huge whip and hold a gun straight.

A very decent Englishman, known by the name of Fred, drives our waggon, and a Kafir drives a third, also belonging to Mr. W., and containing seven very nice fellows, who came out in the *Sweden*, which made the wonderfully quick passage of twenty-seven days from England to Cape Town. There are so many details you would like to know that I hardly know what order to put them in. However, I will next speak of the cooking. Each separate mess divides among its members the labours of cooking and washing up. As M. knows nothing about cooking, and I have developed a remarkable talent that way, I do all the cooking, and he does all the washing up. We have also to provide our own wood and water. The latter has been plentiful all the way, but wood is now a thing of the past. We have a small stock on the waggon, but I have already learnt to build a good cooking-fire out of dry bullock dung, which we shall have to depend on now for a considerable time.

Now, as to the food we get. We have very frequent opportunities of buying sheep, the prices of which have fluctuated at different points on the road from 5s. to 10s. per sheep. M. and I got a quarter of a sheep for 1s. 3d. the other day. Then we carry with us bacon, potatoes, onions, tea, coffee, sugar, condensed milk, biscuits, flour, dried peas and beans, rice, raisins, Cape brandy, a little sauce and pickles, a lot of dried herbs, mint, &c., so that we not only don't starve but live *well*, with the aid of M.'s portable canteen (Silver's), which contains in a small compass every requisite for cooking and eating, for two persons.

Our guns, too, bring in frequent welcome additions to the larder. We have not got fairly into the big game or buck country yet, but nearly all the way we have seen plenty of doves, which are plump and excellent eating. I shot nine one morning, and a grand stew we made of them. Fred, the driver, shot a "duiker" doe one rainy day; it is a pretty little antelope of a quiet dun-brown colour. Last Sunday we bought from some Kafir boys a doe grysbok, rather bigger, reddish brown, with silvery hairs here and there, for 2s.

We have seen many hares, a little smaller than the English ones, rather thinner and more active—hosts of the so-called rock-rabbit, a brown furry little animal, with hardly any ears and funny long black feet, the "cony" of Scripture, I believe, living in holes among almost inaccessible rocks and cliffs. A few big bushbucks and springbucks have been seen, but none yet brought to the waggon by our sportsmen, of whom I and another Yorkshireman, B. by name, are about the keenest. I shot a fine grey partridge two days ago, very like our bird, only rather larger, and slightly darker plumage—very tough birds to kill. We have also seen many pheasants, and got a couple. They are not very brilliant plumaged, and have short tails.

In the dusk, coming up a gully, after shooting by the Fish River, I almost stumbled on to a leopard, or "tiger," as they call it here, which had apparently caught some small beast, and was growling over it. The brute gave a most tremendous growl at me. I stood still for about half a minute, uncertain what to do. Then, having only shot in my gun, I walked quietly away, the leopard growling fiercely at me all the time, but not moving. I was told afterwards that I had acted wisely, and *not* cowardly, as I should not have killed him with the first shot, and he would probably have given me some ugly scratches, if nothing worse.

We have passed through every variety of scenery, plain, scrub, wooded hills, grass lands, mountains, rocks—in fact as beautiful and varied scenery as any man could desire, not excepting a snow-clad peak, the Winterberg, which we saw a day or two ago. We crossed the famous Katberg two days ago. It is a very high and rough mountain, with a winding zig-zag road, very dangerous and precipitous in parts. We came half-way up in the night, then camped out on the slope of a hill, with a fierce driving wind and a terrible quantity of dust, but the next day the wind went down. We have had two regular rainy days, rather unusual for this season, several windy days, and many dusty days. The dust is so fine that it covers one all over, and penetrates everywhere. I must have swallowed my allotted "peck of dirt" on this journey already. Nevertheless we are all very healthy. I have walked nearly all the way, though I often take a little ride on Mr. W.'s waggon, and have a pleasant chat with the children, with whom I get on capitally, having always been fond of the "little folks." I tell them of the wonders of England and Europe, and they tell me of the rough life of the colony, and tales of shooting, fishing, &c.

There are plenty of openings in the colony for anyone coming out with money, and not liking the diggings. Wool-growing is the principal business of farmers in the Eastern Province, and is now paying well. Produce of every kind can be raised by irrigation. There are plenty of rivers.

Ostrich-farming is also carried on successfully; a good adult bird yielding at least 10*l.* twice a year.

The English colonists are capital fellows, very proud of the "old country," and full of kindness and welcome to English emigrants. Our waggons are going to "trek" on this afternoon.

To-morrow being Sunday, my chum and I have gone in for a luxury. We bought on the Queenstown market this morning a big bucketful of beautiful green peas for 1*s.* 3*d.* I also got a bag, over 100lb., of fine potatoes for 4*s.* 6*d.* Horses are good and cheap in the colony. At one place we found a lovely garden and orchard, with lots of oranges, citrons, loquots, apples, and other fruits. Pomegranates also plentiful.

We go about very roughly clad. I find I look like a cross between a bushranger and poacher. Life on the roads is very free and jolly, and no strong man need fear any hardships in this colony.

As we got farther up the country game became more abundant, we often saw droves of graceful springbuck, and two of them were shot by B., after a long and careful stalk. Partridges of two kinds, paauws, knorhaans or lesser bustards, and many other birds and beasts, became very numerous. During the whole of the way, we were hardly a day without passing some " canteen " or " accommodation house," indeed, they were too frequent for some of our fellow-passengers, who could not resist the temptation of " liquoring up " freely at each of these opportunities. The weather was very pleasant during the whole of the journey, we had sharp frosts once or twice at night, but the days were always warm. Plenty of sport, good food, pleasant scenery, plenty of good singing, and " spinning of yarns," all contributed to make the time pass quickly; but still many of us began to grow impatient, and to think we had made a great mistake in adopting such a slow old-fashioned mode of conveyance.

When at length, on the evening of the 30th May, after a rather rough crossing of the Modder River in the dark, we were told on " out spanning " that we were only about eighteen miles from Du Toit's Pan, where most of us had decided to commence digging operations, some of us were too impatient to stop any longer; so four of us started off to walk, accomplished about ten miles, then camped with our blankets among some fine mimosas, and started a big fire. A thunderstorm came on, and we got very wet before morning, but we did not mind that now. On we went, gaily singing, till we came to a Boer farm, where the niggers said we were " not far " from the Diamond Fields, and soon from the brow of a thinly-wooded hill we were delighted by seeing the white dots of tents on a distant ridge, and we waved our caps and shouted lustily for joy, for Du Toit's Pan lay before us.

Passing over a broad plain, covered with stunted grass and here and there a little thornbush, we rapidly neared the camp. We were barely half a mile distant from the nearest tents when I saw four springbuck grazing, and got so near to them that I risked a couple of shots with my revolver, but missed them. Then we got to the "Pan," from which this camp takes its name, a large shallow depression in the ground, which will apparently be full of water in rainy weather. Cattle were grazing all around, nigger men and women of all tribes and colours busy drawing water from two dirty wells, or washing clothes at two dirtier dams, while on a slight rise of ground beyond the Pan stood tents and waggons of every description, and farther up yet rose the huge mounds of earth and gravel thrown up by the diamond seekers, above which a dense permanent cloud of fine dust showed that they were all busy at work "dry-sifting."

In the afternoon there was a meeting of diggers, to hear terms proposed by the proprietors of the adjoining farm of Bultfontein, which had been "jumped," or taken forcible possession of, by a number of diggers. It was an animated scene. Crowds of rough bearded diggers, in various and picturesque costume, many with picks or shovels on their shoulders, stood on the slope of a hill, and listened pretty quietly to the speeches. At last it was declared that the farm of Bultfontein was thrown open to the public at 10s. per claim (thirty square feet), monthly license, and that those diggers who had jumped claims, were to keep them, on the same terms as new comers. As a great number of "jumpers" were present, this measure was advisable and gave general satisfaction; though one or two, who were not "jumpers," proposed that the whole of the claims should be numbered and drawn for by lot, but this was not agreed to.

Well, I see I was wrong in saying that I was fifty days on the road, it was only forty-six, but even that is a great deal too long. Some fellow passengers, per *Roman*, who had gone up by steamer to Natal, and thence by waggon to the Fields, arrived at Du Toit's Pan two days after us, so there is not much to choose between those two routes, except that *viâ* Natal there is much more big game. And it was really vexatious to think that we might have got up in eight or nine days at much less expense.

CHAPTER IV.

PNIEL TO CAPE TOWN BY INLAND TRANSPORT COMPANY'S HORSE-WAGGON.

THERE's news of the waggon—it will be here about twelve," said another digger to me, as we sat at Jardine's comfortable breakfast-table in the Royal Arch Hotel, Pniel. " Glad to hear there is a chance of our making a start to-day," I replied, "but I will have an hour's farewell fishing in the Vaal first." It was Wednesday, the 15th November, 1871, and the waggon should have reached Pniel some days previously, and started on the return journey to Cape Town, according to advertisement, on the 13th. All the places were taken, and diggers and merchants, anxious to reach their homes and friends, had been waiting some days in Jardine's Hotel, impatient and grumbling, some fearing our waggon had met with an accident, others attributing the delay to what ultimately proved to be the real cause, viz., bad management at some of the relay places. It was a hot morning, but rather cloudy and breezy. After breakfast, I and the friend above mentioned wandered along the pleasant, gravelly, willow-fringed banks of the Vaal, down the stream, I casting in my light gut line and paste bait wherever I saw a rapid or eddy likely for the vigorous yellow fish, pausing every now and then to pick up some of the pretty pebbles which are so abundant on the banks of the diamondi-ferous stream. We had been absent from the hotel about two hours. I had caught a dozen tidy yellow fish, from a quarter of a pound to two pounds in weight. It was getting terribly hot and sunny, the fish were off the feed, and I was moving up stream and taking my rod to pieces. I heard a shout, then a young friend came swiftly towards us, and said, "Be quick, the waggon is there, and going to start in an hour." So, quickly we had climbed the hill, passing big stores and busy claims, where the Kafirs were hard at work getting the gravel from amongst the big iron-stone boulders, and when we reached our hostelry it was one o'clock; the waggon stood there empty, the passengers from Cape Town having already begun to disperse themselves in the direction of the different camps, where they were going to try their luck, most of them of course proceeding to the famous

Colesberg Kopje, reports of which had caused such a sensation in the colony. The Inland Transport Company's waggon is a very strong but light vehicle, somewhat resembling a covered waggonette. In front is a seat for the driver, and his two nigger assistants; behind this three similar seats cross the waggon, each holding three passengers, and at the back of all there is a little sort of *coupé*, holding two passengers, with their backs to the horses. There is no glass, but stout curtains can be drawn and fastened across all the windows to keep out wind, rain, or dust; the moderate softness of the seats can be increased by one or two artfully arranged blankets; while those who have a corner seat, which is always preferable, can easily fasten a light pillow to the window-frame in such a way as effectually to secure their heads from the tremendous bumps caused by the jolting of the waggon, if they go to sleep sitting, as they doubtless often will.

I hastily packed my solitary portmanteau, and went in to dinner, after having done full justice to which, the ten other passengers and myself proceeded to instal ourselves as comfortably as possible in our respective seats. And at two p.m., amidst loud cheers and hurrahs, and not a few envious looks from our assembled friends and the whole *personnel* of the hotel, our driver shouted, cracked his long whip, and our ten gallant wiry little Cape horses started off at a canter, which very much resembled a gallop.

Leaving the banks of the Vaal, and the familiar scenes and faces of the last few months; leaving the hard, rough toil of digging, and turning our faces *homeward*, towards relatives, friends, civilisation, and comfort, many of us with good news and well-filled pockets for those at home; what wonder that we all felt a keen exhilaration, as the waggon dashed and jolted along—away over the hills, down on to the plains, and over the level ground—briskly, nay, swiftly and wildly, to the jingling of the merry little bells on our horses' necks, which we in the waggon accompanied with song after song, and chorus after chorus, till we grew hoarse and were fain to rest, and look out upon the hills and plains, and watch for the graceful bounding springbok, the pretty little furry bushy-tailed meerkat, the noisy knorhaan, and many other of the birds and beasts so numerous in this part of the country! We were nearly all young, none of us past the prime of life; several of us had been very lucky, and were taking down big diamonds to sell at Cape Town, or send home to the European markets. Merchants, too, were there, with keen eyes and shrewd heads for successful trading at the Fields.

I was only just beginning to recover strength after the fever which had so lately left me, and the diarrhœa which was still keeping me weak, moreover, I was suffering acutely from opthalmia; but when the doctor had represented to me the trying nature of the journey, and its dangers for an invalid like me, I had replied, "Doctor, I am *homeward-bound!* That thought will be sufficient to cheer my spirits and restore my health. I have set my face straight for Old England, and I am going there straight." And in truth I was not the least merry of the party, and my spirits and health improved, with the exception of my eyes, each day of the rough journey.

At five in the afternoon we made our first halt, at Radloff's farm, called "Sekretaris," where we stopped for an hour, and I purchased a large loaf of bread for a shilling, and refreshed myself also with two cups of milk at 3*d.* per cup.

A few hours later we came to Combrink's, where we could get nothing but sour or thick milk, but even that I did not despise, for I began to have the keen fever-convalescent appetite, and would neglect no opportunity of wholesome food. We outspanned that night at another farm, De Plooi's, sleeping on the ground in our blankets; and as, in the morning, our horses were not ready, and we had to wait till past ten o'clock, we got a rough but substantial breakfast of meat, milk, bread and coffee, at the old Boer's, at very trifling cost.

But as the painful condition of my eyes prevented me from taking my usual copious notes of this journey, I am unable to give more than a general outline of it. We crossed the dangerous rocky bed of the Riet River, camped out by the banks of the broad Orange, having arrived there too late to get the "pont," or huge ferry-boat, which takes waggons and cattle across; crossed on said "pont," at about five a.m. on the morning of the 17th, to the hotel kept by John Rostoll, the owner of the ferry, but did not stay there, for Hope Town was only a mile and a half off, and we reached it before seven. There we had a comfortable breakfast, and then proceeded by Addison's Farm, Steenbok Flat, Kalk Kraal, Skilderspan, Jägerschern, Wonderfontein and Driefontein to Victoria West, which we reached at six p.m. on the 19th. Victoria West is a pretty little town in a valley, between two high slightly-wooded hills. Early in 1871 a waterspout burst over these hills, and a huge body of water rushed down upon the little town, causing fearful destruction to both life and property, which will long be remembered in the colony. It is painful to see how many families there are in mourning.

Enjoying a hasty dinner at Victoria West, we went on past Brackfontein and Devenish's Farm to Beaufort West, arriving there at one p.m. on the 20th. Here we began to get our first glimpse of real luxury. At the hotel (Human's, I believe) the snug cleanliness and comfort of the little bedrooms in which we performed very needful ablutions, were most tantalising, after nights in the jolting waggon, with occasional uneasy naps for an hour or two on the hard ground, when we rested, fed, or changed our horses. Alas, we were not to sleep here! But we got a most sumptuous dinner, with an abundance of green peas, which called forth exclamations of delight from those to whom even a fresh potato had long been an unwonted luxury. Moreover, the pretty ladylike daughters of the host were extremely polite and attentive, and we had not been used to *that* sort of thing. I believe the whole family will have moved to the Diamond Fields by this time, and I prophecy great success and prosperity for them.

Moreover, we discovered here a baker's shop, wherein were wonderfully delicious cakes, in which I immediately invested a couple of shillings, and was also irresistibly tempted by some fine raisins, for diggers are very much like schoolboys in their fondness for "sweets." It was pleasing to find also that beer was decreasing in price; from 3*s.* per bottle on the Fields, Bass, Allsop, and Guinness was down to 2*s.* at Beaufort West.

At Devenish's Farm, where we had breakfasted before proceeding to Beaufort, we had been much pleased at the abundance of running water, trees, shrubs, and gardens round the farm, still more so at the sight of more than a dozen full-grown ostriches, and about three dozen in all stages of infancy, feeding quietly in a large grassy enclosure.

At four p.m. we left the town, and proceeded over a very rough road, which gave us much jolting. We bore all such trifles very good-humouredly by this time. At about six we met the Company's waggon from Cape Town. Both waggons halted; homeward-bound and upward-bound chatted pleasantly, and exchanged news; then we drove gaily off in our several directions, amid loud hurrahs and much cracking of whips and blowing of horns. Then on to a farm called "Uitkeek" (English, "look-out"), which we reached about 1.30 a.m. Slept on the ground till five a.m., had coffee, left at six, on to Rietfontein, where we had a very excellent breakfast. From five p.m. on the 21st to five a.m. on the 22nd we were at Blood River, where there is a decent hotel. We got an excellent dinner for 2s. 6d., chickens, curry, beef, mutton, potatoes, beans, &c. Then we indulged in the luxury of a real bed, for which only 1s. was charged, and we did not at all like being pulled out of it at two in the morning, but "onward" was the word. At six we reached Grootfontein, where we got eggs and coffee; at ten, Geelbek, more coffee, and from twelve to two p.m., stopped at Zoutkloof, where we had an excellent dinner, with green peas and other delicacies, the host swinging a big "punkah" over the table the whole time to keep the flies off. Then we drove on to Patatas River, a little beyond which we got a good supper, with green peas in abundance, at another farm. Thence we went on up high mountains, and after a halt at the unearthly hour of two a.m., which we spent in eating bread and butter and imbibing beer, at a picturesquely situated hotel—in a room which was all papered with *Illustrated London News* pictures—we drove on, through very fine mountain scenery, to the little town of Ceres, most picturesquely situated at the foot of a high mountain, and looking very gay with its white houses and lots of green trees. After breakfasting heartily, and having pleasant chats with some of the inhabitants, all very anxious to know how things were going at the Diamond Fields, we started gaily, at about three p.m., on the last stage of our waggon journey, *viâ* Mitchell's Pass, Darling Bridge, and Bain's Kloof, to Wellington, where we were to take to the railway cars for Cape Town.

The scenery along the whole of this last stage was awfully magnificent; high mountains, deep ravines, fearful precipices, along which a narrow road wound along, bordered here and there with huge stones, to guard against waggons or carts toppling over into the abyss below. A wild torrent dashed along the bottom of the deep valley; here and there lay huge rocks in chaotic masses, and we had to drive very cautiously, for there were many waggons coming up the Pass, and but few places where there was room for two vehicles to pass each other; so our driver's horn kept sounding loudly, waking up the echoes of the grand old mountains, as a signal to advancing waggons to keep out of the way. It was wonderful to see how cleverly the driver guided his eight horses along the sharply-winding, precipitous road, and how very close to the edge of the precipices we often were, in passing other vehicles. And when we had passed the summit, and were rattling down a fearfully steep declivity, some of the passengers were avowedly nervous. But soon we reached a level plain, and then the driver rose up, yelled, and cracked his whip loudly, and the splendid horses rushed away at full gallop along the level road in the bright moonlight, and dashed up to the doors of the hotel at Wellington at nine p.m.

How quickly we then descended from the waggon, and how we exulted at the thought that there was to be no more jolting, no more broken nights, no more coarse food, scarce water, and hard work—for our waggon journey was at an end, and the pleasures of civilisation lay before us. It would have been difficult to find a merrier company than that which was shortly assembled in the spacious saloon of the hotel, discussing a supper of hot and cold viands, with oranges, bananas, and other fruits, and some excellent Cape sherry.

Though we had once or twice fared well on the journey—green peas to wit—our food at the Boers' farms had often been of the coarsest and roughest description. Cooking is certainly not the *forte* of the Boer or his "vrouw." At one place we could get nothing but hard-boiled guinea-fowls' eggs and coffee. A heap of eggs was laid upon the table—no egg cups, no spoons, not even a morsel of bread—and the old Boer took out a handful of salt out of a big jar and threw it down upon the table. But all these things are gradually improving, owing to the immense traffic on the Diamond Field routes. Another Transport Company is now running waggons from Cape Town, and both companies have made efficient arrangements to have no delays with the relays of horses, and to allow frequent and ample time for rest and refreshment. We had found two relays quite unprovided with horses, and had to do one stage with mules and another with *oxen*. But the driver, by dint of much yelling and whipping, and his sable assistants by running beside the bullocks and belabouring them with the terrible "sjambok," managed to overcome the constitutional slowness of these animals, and even "conciliated" them into something resembling a gallop. Altogether, the journey was pleasant enough, nothing very serious in the way of hardship or fatigue; and even I, the invalid, was much stronger and stouter at the end of it than when I left Pniel, in opposition to my doctor's recommendation. But we are not at Cape Town yet.

On the morning of Friday, the 24th November, after a most luxurious sleep, we rose, paid our bills, and got into the waggon for the last time; for a very short trip this time, only to the Railway Station, a quarter of a mile distant from the hotel. Here the waggon was placed upon a truck, and the passengers were presented with tickets for the train, included in the 12*l*. passage money.

What a delight that smooth railway trip was, after the confinement and jolting of the old waggon, which was coming along in solemn, solitary state, on its truck behind us!

We passed through most luxuriant and varied scenery—mountains, plains, pretty little white villages embosomed in green trees, long stretches of bright green vineyards surrounded by hedges of quinces, gardens where flowers of wondrous beauty bloomed in bright profusion, and we thought of the hot, barren, dusty veldt round our mining camps far away in the Orange Free State, and greedily drank in the fair prospect around us, and were thankful.

But this was not all. At a station called Stellenbosch, about half-way to Cape Town, our train stopped ten minutes for refreshments, and then what a sight met our eyes! Negro, Malay, and half-caste girls, in clean white clothing, were waiting for us with baskets of huge oranges, plates of strawberries, cups of hot coffee, and piles of delicious cakes! A wild shout arose from the carriage in which I was sitting with three other diggers, a rush was made for the window, and the carriage was soon full of oranges, strawberries, and cakes, at what seemed to us absurdly low prices. And the oranges looked too large to be good, but they were the most delicious and juicy that I had ever tasted. The strawberries and cakes, too, were deserving of the highest praise, and we enjoyed ourselves more like schoolboys than ever.

And soon we were speeding along in sight of the grand old Table Mountain, fair Cape Town, and the calm blue sea, dotted with the white sails of the fishing boats, with a big craft lying here and there, and a forest of masts and rigging, showing the docks in the distance.

My fellow-passengers were all colonists. They were close to their homes and their friends now: you could see it in their eager, joyous faces; but *I* looked out into the far distance over the broad blue water, and longed to be standing once more on the familiar deck of the good old *Roman*, and fairly "homeward bound."

At 9.15 we were in Cape Town Station, where eager friends and relatives and many of the general populace were waiting in a crowd for the arrival of "the diamond diggers."

I slipped away from the throng, for I had no friends there, and, with one fellow-passenger similarly situated, giving our light baggage to the brown-faced, white-clad, obsequious coolies, we marched gaily across the parade to the Royal Hotel, in Plein Street.

Mr. Lopes, most excellent of landlords, was standing in front of his door, clad in most faultless costume, and looking oppressively aristocratic to our unaccustomed eyes.

And what a figure I was! A dirty old broad-brimmed straw hat, with a blue veil round the crown, a light brown canvas jacket much the worse for wear, bright yellow trousers, a striped shirt, a big red sash round my waist, and a pair of rough brown "veldt-schoens" on my feet—altogether wild-looking, haggard, and travel-stained. No wonder that Mr. Lopes looked at me somewhat dubiously at first, but in an instant he thought of the arrival of the Diamond Field train, and was re-assured.

With the utmost politeness he ushered us into a comfortable, nay luxurious, bedroom, and proffered warm baths, and every possible comfort.

We hastily made a trifling change in our apparel, and then descended to the saloon, to enjoy a breakfast of the most delicious fresh fish that mortal man could desire. Then we went out, bought civilised "toggery," and commenced to enjoy ourselves.

Our first ardent desire was to eat ices, our next to drive in a Hansom cab; after the satisfactory accomplishment of both of which, I settled down to the perfect enjoyment of luxurious, placid *dolce far niente*, for I was still far from well, and did not want to do anything, not even to fish.

I had to wait ten days at Cape Town, and the time passed most delightfully. I don't believe there ever was a more comfortable hotel than the Royal, with its large, high, cool, luxuriously furnished drawing-rooms, its pleasant lounge beneath the verandah between the green trees in front, its abundant table and most excellent *cuisine*, and the attention of such a host and hostess as Mr. and Mrs. Lopes. We were lively too; returned diggers, naval officers from our men-of-war stationed in the neighbouring Simon's Bay, travellers and hunters from the interior, enterprising wealthy merchants of Cape Town, all hearty, genial, and kindly—the time could never hang heavily in such company.

Then there was a grand ball given by the officers of a Swedish man-of-war, to which came most of our naval officers, and plenty of fair English girls and matrons.

There were plenty of delightful rides and drives to be made, the neighbourhood of Cape Town affording an endless variety of most lovely scenery; and the best of horses and neatest of carriages were easily procurable, but I was too lazy. I strolled sometimes through the beautiful Botanical Gardens (liberally thrown open to all travellers) and I visited the Museum, delighted with its admirable collection of birds, beasts, fishes, minerals. &c., &c.; specially interested in the fine collection of pebbles from the Vaal River, containing beautiful specimens of agates, cornelian, chalcedony, garnets, crystals, jasper, and amygdaloid. There is also a pure nugget from the Tatin Gold Fields, a model of the first South African diamond, and many diamonds lent for exhibition. A careful inspection of the treasures of the South African Museum will well repay any intending digger.

The population of Cape Town is very mixed—English, Dutch, Germans, and other Europeans; negroes, Malays, half-castes of every shade of colour, many of the girls of great beauty, and dressing picturesquely, generally in white. The European population follow closely upon the London and Paris fashions, and generally dress remarkably well. Our soldiers, with their white trousers and helmets and red coats, look very neat and cool; so do our policemen. The Malays wear immense broad-brimmed straw hats, of a pyramidal shape, and very curious wooden sandals, only held on to the foot by a big wooden button between the big and next toe. They are large dealers in fish, which they bring round in carts, blowing a very loud and discordant horn. The markets are abundantly supplied with the best of meat, game, fish, vegetables, and an endless variety of fruit, of which there is always some in season.

The climate of Cape Town is delightful; it seemed quite cool after the Diamond Fields, and the heat was never at all oppressive during my ten days' stay there, though the summer season had fairly set in. The warehouses, stores, and shops of Cape Town are magnificent, the import and export trade being very large. There are occasional performances at the theatre—concerts, fêtes, balls, &c.; and for riding and driving, boating and fishing, there could not be a more delightful residence. The neighbouring vineyards of Constantia—Cloete's, and Van Renen's—will well repay a visit; and, from samples I have tasted, I think Cape wines are much calumniated in England, and will one day be appreciated at a high value. There are plenty of omnibuses about Cape Town and neighbourhood, and an abundance of Hansom cabs.

Cape Town is a perfect paradise to a returned digger. I know of no place where better living, or more pleasant society, is to be found. I spent one day most pleasantly at the country house of a friend from the Fields, a lovely little place at Claremont, and we drove about in the afternoon among gardens, parks, and vineyards, all of the most bewildering luxuriance.

But now it is time for me to leave fair Cape Town—though I could linger over its pleasant reminiscences for hours—and go on board the old *Roman*, in which I have secured my passage for England, and the same berth I occupied on the voyage out, No. 1, about the best situation in the ship—being far away from the noise and shaking of the screw.

Pleasant Cape Town, and grand old Table Mountain, *au revoir!*

CHAPTER V.

DIARY ON BOARD S.S. "ROMAN," CAPE TOWN TO SOUTHAMPTON.

5TH December, 1871.—" Once more on the deck I stand—of my own swift gliding craft." She is not "my own," though, and she does not go in much for " gliding ;" *rolling* is more her form, I know, but she is a splendid old sea-boat, and familiar to me as home. Familiar faces all around me ; here is the genial, gentlemanly captain, the jovial, hearty officers, the attentive stewards, the sturdy, merry crew, aye, and even the same two dogs, old " Lion," the big black retriever, stately and dignified as ever, and little " Charlie," the black and tan terrier, who enjoys the tropics with an intense laziness, and will shiver piteously as we draw near the chills and fogs of Old Albion. But I am going ahead too fast; now let me stick to my diary. Steamed out of Table Bay at 4.15 p.m. Fair breeze outside, sails hoisted at 5.15. Few passengers, two parsons aft and one forward. Several returned diggers —among them two lucky ones from the Colesberg Kopje. Also a young Oxonian, who has been hunting up in the big game country, had grand sport, and proves very companionable, his conversation being amusing and instructive to a high degree.

6th December, six a.m.—Fair breeze continues, we are bowling along rapidly, ship quite steady ; by noon 187 miles run from Green Point (corner of Table Bay); weather fine, but cool.

7th December.—Clear, sunny, but not warm. Fair breeze all day ; 229 miles run by noon. One of our lucky diggers comes out very strong as a banjoist and vocalist, we have very pleasant times in the smoking room, quiet whist and écarté, chess, and plenty of good singing and music. In the evening our musician plays and sings on the poop for the gratification of the ladies— pity they are all married ladies—and lots of children, some of the latter terrible squallers. Development of Herod-like feelings among some of the male passengers and ship's officers, deprived of natural and needful rest by incessant howling of some of the youngsters.

8th December.—Breeze has died away, **or rather there is just a** faint breeze ahead, nearly a dead calm. Noon. Breeze has got round again, sails set forward. 217 miles run. Much music in saloon; chess, &c.

9th December.—Favourable breeze fresher, more sail, slight ripple on; 237 miles. Afternoon and evening stronger breeze, ship rolling a good deal. Music and whist.

10th December, Sunday.—A grey morning, some sea on, and much rolling. Captain read prayers in saloon. 241 miles run. Quiet, slow day.

11th December.—Grey morning, inclined to rain; much rolling still. Bathed, water just right temperature, "with the chill off." 224 miles run, 360 from St. Helena. Music and yarns in smoking-room.

12th December.—Up at 7.30; bathed. Breeze a little fresher, slight rain. 228 miles run, 145 from St. Helena. Music in saloon in the afternoon, and on poop in the evening.

13th December.—Up at six; just cast anchor off St. Helena. Quarantined because of measles at Cape Town. Tried to fish; hooked a gar-fish, but lost him half-way up. Boats come off with fruits, birds, and curiosities, but are not allowed to come alongside. After breakfast we get *pratique*, but as we are to sail in two hours, and it is raining, don't think it worth while to go ashore. Boats now alongside, and birds, shells, beads, baskets, and sundry curiosities offered for sale, and sold at half the prices asked. Pears sixpence a dozen, hard and flavourless. Two fresh saloon passengers, and eight marines for Ascension. Lovely flowers brought on board, also cabbages and other vegetables for Ascension, which must be a barren place. Anchor up and off at noon, with fair breeze. Several homeward-bound ships passed us while anchored. The *Marc Antony*, of the Cape and Natal Company, is lying off St. Helena, boiler having broken down, and will be very late at the Cape, instead of the magnificent quick run she was expected to make.

14th December.—Warm, cloudy day, one light shower in morning. 244 miles run. Music and singing in afternoon.

15th December.—Rather warmer; flying-fish about. 233 miles run; distance from Ascension 226. Very quiet, dull day.

16th December.—Ascension in view at 7 a.m; good-sized island, fine bold outline, one high peak. Pass sandy (?) beach, where turtle are caught at night. Round a point, and got to anchorage in a large bay about 11.30. No guns fired here, for fear of scaring the turtle. An old man-of-war hulk stationed here; two merchantmen lying in the bay. Many peculiar birds flying about, very close to the ship, "boobies" I think, One big fellow settles on jib-boom, and is all but caught by a passenger, not flying away till the man actually touches it. Picturesque little settlement ashore, at foot of high mountain. Many large barracks, officers' quarters, forges, condensing factories, a large canteen, a church, a reading-room, and a "Theatre Royal," all painted a uniform yellowish brown.

Went ashore at one p.m. Found the island apparently all composed of volcanic scoriæ and lava, but here there is one part where vegetation grows, and game, pheasants, partridges, and wild goats abound. At the settlement, however, the only specimens of vegetable life I saw were two miserable stunted nondescripts, a few inches high, surrounded by a most imposing amount of wooden palisades. I judged this arrangement to represent the Botanic Gardens of Ascension, as it was situated in the middle of a fine parade-ground. Finding the canteen closed, Captain H. and I strolled on to the beach, and found it entirely composed of water-worn fragments of shells and coral, most beautiful on close inspection. We found many beautiful entire shells, of seven or eight varieties, also handsome *echini*, or sea-urchins. Going down to the rocks, found the pools amongst them marvellously rich in life. Small fish of various species, a great many like our fresh-water perch, barring the back fin, with very marked black bars down the sides; also thousands of weird-looking crabs, black with many round white spots, of wonderful agility, running over the rocks much more quickly than I could follow them, and often *jumping* small distances. One of them, jumping into a pool to avoid me, was hotly pursued by a hideous *poulpe*, octopod, or "devil-fish," which darted out from a crevice in the rock, but missed the crab. In deep, clear water, outside the rocks, and in some pretty inlets, were numerous fine fish, of very dark colour, from 1lb. to 3lb. each, one or two still larger. How I wished for a rod and line! The bottom of the pools was thickly studded with *echini*, also with three kinds of coral, some pieces of which I managed to break off, with the aid of a good stone. Innumerable shells, tenanted some by their natural owners and some by hermit crabs, added to the beauty of the sub-aqueous landscape. With a good collection of shells and coral, we returned to the canteen, and found it pretty well supplied with everything, like a store at the Diamond Fields. Marines, workmen, and other people connected with the fort and station, kept dropping in, and were eager for any news brought by our steamer.

Returning to the little jetty, I noticed a small flock of goats, in tolerably good condition. These animals are reported to subsist entirely on old canvas and paper collars, the latter being extensively worn on the island. A reverend gentleman, one of our passengers, saw a goat devouring a piece of old canvas with apparent satisfaction. On the parade ground, I saw a game of cricket played by some of the officers on a ground *paved* with some kind of concrete stone—grass, or herbage of any kind, not existing in this part of the island. Many Kroomen, or Krooboys, act as servants, seamen, &c. They are a fine looking race of negroes, very well blacked, their countenances all looking as if they had been lately operated upon by one of the London Shoeblack Brigade, with a liberal supply of Day and Martin. It was currently reported on our ship that there are two good looking young ladies on the island. I saw a female on the jetty, but she could not have been one of those.

We brought for the officers' mess some cabbages and carrots from St. Helena, also a large supply of liquors and beer. A huge turtle, weighing I should think 1000lb., was sent on board our ship, so I look forward with pleasure to some aldermanic treats. At 4.30 we went on board again, and by 6 p.m. were leaving Ascension far behind. I could have spent a few days there very pleasantly in fishing and exploring. The heat is rather intense there sometimes, and it is the driest place I ever saw.

17th December, Sunday.—Very hot and sunny. 173 miles run by noon (from Ascension). A flying-fish, nearly the size of a mackerel, came on board in the evening. All officers and passengers in very light costumes, Bath water almost tepid.

18th December.—Warm, but cloudy. 218 miles run. In the evening, in honour of crossing the line, two rockets sent up, and a blue light burnt. About 9.30 the phosphorescent animals or zoophytes in the wake of the ship wonderfully brilliant; small coruscations and large bodies of light revolving in the wash of the screw, some of them visible a long way off, and the water lighted up from below by the countless animals swimming a foot or two down, so that the slight ripple on the surface had a marvellously beautiful appearance.

19th December.—Hot and sunny. The breeze has left us, but there are signs, I fear, of another springing up-heading us. 215 miles run. Very hot, close day and evening. Much singing in evening. No lights in the sea at night.

20th December.—Almost dead calm. Slight rain. Waterspout seen about seven a.m. Several Mother Carey's chickens about. Run 192. Very hot. In afternoon a three-masted schooner seen. Too far off to speak.

21st December.—Hot, sunny morning. Met a French brig, white hull, the *Navigateur*, apparently bound for the Cape. Breeze getting up ahead, making ship rather cooler. 190 miles run. Freshening breeze ahead. Much singing on poop in evening; whist, &c.

22nd December.—Much cooler, strong N.E. trade; ship pitching a good deal, and shipping seas forward; going seven knots. Run 176. In the evening rehearsal in the smoking-room for amateur Christy Minstrel performance for to-morrow, Saturday, to be kept as Christmas Eve.

23rd December.—Fresh morning; wind N.E. a little on our beam, so hoist sails, which help us on a little. Run 172. A ringdove came on board, was caught and caged. About 6.30 p.m. we pass the two lights of Goree, Cape Verde. At seven p.m., grand Christy Minstrel performance in saloon. Tables and lamps cleared away for stage. Seven performers, well blacked, and most excellently and comically costumed; songs, riddles, &c., really a very creditable performance. During the singing, champagne and brandy-and-soda handed round among the audience, presented by the captain. The captain thanks the performers, and announces a "wedding" for Christmas Day. Our big turtle was killed this evening.

24th December, Sunday.—Some pretty tall drinking going on; "experienced surgeon" comes to much grief—gets very tight, tumbles out of berth and cuts forehead, has to be tied down and locked up. Run 146.

Christmas Day.—Cool morning, very calm; turtle steaks to breakfast. Fine scrolls, with beautifully painted devices, and suitable inscriptions, by a talented lady passenger, decorating the saloon. Quiet morning; Church service in saloon. At lunch, a fine Christmas cake. Excellent dinner at five, turtle fins, turkey, fowls, roast beef, &c.; champagne and other suitable liquors circulating freely. At 7.30 grand performance in saloon of "The Wedding," an original burlesque, very well got up by the first and second officers and several of the passengers. Costumes would have done credit to any stage, and must have taken an immense deal of preparation. The first officer, as the bride, looked very like Miss Anna Swann, the Nova Scotian giantess,

—only much bigger! Songs and dances, all very funny and grotesque. We were in soundings to-night, heaving the lead: dangerous part of the sea. At 7.30, found no bottom at seventy fathoms—two hours later, bottom at only about twelve fathoms. I was on deck till midnight; cutting cold wind and intensely cold air, heavy dew.

26th December.—Cold, clear, sunny morning. Cape Blanco, and a long, low, rugged coast line in view some ten to twenty miles off. Sea calm. Bath very refreshing. Many birds about. Run 161. In sight of land all day. Rocky coast, big breakers dashing up the cliffs; apparently nothing but a waste of sand behind, said to be inhabited in the interior by savage Arab tribes. In the evening magnificent moonlight effect over long rolling swell.

27th December.—Heavy swell on, but light wind, still ahead. Good bath. Ship rolling much. Run 173. Distance from Peak of Teneriffe 220. Singing and whist in evening.

28th December.—Not so cold. Light breeze still ahead. At 11.30 I made out the Grand Canary. Run 165. 325 miles from Madeira. At two p.m. the Peak of Teneriffe plainly visible above the clouds, covered with snow. In the evening, singing and playing, as usual. Fine moonlight view of the snow-clad Peak. Revolving light on farthest headland of the island. Saw a faint light of the little town at Santa Cruz. This afternoon there was a very good auction sale in fore-cabin; karosses, lion, leopard, jackal and other skins, diamonds, curiosities, &c., &c. Very good prices realised, for diamonds especially.

29th December.—Fine fresh morning, jolly cool bath. Run 174. Distance to Madeira 153. Auction on quarter deck in afternoon; skins, curiosities, &c. Music and whist in evening.

30th December.—Madeira visible at sunrise (about 6.30). Heavy swell on. Rather cold morning, but bath still bearable. Anchored at 11.30. Went ashore. Dined at Neal's Hotel, on top of a hill. Painfully hard walking, all stones. Splendid fruit, vegetable, and fish markets. Bananas, oranges, guavas, custard apples, &c. Plenty of green peas. Immense albicores in fish market, live turtle, and large quantities of horse mackerel. Left about 5.30.

31st December.—Fine morning. Heavy swell on. Rather cold. Run 118 from Madeira. In afternoon large three-masted steamer seen and spoken, the *Mariana* or *Miranda*, for Buenos Ayres. Great rolling; occasional light rain. Saw Old Year out on the poop.

1st January, 1872.—Cool damp morning, with very heavy swell. Bath getting rather cold. A fine rainbow. Signs of a favourable breeze getting up. Run 182. In evening singing, écarté, and whist, in smoking room. Stayed on poop till twelve. Hardly any sleep all night, owing to rolling and noises.

2nd January.—Wind ahead (N.E.) All sails furled. Heavy swell on. Ship rolling very much, especially at breakfast time, spilling gravy, &c. Run 205. Sighted many ships to-day. Among others, spoke the *Dolphin*, of Shoreham, bound to Falmouth. Wind nearly dead ahead. Whist, singing, &c.

3rd January.—Cold, damp morning. Rain before breakfast; fine afterwards. Wind still ahead, but hope to reach Southampton by Sunday. At about ten land in sight—Spanish coast. At twelve off Cape Finisterre, and a long stretch of coast very distinctly visible; also a fine three-masted screw steamer, going coastwise. Run 195. Only 625 miles to Southampton. Fine bright day, many sea-gulls around, and one or two lesser albatross. In afternoon, wind round to S.W.—fair for us—roughish sea, rather thick weather. Usual music, whist, &c., in evening, but under difficulties; wind freshening, ship rolling tremendously. At night had to shorten sail, and soon after turning in, at 10.30, she gave some tremendous rolls. Smashes of crockery were heard, and heavy articles of furniture and luggage rolling and banging about. Everything in chaos on the floor of my cabin. Bottle of wine and one of *noyau* smashed in saloon, and some of the liquid splashed into C's. berth.

4th January.—Rainy morning. Wind not quite so strong. Going about eleven knots. Some good *rolls* just about breakfast time, and coffee and gravy spilt here and there. Lots of gulls and lesser gulls about. Fine sea on; rough, but not so much swell. Run 244 by noon, sea getting up, wind still fair. In evening, regular Bay of Biscay weather; gale from S.W. At dinner many small mishaps—soup, gravy, &c., in undesirable places; biscuits, nuts, apples, and oranges, flying all over the saloon. At about eight, main topsail carried away by gale, and split to ribbons, whereby ship rolled tremendously. Great running on deck, mate shouting for men with axes and tomahawks to cut away the *débris*. Great hauling of ropes, in which I assisted, getting swung about and one foot stamped on, so said " I wouldn't play," and retired to saloon. Some of lady passengers turned rather pale, and some of males required a good deal of "Dutch courage." Continued heavy rolling and tremendous thumps from big seas all evening. Turned in at 10.30, rolling tremendous. Wedged myself in berth with extra rugs, &c.; got to sleep, unlike most of the other passengers, and slept till six a.m.

5th January.—Sunshiny morning. Breeze has shifted to W. by N.W. Very good for us. Heavy sea on still. Passengers all more cheerful, though few have slept. Plates, dishes, &c., very lively at breakfast. Difficult to get from one part of ship to another. Big rent in main topsail from last night's gale. There was a squall and heavy hailstorm about 6.30 a.m. Land in sight at ten, and by eleven in good view of the Lizard Lighthouse, a fine large white building, and one or two scattered farmhouses on the neighbouring headland. Good breeze, grand heavy green sea and white waves. After lunch, wind backed again to W.S.W., and weather became thick and hazy, with squalls, Lots of sea-gulls about, and one or two wild-ducks seen. Run 222. Sighted Start Point in afternoon. Thick haze and rain. Wind rather less. At dinner-time heavy thunderstorm and vivid lightning, and "St. Elmo's Light" visible on mainmast head; this disappeared on a fearfully bright flash accompanied by a crashing peal of thunder. Evening calm, going slowly. Numerous craft about. Music, singing, and tall drinking in smoking room. Turned into my berth at eleven, for the last time.

6th January.—Off the Isle of Wight at daybreak (seven a.m.) Pilot on board before eight. Hurrah for Old England! In Southampton Docks at ten, pouring rain, waited some time for it to leave off, but it seems it never does. Finally went ashore in it, and it has been raining nearly ever since.

PART III.
SKETCHES OF LIFE AND CHARACTER ON THE FIELDS.

CHAPTER I.

DIAMOND DIGGERS.

AMONG the mighty concourse attracted to the banks of the Vaal and the interior of the Orange Free State by the wonderful riches which have been discovered there during the past two years, there are of course to be found men of numerous nationalities, of every grade in the social scale, and every type of character and manners. A large proportion of the diggers are Cape colonists, and Natalians, then come the Dutch Boers, both of whom have, of course, facilities for trying their luck at the diggings at little expense, owing to the small cost of the journey. Then come Englishmen, Australians, and Americans, the former in very large and continually increasing numbers. A good many Germans, with a sprinkling of Frenchmen, Italians, and Spaniards, are also to be found among the diggers.

An Englishman will get on very well among the colonists when he comes to know them, and succeeds in rubbing off some of their prejudices. I found a very general feeling amongst them that the South African colonies, their productions, and their people, were not properly appreciated in England, and there really seems to be some little foundation for this feeling. But to anyone who speaks well of the colony, as it deserves, they are very friendly, hospitable, and generous. They are a very fine race of men, generally tall and well built, tough, strong hardworkers, energetic, steady, and sober. All, or almost all of them, speak Dutch or Kafir, or both. They get along very well in business and other necessary intercourse with the Boers, without feeling any great liking for them. Some of the Natalians, especially, have rather too much of the "nemo me impune lacessit" style about them at first sight; but this will soon wear off on a closer acquaintance, and beneath the hard, rough shell of manners which are not those of the most refined civilisation, will be found the wholesome kernel of an honest, warm heart, of manliness and good feeling. The colonists, as a rule, dress after the latest English fashions, the dwellers in towns especially, but of course at the diggings everyone dresses "just how he darn pleases;" and it will be difficult to distinguish the colonial-born from the recently-arrived English by the dress, except that perhaps the latter are a little more inclined to disguise themselves, or "come out strong." The corduroy trousers, the light flannel shirt, the broad felt hat, or pith helmet, and the broad belt, with its partitions for diamonds and gold, are common to both; but the brim of your Englishman's hat may perhaps be a little broader, his "puggeree" more showy, and his belt of a handsomer pattern than those of his colonial friends. But, on the other hand, I think the colonists come out the strongest in feathers. Large ostrich feathers, worth perhaps ten shillings each out there, are frequently to be seen curling gracefully round the slouched felt hat of some stalwart young farmer from Natal or the Cape colony—wings of birds of gay plumage, shot on the way up, immense long feathers of the Kafir crane, all these and many more make gay their head-covers; nay, I have seen a broad strip of the soft fur of a silver jackal, or some other animal, going right round the crown of a hat. Red sashes, of silk and other materials, and of great length, like the Eastern "cummerbund" are very extensively worn; not only because they are ornamental, and softer and pleasanter wear than a leathern belt or strap, but because they are considered to be of some use as a preventive against diarrhœa and other disorders of the bowels. Green veils, blue veils, red and white puggerees, and divers other arrangements for coolness, shade, or ornament, are also very prevalent among all the diggers; so that with the numerous suits of brown or yellow cords, with "white ducks" here and there, the gay colours and variegated patterns of the shirts, and the eccentric but highly ornamental character of the headgear, an assemblage of diamond diggers has in it many elements of the picturesque, and a good deal of vivid colouring. The diggers are, as a rule, a good tempered race, and respecters of law and order. Revolvers are *not* carried, at any rate never openly. I remember a time, though, when one or two daring highway robberies in the neighbourhood of Du Toit's Pan caused me—as well as many others—to take out my six-shooter at night, but I am sure I should have got along just as well without it.

The Australian and American diggers generally do well, having had previous experience of mining. An Australian, with his wife, worked near me at Du Toit's Pan, employing no Kafirs, he digging and sifting, she sorting, and they had very fair luck, making about 800*l.* in three months. They got early news of the "new rush" (Colesberg Kopje), and went over there. The man was employed in sinking a well there, and had got down to a good depth, in a hard stratum where blasting was required. One day, owing, it is believed, to imprudence in using a steel rod for "tamping" instead of a copper one, a charge of powder ignited while this Australian and another man were below. A terrific explosion took place, the Australian was killed instantaneously, the other man severely injured. His widow, I hear, was very soon consoled.

American diggers "go-ahead" well at the Fields; I knew some very nice fellows amongst them, and some very lucky ones too. One party, not satisfied with the ordinary way of digging and sifting, brought up a large steam-engine, with a rotary cylindrical sieve, by means of which they were to sift I don't know how many cartloads of stuff a day, and to work out a whole claim in three weeks or a month. They got about a dozen Kafirs to work out the stuff quickly, and bring it to where the machine stood, close to their tents. Great was the crowd collected, and loud the admiration expressed at the working of the machine, which appeared to go on smoothly enough, though one or two wary old diggers shook their heads and expressed disapprobation. When the steam-whistle sounded, the Kafirs and Boers standing round jumped with fright, but stood their ground. But when the engine blew off steam, the strange sight and sound were too much for uncivilised human nature, and there was a regular "stampede" of Kafirs and Boers too. They soon got used to it, of course. The machine went on working for a week or two, but soon it was found that if the sieve was turned at full speed, all the stuff, by centrifugal force, stuck to the sides of the cylinder instead of getting properly sifted, and if turned slowly it got through no more work than a couple of Kafirs would do in the same time; so soon the engine and cylinder were advertised for sale, and found a purchaser at a fair price, as it could be applied to many other purposes. My Yankee friends, in nowise discouraged, went on steadily digging, and will probably ere long set sail for Columbia with a "pile."

I have little to say about the Germans in this chapter. More of them are to be found amongst diamond buyers than amongst diamond diggers. Frenchmen, Italians, and Spaniards are but few in number. They soon get merged in the great mass of English-speaking diggers, and lose many of their most apparent national characteristics.

But the Boer, the omnipresent, cordially detested by the English, surely I can find much to say about him. In the first place, to borrow from my Yankee friends what appears to me a very suitable expression, he is a "mean cuss." Most emphatically and thoroughly mean is your average Boer, with his stolid ignorance, his contempt for civilisation and refinement; living, though perchance a man of considerable wealth, in a way that would disgrace a farm labourer, in a barely furnished one-storied house, the floor plastered with cow dung, feeding like pigs, living often on meat and mealies, satisfied with breeding cattle and sheep on the scanty "veldt" that surrounds his farm, not even thinking of fencing in a bit of ground to grow a few vegetables, and seldom, therefore, getting either vegetables or good bread to eat. There are exceptions though; the Boers in the neighbourhood of the Fields are beginning to find out how well it pays them to bring vegetables, eggs, and other small luxuries on the Du Toit's Pan and Colesberg markets; while those of the Transvaal country, impelled by the wondrous fertility of that region, have long been large growers of corn, maize, tobacco, and many other important marketable commodities;—but even in the houses of such as these I will warrant that you shall find neither abundance nor comfort.

But it is with the Boer digger that I have more immediately to do. Who digs so cheaply, who risks so little capital, as he? He starts for the Fields with his big waggon, his team of oxen —slow and stolid as himself—perchance a flock of sheep, too, and a good stock of maize, flour, tobacco, and "Boer brandy"— for he is not going to be swindled by the high prices at the Fields, not he. Moreover, he has with him not only his "vrouw" and "kinders," *i.e.*, wife and children, but a lot of Kafirs, whom he has obtained in the interior at about the wages of *a cow*, or 3*l.* per year. So he comes to the Fields, lives in his waggon, or in a tent which his Kafirs and his "kinders" make for him, spends no money at all on the Fields, living on the stores he has brought with him. See him dig—well, you can hardly call it digging; the brutal old patriarch will sit at the sorting-table all day with his pipe—*perhaps* allowing the "vrouw" to do likewise—while half-naked Kafir boys (aye, and young girls, too), and his own children, from the long, pasty-faced, half-idiotic lout of twenty, down to the little four-year-old, who can scarcely toddle, are all toiling hard under the broiling sun, picking, shovelling, hauling, breaking, and sifting. One old couple I have often seen sitting solemnly at the table—long after all the English diggers had knocked off work for the day—while a young Kafir girl, of most graceful figure, and a still younger Dutch girl, were toiling hard at a big sieve, evidently thoroughly tired out. Another, working quite near my claim, used to rouse my indignation, and that of many other Englishmen too, by the amount of labour he got out of a most active little girl of about ten and a poor little toddler of five, hardly able to lift the tools they worked with. The Boers are an intensely stupid race, but have a kind of low cunning withal. Many of them sold diamonds very cheaply during the early times, but they have grown pretty wide-awake now, and ask enormous prices. They have a very great animosity towards Englishmen, which, as they are too cowardly to show fight, now takes the more profitable form of cheating them on all possible occasions. Proud indeed is the Boer who has performed a successful swindle on a "verdomd Engelschman." I must admit that if they apply this objectionable participle to us, we English are, in return, no less emphatic in speaking of the Boers. Many of the latter have been very lucky, and were particularly fortunate in finding big stones during my stay at Du Toit's Town. At that time, whenever the report spread through the camp that another 50, 80, or 90 carat stone had been found, the natural inquiry would be, "Who found it?" and the almost invariable reply was, "Another —— Dutchman!"

Some of the Boers used to cause particular irritation amongst the storekeepers by the amount of silver they took out of the camp, small change being in great request and very scarce. One old fellow came in with a waggon-load of oranges, which he retailed from his waggon at ten for a shilling, and absolutely refused to take anything but silver in payment, so it is estimated that he must have taken something like fifty pounds worth of silver with him when he "inspanned" his oxen and trekked away from the camp. Others, to avoid the expense of a tent or store, having brought a waggon-load of "Cape Smoke," wine, &c., would sell it from the waggon at a little lower than store prices.

The Boers are—or rather used to be—awfully noisy fellows at night. Besides a very regular business of psalm singing, very edifying to *them* no doubt, but by no means gratifying to an English ear, they would have grand jollifications whenever one of their number found a big diamond—which was pretty often. Their chief delight on these occasions was to let off all the crackers they could buy, and fire an indefinite number of guns and rifles. I say "indefinite," though I was at one time inclined to think they fired a shot for each carat of the diamond found, but I was always too lazy to count. I should have premised that the noisy part of the business always took place late at night, after a Homeric repast had been eaten, and numberless glasses of Boer brandy been consumed by the men, and "kommetjes" of coffee by their fair and fat spouses; and, in their excited state, they would often forget that, in order to make a noise, it was *not* necessary to put a *bullet* into the rifle; so, after a horse had been accidentally killed, and several diggers had complained of bullets whistling through their tents in rather unpleasant proximity to their persons, our active *Landdrost* or police magistrate issued all over the camp notices forbidding the discharging of firearms within the precincts of the camp after sundown. Some of the lucky Boers still persisting in their usual expression of exultation in spite of this edict, the police one night made a raid on a lot of the demonstrators, caught them *flagrante delicto*, and seized their guns, most of them old "roers" of portentous strength, but some excellent new sporting rifles among them. The said weapons had to be ransomed next morning at the police-office by their chopfallen owners on payment of a fine of 5*l.*—Most distressing; for of all things that a Boer most detests, "*parting*" is the worst, however rich he may be. Catch him saying, in the words of the poet, "*parting is such sweet sorrow.*" He sees in that operation all sorrow and no sweetness. Occasional instances have been known of temporary aberration of intellect, caused by large "finds," prompting a Boer to acts of unwonted liberality or lavishness; as in the case of the middle-aged Dutchman who, when a "merry-go-round," with its beautiful and exceedingly piebald wooden horses, was first put up in the market square of Du Toit's Pan, was so astonished and delighted that he straightway mounted one of those fiery steeds, sternly refused to descend at the termination of the regular "round," and remained triumphantly seated, to the admiration and amusement of all beholders, till sundown, when finding that he had had thirty shillings' worth of equestrian exercise, he paid it "like a lamb." As other anecdotes of Boers will be found in other pages of this work, I will now return to the consideration of Englishmen, or British-born colonists, at the diggings, and will for the present class them together.

A most true and striking contrast may be drawn between the wealthy and successful and the poor and unsuccessful digger. The rich man has everything that wealth can procure to replace, as far as possible, the comforts of civilisation—a spacious well furnished tent, with shady trees around it, a soft and luxurious couch, good and abundant food, servants to cook it for him. As to work, he need do very little of that. He has a claim at each of the rich diggings, with a trustworthy person to work it for him. Elegantly dressed, mounted on a thoroughbred horse, he canters merrily from one camp to another, hears the reports of diamonds found for him, sits down at a table now and then to amuse himself for half an hour by sorting, rides back at evening to his tent or to an hotel, enjoys an excellent repast, washed down by the wines and ales of Europe, goes to call on a few friends in the evening—when the result of mutual inquiries is that a few bags containing from half a dozen to fifteen diamonds are thrown carelessly from one to another of the gay party, and shown as the results of the day's or week's work. He smokes the best Havannahs, lounges into a billiard room, reads a novel, or finds a thousand other ways of amusing himself, and turns in about midnight, to lie in a soft bed till his black boy brings him coffee in the morning. Not very hard, such a life as that, you will say.—True, and there are many such, and generally the richest men are the most fortunate, partly, of course, because they employ the greatest amount of labour, and get through the most ground.

But now look at the poor man!—With the earliest dawn, or even sooner, he rises from the hard ground, or from one or two wretched buckskins on which he has been lying—in a poor shaky little tent, affording hardly any protection against wind or rain. He cooks his own rough food with the dung fuel he has gathered himself, eats hastily, then hurries to his claim. Sometimes shivering beneath the cutting winds and pelting rains, at others scorched or melting beneath the burning sun, still he works on manfully, for he cannot afford to employ any Kafirs. Deeper and deeper he burrows into the very bowels of the earth, load after load of stuff he painfully gets to the top of his claim;

wearily, mechanically, month after month, he goes through the monotonous work of sorting table fuls of the same dry stuff—with never the sparkle of a diamond to cheer him—and feeling, ah, how bitterly, that "hope deferred which maketh the heart sick"—as he thinks of his struggling wife and children at home, and of the poor yet certain employment which he left for dazzling dreams of Golconda. But "luck must turn," he thinks; so he works on fiercely, with wild untiring energy, heedless of wind, rain, hail, lightning, frost or heat, grudging even the brief time he gives to the consumption of his coarse food, and the recruiting of exhausted nature by a few hours' sleep. And perchance the tent will blow in upon him, and he will wake to find his clothing wet through, his little store of provisions spoilt, everything in a horrid chaos of water and mud, and the rain pouring in upon him, and the pitiless wind piercing through him, as he looks out on the gloomy prospect around him—a leaden sky, the barren "veldt," a few bedraggled quivering tents among pools of water, and flooded claims where no work is possible for that day.

And, perhaps, after a long and patient endurance of these and a thousand other hardships, still finding nothing, but seeing rich men around him add big diamonds to their riches, the man—either struck with sudden sickness, the *malaria* of our camps, or wearied out to utter hopelessness—sells his claim, where his hard labour has been so long unrequited, and turns his pale face and his weary steps homewards. And he will learn probably, soon after he reaches that home where he brings so little of comfort to the dear ones he left behind, that the man to whom he sold that old claim for a few shillings or a couple of pounds, found a large diamond in it the very next day, and is now finding almost daily.

This is no picture of exaggerated sentiment, such instances are of only too frequent occurrence.—I knew of an old man who worked in a claim almost day and night for many months, till at last he gave it up in despair, sold the claim for 10*s*.—and the purchaser found a large diamond the next day only a few inches below the depth the old man had reached.

But, as a rule, our diggers lie in most respects between the two extremes I have quoted, and are a merry, good-tempered, hopeful lot, full of fun and frolic. When a big rain has washed us nearly all out of our tents and claims, and in a half-drenched state we congregate in the hotels and canteens, many are the glasses drained to "luck"; many the songs sung, and the merry tales related, and few, very few, are the disputes and fights.

And I really do not think that the diggers are an intemperate lot upon the whole—I am sure they were not at Du Toit's Pan— but the sudden riches of Colesberg Kopje have turned a few heads, and brought the canteen-keepers some *too good* customers. I have seen some ludicrous and shameful examples of the effects of intoxication. One white man I saw seated in the middle of the road, leaning upon a naked Kafir scarcely less drunk, while they both sang, shouted, threatened, and laughed at the crowd that surrounded them, and passed the bottle of "Cape Smoke" freely from one to the other, till they both became "maudlin," then dead drunk, and finally lay down to sleep in the hot sun, in the middle of the road, and had to be dragged out of the way of an advancing waggon.—I never saw black and white so equalised by any other medium.

Many of our diggers are military men—who can tell brave tales of campaigns in India and the Crimea, over the evening smoke and "nightcap"—professional men of every grade, clerks, tradesmen, artisans, all are here represented. Men of high standing and authority from different parts of the colony are to be found at the diggings, and the local colonial papers frequently have paragraphs exulting at the success of local worthies and "big-wigs." Deserters from the army and navy are numerous enough. Sometimes the most dissipated, those who do the least amount of hard work, are the most successful. Early in 1871 a wild Irishman used regularly, whenever he found a diamond, to betake himself to a canteen, and there remain till he had drunk what *the landlord* estimated as the value of the gem. And the man was wonderfully lucky. When he had drunk his last bottle, and slept off the effects of his last carouse, he would go off to work again, and generally return in a few hours with another diamond, to recommence the same miserable round. I do not know what has become of him, but should think he must be dead by this time.

The diggers are an open-handed lot. Subscriptions for the benefit of a brother digger who has met with any accident, for churches, hospitals, and other charities, are soon filled with liberal donations, No one who is willing to work, and has been long enough at the Fields to be known among a good many diggers as being honest and steady, need fear poverty; for even should he exhaust his own little resources before he finds anything remunerative in his claim, he will be sure to find plenty of chances of working good claims for richer diggers "on shares." A digger may be going down to the Colony for a month or two, or home to England for a short time, leaving a rich claim at the Colesberg Kopje, and is glad to give an honest, hardworking man a third, or even half share of the finds, to work the claim for him during his absence. Sometimes, too, a man will own two good claims in different camps, and want a representative to take entire charge of one of them; or, a capitalist may wish to buy several claims on a rich kopje, but, as according to Diggers' Regulations he cannot himself hold more than one claim, he will get a working man to take out a licence for him, re-buying the claim, paying all expenses, and giving the man who works the claim for him, and puts his name on the licence, a good share of the profits. I have even known a half-share in a good claim, *plus* 6*l*. per month regular salary, given to a man for working a claim and bringing two Kafirs with him. I will now endeavour to cull from one or two colonial newspapers of the very latest dates, any items that may bear on the life of a diamond-digger as it is.

The bachelors at Du Toit's Pan gave a ball last week at the Masonic Hotel—a very large room and a splendid floor for dancing—which commenced at nine o'clock, and terminated at four a.m. The music was good, and the arrangements excellent and liberal. There was certainly no want of ladies; indeed, some persons thought that the proportion was too large, as many gentlemen did not dance. To the credit of the digging community, let it be recorded that, so far as my observation went, there was not a case of anyone taking a little too much. This is saying a great deal, because there was a *buffet* where liquors of all sorts were to be had the whole evening for the asking. Thus, something like sixty bottles of Hennessey (French brandy) were disposed of, about fifty dozen of soda water, and everything in proportion. There was no supper, but substantial refreshments for all. The bachelors at Colesberg Kopje will have to return the compliment.

All the camps on still, quiet nights are lit up, especially in the business part of the town, so that it is nearly as light by night as in London. The shopkeepers burn paraffine, and I was greatly surprised to see the lively appearance "the city of the Pan" presented by oil-light and candle-light. As most of the diggers are at work in the daytime, a great deal of shopping is done in the evening. Of course, those substitutes for the London gin palaces are nearly as bright and radiant with light as day, and the many votaries of Bacchus are flitting about, bat-like, after the shades of evening have fallen. Some have represented the diggings to be a place for deep drinking of alcoholic liquor. I can't say, taking into consideration the population and the style of living, that such is the case. We do occasionally see an old *rooi*, or a policeman, the worse for liquor, but that you must expect to see on these Fields. But I maintain that the great majority are a sober, industrious, plodding sort of folks; and if they do now and then "take a drop too much," they have the sense to keep it to themselves.

At night as by day, the camps are very orderly, which speaks volumes for the quiet and peaceable character of the diggers. Rows are not of frequent occurrence, and everyone is allowed to pursue the even tenor of his way unmolested. Psalm singing is carried on to an alarming extent in the Boer quarter, which, although decidedly unpleasant to the human ear on earth, may be duly appreciated elsewhere.

One day last week the camp rang with cheer after cheer. I went to inquire what luck, and found that two poor men, who had been working long without success had found a splendid stone of ninety-seven carats—their fortune made in five minutes. Such circumstances make all hopeful.

I saw a person last week, who told me he had just given 450*l*. for a quarter claim, and, before night, had got diamonds enough to pay for it, and 500*l*. over.

One day, as I rode in the passenger cart to Du Toit's Pan, a fellow-passenger was a working man, and he shewed me a large stone he had got that morning, weighing about fifty carats, besides another of ten, and another of seven, all before breakfast. He said, "Yesterday I was a poor man, now I am a rich one." But at that early hour of the morning he was showing symptoms of having drank too freely; but it is not very surprising that such success should throw a man off his balance a little. These circumstances are of daily occurrence, but on the other hand there are many unsuccessful—it is a complete lottery. One person finds ten and even twenty stones in a day, whilst another, working not three feet from him, finds nothing. Still they are all hopeful, and I am happy to say there is no sign of distress. Only one man asked me for alms, so I gave him his breakfast, and a trifle; but an hour or so afterwards, seeing him in a state of intoxication, I took it he was not really in want, but was too idle and dissolute to work. There is no difficulty for anyone who is willing and able to work to get employment; but in a population of so many thousands it would indeed be extraordinary were there no idle and worthless characters.

The amount of money in these camps is something beyond belief. No one comes to make a purchase without a pile of bank notes; and the short time I have been here I have seen more ready money than the whole eleven years I have been in Natal. The great difficulty people seem to have is to find something to purchase with their money. Yesterday, a man, with all the appearance of a day labourer, came into my store intoxicated, and asked for a bottle of pickles. I served him, and said the price was 2*s*. 6*d*. He replied, "Who the ——— asked you how much it was?" untied a dirty handkerchief, and disclosed a bundle of bank notes as large as a pudding basin, value from 5*l*. to 50*l*. each. He chucked them down, saying, "There, take your choice out of them, and if you don't like that lot I've got plenty more."

Again, another day, a woman and her husband came in and bought a few pounds worth of goods, and for payment drew from her bosom a bundle of bank notes as thick as my wrist, and had difficulty in finding one small enough to pay my account.

"How many have you found?" appears to be the question of the day. No one thinks now of asking people from the "New Rush" if they have found anything. We take it for granted when we see a *rusher* of the *new* sort come to town, that he comes either to sell or to ship.

Babe's party were in yesterday, the same who found the 83½ carat stone. Their answer to the question, "What have you found since you were here last?" was, "A little." "What is your largest?" "Only a 16."

I

But it is not only at the "New Rush" that they are finding large stones. Messrs. Young and G. Cronan were in yesterday, and they brought me evidence that Gong Gong is looking up again.

This chapter would become of unwieldy length did I attempt to give any detailed description of individual diggers. I will just glance at the peculiarities of a few. H., who worked near me, a tall, stalwart man from Lancashire, was noticeable for the splendid belt of many colours he wore (I hardly ever saw him with a coat on, never with a waistcoat), for the beautifully neat way in which he worked his claim—the walls and floor of it being kept as smooth as those of a house—and for his contempt and hatred for —— Dutchmen. He would omit no opportunity of "chaffing" a Boer, and would have been delighted had his taunts been resented by even half a dozen of them at a time, but none of them dared raise a finger against him, and it would have been very bad indeed for them if they had.

S., another neighbour, was particularly fond of pets; frequently he brought a young baboon down to his claim and amused his niggers by insisting that it was "their brother," another time it was a tame "meerkat," another time a bull-pup, and so on. S. didn't like Dutchmen, either; in fact there was a pretty strong British *clique* round my claim.

R., a sturdy, brown-faced, bearded, very thick-set digger, generally very quiet and temperate, once got slightly thrown off his balance by the finding of a 20-carat; and in one of the billiard-rooms that night he was dancing all round the table, to the great discomposure of the players and the crowd of spectators and loafers, dancing round, elbowing every one out of the way, and vociferating the chorus of the "Marseillaise."

Another neighbour of mine, an old sailor, used to work very hard and very regularly, but could not resist going on the spree whenever he found a diamond, or whenever he met a brother seafaring man.

I have seen various classes of diamond diggers very variously affected by the rough life at the Fields, or by sudden acquirement of wealth. I have seen a very decent gentlemanly young fellow, after sudden rich finds, become intensely affected, cut nearly all his acquaintance who had not been equally lucky, go in for extravagance in dress, gambling, and drinking, and in his general demeanour affect the "haw-haw" swell to a ridiculous extent.

I have seen others, apparently of the station of gentlemen, become so used to the freedom and absence of restraint, the loose style of clothing, and coarse vulgarity of speech prevalent on the diggings, that on the voyage home, though they had plenty of money, and were by no means economically disposed, they took a second-class passage, saying that they would be much more jolly, and shouldn't be half so comfortable in the first cabin. On the other hand, some fellows who couldn't possibly have been anything but farm labourers at home, and still preserved the loutish appearance, manners, and talk of a ploughboy in spite of the fine clothes their suddenly acquired wealth enabled them to wear, and in which they looked so singularly ill at ease, took a first-class passage—and how miserable they seemed among ladies and gentlemen, with whom they had nothing congenial! They were driven sometimes to drinking and most reckless gambling, sometimes to the society of the common sailors, for only in such things could these poor "fish out of water" find comfort. Money they had plenty—manners they had none. But still there are plenty of men whose minds are strong enough to bear sudden reverses or accessions of fortune with perfect equanimity, and I doubt not that each of my readers thinks that he, at any rate, would be very glad to try the experiment of the latter in the finding of a big diamond of pure water.

CHAPTER II.

DIAMOND BUYERS AND DIAMOND BROKERS.

First and foremost amongst the ranks of diamond buyers on the South African Fields must certainly be placed the German Jews. There are very few Englishmen amongst them. The dealers in diamonds may be divided into the following classes :—1. The large buyer, who is a diamond buyer, and nothing else ; 2. The storekeeper, who buys diamonds ; 3. The small buyer ; 4. The diamond broker. Of the first class we can hardly take a better example than Mr. Moritz Unger, one of the earliest and largest buyers on the Fields, being backed up with an immense capital by an Amsterdam house. He has many enemies, as any man in such a position, among such a host of competitors, is sure to have ; but I have heard many diggers say that he gives as fair prices as any man on the Fields. He is established in a substantial and comfortable house and office at Klip Drift, having his family with him. He is a good judge of horseflesh, and owns some remarkably fine horses. Formerly he used frequently to ride from one camp to another, visiting the claims, asking each digger if he had any diamonds to sell, doing business in the hotels and canteens, and, in fact, everywhere, with untiring energy. Now that the camps have become so numerous and so large, he has found it impossible to continue this system, but generally remains at his office at Klip Drift, to await the numerous sellers, and visiting occasionally the big camps of Du Toit's Pan and the Colesberg Kopje, at the latter of which places he has established an agency. He is not famed for excessive politeness, but is somewhat cheeky and slangy. This, however, is no very serious drawback to business or social intercourse in the eyes of most of the diggers, chaff and slang being very current. Like most diamond buyers, Mr. Unger affects rather a loud and dashing style of dress, such as a velvet jacket, white cord or buckskin breeches, and long tight-fitting well-polished boots, adorned with glittering spurs. A handsome courier bag is slung to his side, the contents of which would often be a moderate fortune to many of us.

Diamond buyers of this class almost all wear long boots, partly because they are much on horseback. Ostrich feathers, red silk "puggerees," or green veils, round their hats, elaborate ties, white waistcoats: all these gay and festive articles of dress are much favoured by the diamond buyers.

Besides buying, for cash, diamonds of every size and quality, and "boart," Mr. Unger and others of his class will, if desired, receive consignments of diamonds to send to European markets for sale, and will make liberal advances upon really good stones. Many of these large buyers content themselves with staying quietly in tent or office, awaiting sellers. Others again perambulate the claims, frequent the canteens, and canvass everywhere for business. Whenever a loud shout proclaims the finding of a big diamond, two or three of the diamond-buying fraternity are quickly on the spot, and cash offers are made, sometimes very good ones too. In fact, I believe, that often higher prices have been paid on the Fields, for large *off-coloured* (*i.e.* yellowish) stones especially, than would be realised at home; but the latest news from London, to the effect that large yellow stones are almost unsaleable, has already affected all the buyers in the colony.

Many of the buyers have often immense sums of money at their command, and immense numbers of fine diamonds in their possession. I know that Unger once showed a gentleman a *hatful*. But so many exaggerated stories were at one time current in this respect, that the following absurd *canard* was circulated to ridicule the public credulity. It was related of a well-known rich buyer, occupying an office at Du Toit's Pan, that when he had weighed a parcel of diamonds, and paid the price of them to the seller, he would throw the diamonds into a bucket which stood on the counter: when the bucket was full he would empty it into a *muidsack* (grainbag, containing about 200lb. weight) which stood in a corner, and when the *muidsack* was full, it was taken into an inner room, wherein were dozens of other muidsacks already filled with the glittering gems; while in another room numerous deep cupboards were crammed with rolls of bank-notes, all of high values. Such was the "yarn" over which we used to laugh, but which many of the Boers firmly believed to be true. But Boers will believe anything. (See, in my diary, a brief account of the proceedings of a fortune-teller.)

When a digger comes to a buyer with a stone, or lot of stones, the latter weighs them carefully, examines them minutely through a powerful glass to detect any tinge of colour or any flaw, then asks, "How much do you want for them?" The digger names a figure. The buyer laughs contemptuously, and offers half. Digger pockets his diamonds, walks out, goes and sees several other buyers, perhaps they offer him still less, in which case he goes back to the first, and clenches the bargain; or, perhaps one will give him a little more than the first buyer offered. Buyers who have large capitals at command generally make very large profits. Mr. Unger must be making a fortune. Most of the storekeepers, large and small, advertise that they are "Diamant Koopers," or "Diamond Buyers." One man combined in his own person the various functions of dissenting minister, dentist, watchmaker and jeweller, homœopathic chemist, and diamond buyer; and he made money too, and gave very fair prices for diamonds. The storekeepers, in fact, all buy diamonds whenever they see a chance of buying *cheap*; and I should advise everyone, diggers included, to do this. I think that the storekeepers, on the whole, give somewhat lower prices than the regular buyers, and should always recommend a seller to go to one of the largest of the latter. I do not propose to enter here into the question, so often raised, as to whether it pays best to sell diamonds on the Fields, at Cape Town, or in Europe. I certainly saw many auction sales of diamonds in Cape Town, and they seemed to realise better prices than they would have done on the Fields, but then the bad news from England had not come. This question depends much on fluctuations in the European market, and would probably have a different answer for different qualities; but one thing is certain, that pure *white* stones of good shape command pretty nearly their full value everywhere.

The hotel keepers and canteen keepers have many facilities for diamond buying; they, with the storekeepers, generally buy diamonds, and also have a party working some claim or claims for them, so, with these three strings to their bow, they can hardly fail to make money. Some of the smaller store and canteen keepers have occasionally been known to yield to the temptation of buying diamonds from natives. No native is allowed to dig on his own account, and every diamond he may find, either in his master's claim or elsewhere, belongs to his master. If, therefore, a nigger offers you a diamond for sale, you know that it is stolen. Your proper course is to collar the nigger and hand him over to the police; it will soon be ascertained whose nigger he is, the rightful owner will get the diamond, and the nigger will get what is so good for him, viz., the "cat," and a long dose of "chokey" (prison).

But, alas, human nature, especially in the keepers of low canteens, is weak; the conscience blunted by a long series of drinking and card-sharping, which is very freely and unscrupulously indulged in by that class of the community. Our canteen keeper has come to regard diggers and the general public as a natural and proper source of profit, to be "skinned," if possible. " Rem recte si potes, si non, rem, quomodo rem," sang dissipated old Horace nearly two thousand years ago ; and I have heard one of the class I am now speaking of—who certainly never could have read Horace—say, very plainly, and with an air of conviction, " The proper motto for the Fields is—'make money—honestly, if you can —but, anyhow, make money.' I was sometimes swindled when I first came on the Fields, so I will do my best to 'skin' others.'' The consequence is that, when a felonious darkey presents himself at the counter of a grovelling scoundrel of this stamp, he frightens him so by threats of giving him in charge, &c., that the wretched native is glad to part with the diamond (perhaps a large one) for the merest trifle, for a bottle of grog, or perhaps for nothing at all, and the swindling canteen-keeper, if all keeps " dark," has made half a fortune. Should any little transaction of this kind come to light, the receiver of the stolen diamond will be arrested, tried, and fined heavily. In the old times of Lynch law, he would have been " dragged through the river," and expelled the camp, if nothing worse. Here is a brief mention of a case of the kind, in a letter to the *Natal Colonist* of 24th November, 1871 :—" A man going by the name of Rogers decamped from his canteen at Colesberg Kopje, and it subsequently transpired that he had recently bought a diamond of fifty odd carats from a native. A hot pursuit was the result, and it is to be hoped he will be quickly here again and get his deserts. By the way, I am reminded that he is a deserter, from the 75th, I believe."

Now, here is a pretty thing! Here is a scoundrel decamping with a fifty-carat diamond, which might have been a little fortune to some poor and long unsuccessful digger ; no one knows who it belonged to, it *may* have been *mine;* every digger feels tremendously "riled" at such a case as this. Each one thinks, "By Jove, suppose it was one of *my* 'boys' he got the stone from." And I have reason to believe the villain in question got clear off, and is now in England.

There is a class of small, very small buyers, who commence the business of diamond buying with hardly any capital. It is a current saying on the diggings, that to be a "diamant kooper," all a man wants is *a pair of long boots, a courier bag, and half-a-crown!* This is, perhaps, hardly enough. But a very little money certainly suffices. The small buyer, generally an energetic, 'cute, active little party, perambulates the claims freely, and buys a few small stones when he can buy cheap. Perhaps, in his day's work, he may buy 20*l.* worth, and sell them again to one of the large buyers for 22*l.* 10*s.*, or, if he has made a good bargain, for 25*l.* Many small parcels of stones, and some large diamonds, pass through a good many hands, and leave a good many small profits sticking to different people's fingers, before they finally leave the Fields on their way to the European markets.

To be a successful diamond buyer, a man must be a very keen judge of diamonds, with a sharp eye for the slightest defect in shape or colour—he must also be able to drive a hard bargain; novices often make lucky hits at diamond buying, but they also often find themselves sold if they go in for it on too extensive a scale, and without due caution. The intending diamond buyer should make himself thoroughly acquainted, before leaving England, with the latest prices of diamonds of every size and quality, on the London and other European markets.

Diamond *brokers* are a class that have only sprung up quite lately on the Fields, and when I left there were very few of them; but those I knew were making fair profits, without risking capital of their own, by getting acquainted with different large buyers, finding out where the best prices were to be obtained, and then selling, for a trifling commission, diamonds entrusted to them for that purpose. They are very generally buyers also, on a small scale at first. Of course, a man must be pretty well known on the Fields, and bear a good character, before he can expect to do a large business as a diamond broker.

One or two sales of diamonds by auction have taken place, and diamond auctions have probably by this time become a recognised institution on the Fields; but the great place for diamond auctions is Cape Town, where each of the principal auctioneers generally holds a bi-weekly sale, either at his own rooms or in the Commercial Exchange, of the stones consigned to him for that purpose by diggers and buyers. These sales are nearly always attended by the same class, in fact by the same individual buyers, most of them being Cape Town merchants, who dabble a little in diamonds, and have correspondents in London, Amsterdam, or Hamburg. I attended several of these sales in November, 1871. The diamonds may be inspected previous to the sale, when intending buyers examine them carefully, and put down against each numbered lot in the printed catalogue their remarks—often in cipher—on the size, shape, and quality of the stones which compose the lot, and the price they consider it worth. Nearly all the diamonds I saw put up realised more than the reserve prices which had been put upon them by their owners, until decidedly unfavourable news, as to the unsaleableness of large "off-coloured" stones, arrived per mail steamer *Saxon*, and the next day a great many of the diamonds offered remained unsold, not nearly the reserve prices being offered.

From the sales I saw I should put the average of diamonds sold by each of the three large auctioneers at each bi-weekly sale as 2000*l.*, so that even on a small commission your diamond auctioneer evidently makes a pretty good thing of it, and can afford to drive the "slashing turn-out" frequently to be met in the lovely suburbs of Cape Town, or to stand all hands in his auction-room, whether actual customers or not, brandy-and-soda all round at the conclusion of a sale, as I saw the liberal Mr. Caffyn do. The total weight of diamonds sold by public auction during the fortnight previous to my departure from Cape Town was $4512\frac{10}{16}$ carats, and the sum realised thereby was 20,189*l.* 16*s.* 3*d.* This is only a very small proportion of the diamonds weekly sent away from the South African Fields—only very few of them stopping to be sold at Cape Town—but some idea may be formed from even this of the immense value of those Fields. To give the reader a better idea of one of these auction sales, I subjoin literal copies of the catalogues of a sale held by Messrs. Caffyn Brothers which I attended. The "remarks" I made were merely the result of a very cursory inspection as each lot was put up. not having had an opportunity of previous close inspection. The letters in the left-hand corner are the initials of the owners, in many cases of the actual diggers, of these diamonds :—

CATALOGUE NO. 1.

CATALOGUE OF DIAMONDS

To be Sold

THIS DAY (TUESDAY),

At Half-past Two o'clock, p.m.,

BY MESSRS. CAFFYN BROTHERS,

IN THE AUCTION ROOMS.

	No.	No. of Diamonds.	Weight Carats.	Sold for £	s.	d.	REMARKS.
S.	1	4	$9\frac{9}{16}$	50	0	0	White, good stone
	2	1	$3\frac{9}{16}$	27	10	0	,, ,, ,,
	3	6	$10\frac{13}{16}$	71	0	0	,, ,, ,,
	4	9	$9\frac{7}{16}$	45	0	0	Some slightly off colour
	5	1	$3\frac{1}{2}$	21	0	0	White, good shape
	6	4	$5\frac{1}{4}$	13	0	0	,, bad ,,
	7	25	$12\frac{3}{16}$	42	10	0	Mixed colours
	8	11	$4\frac{3}{32}$	15	10	0	Good little white stones
	9	1	$2\frac{7}{16}$	16	10	0	Slightly off colour
	10	2	3	17	0	0	One slightly off colour
	11	1	$8\frac{1}{2}$	27	0	0	Slightly off colour, bad shape
	12	1	$9\frac{11}{16}$	22	0	0	,, ,, ,, ,, ,,
	13	1	$8\frac{7}{8}$	28	0	0	,, ,, ,, flat
	14	1	4	16	0	0	,, ,, ,, good shape
	15	1	5	17	0	0	White, good fragment
	16	1	$7\frac{1}{5}$	24	0	0	White, bad shape, black spot
	11	6	$8\frac{1}{16}$	32	0	0	Mixed colours, good stones
	18	5	$11\frac{3}{8}$	22	10	0	Bad shape, off colour
	19	38	$25\frac{5}{8}$	51	0	0	Good little stones
	20	10	$14\frac{1}{4}$	13	10	0	*Boart*
B.	1	5	$10\frac{7}{8}$	30	0	0	Slightly off colour, good shape
	2	18	$12\frac{4}{5}$	42	10	0	Nearly all white, mixed sizes
	3	19	9	16	0	0	Chips, mostly white
	4	10	$6\frac{1}{3}$	7	10	0	*Boart*
	5	1	$6\frac{7}{8}$	64	10	0	White, good shape, slight flaw
	6	1	$9\frac{3}{8}$	60	0	0	Off colour, good shape

CATALOGUE NO. 2.

CATALOGUE OF DIAMONDS

To be Sold

THIS DAY (TUESDAY),

At Half-past Two o'clock, p.m.,

BY MESSRS. CAFFYN BROTHERS,

IN THE AUCTION ROOMS.

	No. of Diamonds.	Weight Carats.	Sold for £	s.	d.	REMARKS.
R. No. 1	1	$8\frac{7}{8}$	43	0	0	Off coloured, fine stone
R. 2	15	$9\frac{1}{3}$	22	0	0	Mixed, chips, &c.
R. 3	9	$9\frac{3}{4}$	32	10	0	Good stone, some slightly off coloured
B No. 1	29	$11\frac{1}{3}$	23	0	0	White chips
2	1	$11\frac{1}{4}$	30	0	0	Off coloured, bad stone
3	2	$5\frac{5}{8}$	35	0	0	White, good stone
4	2	$12\frac{3}{4}$	51	0	0	White, one good shape, one fragment
5	7	$6\frac{1}{4}$	20	10	0	Mixed colours
6	1	$7\frac{9}{16}$	45	0	0	Slightly off colour, very good shape
7	4	$5\frac{3}{16}$	28	10	0	White, fair stones
8	1	$7\frac{7}{16}$	16	10	0	White fragment
9	2	$10\frac{1}{4}$	14	10	0	Off colour, bad shape
10	1	$6\frac{1}{4}$	43	0	0	Slightly off colour, good shape
11	3	$7\frac{11}{16}$	16	0	0	Fragments
12	2	$7\frac{3}{8}$	60	0	0	Nearly white, good shape
13	3	$8\frac{1}{3}$	34	0	0	Off colour
14	1	$5\frac{7}{16}$	41	0	0	Slightly off colour, good shape
15	6	$4\frac{7}{8}$	4	0	0	*Boart*
D. 16	9	$33\frac{7}{16}$	80	0	0	Nearly white, bad shape
17	34	$30\frac{7}{16}$	129	0	0	White, good little stones
18	10	$9\frac{1}{3}$	9	10	0	Bad chips
19	22	$13\frac{3}{8}$	24	0	0	Rather better chips
20	3	7	25	0	0	Off colour
21	1	$1\frac{13}{16}$	4	0	0	Off colour, bad shape, bright
22	2	$5\frac{1}{2}$	6	0	0	Off colour, bad shape
A 1	10	$11\frac{1}{4}$	30	0	0	Mixed chips
A. 7	9	$13\frac{1}{4}$	25	0	0	Large mixed chips
T. V. 26	12	$11\frac{9}{16}$	31	0	0	White, bad shape
T. V. 27	1	$10\frac{4}{16}$	64	0	0	Off colour, good shape
P. No. 1	1	$7\frac{3}{8}$	49	0	0	Good shape, slightly off colour
2	1	$11\frac{3}{16}$	46	0	0	Slightly off colour, flawed
3	10	$12\frac{5}{8}$	56	10	0	Good stones
4	2	$11\frac{3}{4}$	55	0	0	Off colour, good shape
5	3	$13\frac{5}{16}$	39	0	0	Off colour, largest bad shape
6	1	$7\frac{11}{16}$	40	0	0	White, bad shape, flawed
7	18	$17\frac{1}{3}$	35	10	0	Some large, bad shape, off colour
8	1	$5\frac{3}{16}$	43	0	0	Slightly off colour, good shape
9	1	$6\frac{1}{4}$	22	0	0	White, slight flaw
10	17	$15\frac{3}{8}$	50	0	0	Mixed
H. E. ..	40	43	..	..	..	Not sold; £4 19s. per carat offered, £5 15s. wanted
H E. ..	15	$57\frac{1}{4}$	..	..	..	
H. E. ..	25	130	..	..	..	Not sold Off coloured but good stones; £600 offered, £1000 wanted

Since my arrival in England I have learnt that the small prices now given for our large stones, which are mostly off-coloured, is *not* due so much to the fact of the prevalent yellowish tinge, as they often cut to very fine brilliants, but to the fact of the immense number of large stones now constantly arriving from South Africa having completely revolutionised the market. There is no demand for such numbers of these immense gems at anything like original diamond prices; as there appears to be every probability of a constantly increasing supply of large stones, diggers and colonial buyers will have to make up their minds to receive comparatively low prices for these large stones, as otherwise there is no market for them. For instance, I believe that in one case 8000*l.* would now be taken for a diamond which was priced last year at 33,000*l.* according to the old scale of valuations.

The Diamond trade in London appears to have been, until lately, in the hands of very few persons, and an immense amount of stock having accumulated within the last six months, owing to the difficulty of ready sale for numerous large diamonds, and the slowness of the operation of cutting, consignors have frequently been disappointed not only in the time that elapsed before they received account sales, but in the prices realised. Many of the London consignees have begun to think that it would be better for everyone's interests to submit to the public a merchantable article ready for the jeweller rather than to sell the rough diamonds privately to one of the few dealers who trade in such things.

Sales by auction afford a very advantageous medium for the disposal of diamonds, whether cut or in the rough: those held monthly by Messrs. Debenham, Storr, and Sons, of Covent Garden, have already been noticed in the *Times* as being of public interest and importance, and they are beginning to attract a good many buyers from the provinces and the Continent. It is to be hoped that fair prices may continue to prevail in Europe, though the market certainly rules rather lower this year than in 1871.

Small stones of good quality are still in demand at fair prices, and so are *good* yellow diamonds, but stones with black spots or flaws are worth much less than formerly.

The dealers seem at a loss to fix the value of stones of 10 carats and upwards, few of which are of good form and spotless lustre. For these no scale of values, such as we constantly see in print, is of any use. Each stone, with its special beauties, or its special defects, must stand on its own merits; and its value be determined by men who thoroughly understand brilliants, and know the public taste concerning them. *Bad* stones of large size are certainly not worth more than one-third their former price, and it is by no means easy to sell them even at that.

All this, coming to the knowledge of our colonial buyers, will tend to make them very cautious in their offers for the numerous large stones which will probably long continue to be found in West Griqualand.

I am inclined to think that the system of public competition at auction sales, which now prevails so extensively both in the colony and in England, will prove, in the long run, more satisfactory to diggers and their consignees than the method which formerly prevailed, of selling through dealers and brokers.

We may feel disappointment at the falling off in the price for large stones, but we can hardly feel surprised. The *rarity* of the gem has as much to do with its value as its *beauty;* so, in the presence of the immense discoveries of this one gem, and the great proportion of large stones, it is only natural that the value should be lessened. Rubies, emeralds, sapphires, and pearls still maintain their old values, because the supply does not equal the demand for them; but it would certainly be absurd to suppose that there should be a constant demand for diamonds of 50 to 100 carats at the old scale of prices, making them each worth a comfortable fortune.

The following paragraph from the *Times*, of Feb. 1st., 1872, showing prices realised in London for rough and cut diamonds, will be of appropriate interest here :—

CAPE DIAMONDS.—The largest sale by auction of these gems that has yet been known in this country, was held yesterday at the rooms of Messrs. Debenham, Storr, and Sons, of King Street, Covent Garden. The auction comprised upwards of one thousand carats of cut brilliants and rough diamonds as found. The following quotations may be interesting in the present fluctuating state of the market for rough stones. Lot 741. A white diamond, 9½ carats, £60. 742. A ditto, slightly off colour, 7¼ carats, £37. 750. Seventeen ditto, of pure water, 17 carats, £60. 756. A large dinmond, of drop shape, 14½ carats, £42. 761. Six diamonds, of fine colour, 10 carats, £68. 762. Six ditto, about 9 carats, £48. 767. An uncut diamond, about 45 carats, described as a crystal of the highest promise, £570. 769. A native diamond, in the matrix, a curious cabinet specimen, £14. 771. Five uncut diamonds, together about 25½ carats, £100. 772. An uncut diamond, 18¼ carats, and four others, smaller, total about 23 carats, £96. 773. An uncut diamond, 15 ½¼ carats, of good colour, adapted to form a drop, £75. 774. Ten uncut diamonds, about 32 carats, £160. 776. Four ditto, 28 carats, 105 guineas. 777. Twenty-five ditto, about 39 carats, £250. The cut brilliants sold remarkably well. Lot 724. A magnificent and lustrous brilliant, about 8 carats, 430 guineas. 727. A fine yellow brilliant, of great lustre, about 7½ carats, 140 guineas. 728. A brilliant, of great spread and good water, about 7½ carats, 140 guineas; and lot 738, a large and lustrous brilliant, of fine colour, weighing about 7 carats, 480 guineas. Among the bijouterie we remarked the following items:—Lot 592. Five stars, set with lustrous brilliants, 100 guineas. 629. A single-stone brilliant ring, £90. 659. A court tiara, of five graduated brilliant stars, 185 guineas. 660. A brilliant necklace, of 40 graduated collets, £300. 662. A brilliant pendant or brooch, the stones of the purest water, 105 guineas. 663. A pair of elegantly designed brilliant ear rings, 112 guineas. 684. A pair of magnificent three-stone brilliant ear rings, 120 guineas; and 685, an emerald and brilliant bracelet, 460 guineas. The total realised by the sale was about £9730.—*Times*, Feb. 1st, 1872.

CHAPTER III.

HOTEL-KEEPERS, STORE-KEEPERS, AND AUCTIONEERS.

OUR hotels, on the Fields, though many of them are large and spacious, will not recall, in many particulars, the Westminster Palace, the Langham, or the Grosvenor. They are big *caravanserais*, built generally either of wood or of corrugated iron, possessing a few bedrooms, possibly, but dealing far more extensively in "shake-downs," *i.e.*, one or two blankets or antelope skins spread on the floor and on the table, by no means disdained by the "washed-out" storm-beaten digger, who may be considered as the "casual," while the "diamant kooper," or merchant, is the more frequent and regular visitor, and therefore the more desirable person to propitiate with four square yards of green-baize partition, an iron bedstead, and a mattress.

The prominent feature of an hotel on the diggings, and certainly its most paying element, is the spacious bar, behind which the landlord and his assistants, polite or slangy, civil or bullying, as the case may be, dispense from apparently exhaustless stores the *liquids* of Europe, and *the liquid* of Africa (*i.e.*, the baneful Cape Smoke) to an incessant crowd of rough diggers, in picturesque working garb, whitened by the horrid limestone dust, which dries the palate, chokes the throat, oppresses the lungs, and drives men to desperation and—the liquor bar. Let us take a well-known hotel at Du Toit's Pan, as it was during my stay at that camp, as an example of the class. It is a huge barn-like wooden building, very scantily furnished, with one big dining-room, along the sides of which a dozen of tiny bedrooms are formed by slight wooden and green-baize partitions—a spacious bar in front, with numerous strong shelves well filled with bottles of wine, brandy, beer, syrups, &c., &c., &c., and adorned with one or two fine heads of blesbok, springbok, and other antelopes. Behind the counter stand the busy landlord and his assistants, dispensing fluids of every kind to thirsty diggers, diamond buyers, and transport riders, at such prices as the following:—2*s*. 6*d*. or 3*s*. for a bottle of beer, 9*d*. for a glass of draught ale, 9*d*. for lemonade, soda-water, or foreign wine, 6*d*. for Cape brandy and Cape wines, one of which, Pontac, a wine much resembling a rough new port, is much affected up here, as it is believed to act as an astringent. " Long drinks " are continually called for. such as brandy and soda. lemonade and sherry, ginger-beer and pontac. " Tommy Dodd" and games of " twenty-fives " are freely played for expensive "rounds" of liquor. A *case* of champagne is no unusual "call." Diamonds are freely shown. as the lucky diggers warm with their drinks ; here and there is a loud inharmonious song, a hot argument or dispute, rarely terminating in a regular row. but frequently in "glasses round."

The presiding genii behind the bar generally refuse 5*l.* notes, or charge 2*s.* 6*d.* for changing them. very often even refuse 1*l.* notes, *or* if they *do* condescend to change them, will very probably give several little slips of paper, with some such an inscription as "Good for one shilling—T. B.," as an equivalent of part of the change, to be redeemed when they are more flush of small coin, or, far more frequently, to be passed over the bar again in five minutes time for " another fluid."

Coppers are altogether unknown on the diggings ; the threepenny-piece, known as the " ticky " is still in currency, but there is a considerable scarcity of these small coins, and a cigar, or a couple of boxes of those thin Swedish matches known as " Tandstickors," are regularly given in change as the equivalent of a " ticky," and received without a murmur. The little " good fors," as the above-mentioned slips of card or paper are called, are rather objectionable, being easily lost, especially the paper ones, the recipient of one of which generally feels it incumbent on him to turn it into liquor as soon as ever he feels at all thirsty again, lest he should lose it, and fail to get any value.

At the entrance to the bar are generally standing a few loafing Kafirs, in expectation of a job, or of a "tot" of Cape Smoke from some over-generous inebriate.

There are generally three *table d'hôte* meals per day—breakfast, tiffin, and dinner—at eight, one, and six. There is but little variety in the viands placed upon the long, rough, deal table, but such as they are, there is plenty of them. Abundance of mutton and beef, frequent venison, fair curries and stews, very few vegetables, plenty of bread, white and brown, of rather indifferent quality, and any amount of coffee and tea—such is diggers' hotel fare. The company assembling at such a table is very varied. The rough digger, in his shirt-sleeves, corduroy trousers and jackboots, sits side by side with the rich diamond buyer, "got up regardless of expense," or with the Church clergyman of the camp. All are free and equal, free and easy too—dress makes not the slightest difference in the prompt attention, but very scant civility, shown to all the guests alike by the saucy, bustling waiters, whom the landlord swears at, who swear at the landlord in return, and who probably have shares in rich claims.

The general charge for breakfast and tiffin is 2s. each, for dinner 2s. 6d.; but lower prices may be found at some establishments, even on the Colesberg Kopje.

The hotels are frequented by a lively class of regular customers; and when an occasional spell of bad, wet weather drives diggers from tents and claims, they congregate thickly in the hotels, filling bar and dining-room alike. A bed is charged 2s. or 2s. 6d., a "shakedown," 1s. or 1s. 6d. Some diggers, at the Colesberg Kopje especially, board and lodge regularly at hotels; but it is a very bad practice, being very expensive and greatly promotive of loafing, and leaving claims too much to the Kafirs.

These hostelries are the regular starting-places and booking-offices for the post and passenger carts to different parts of the colony, and for the omnibuses and carts which ply between the different camps.

The hotels at the little towns of Pniel and Klip Drift, which are looked upon as permanent, afford greater comforts to the traveller in the way of sleeping accommodation, and a better *cuisine*, than the temporary wooden and iron structures of Du Toit's Pan, De Beer's, and the Colesberg Kopje.

Jardine's Hotel, at Pniel, the booking-office of the Inland Transport Company's passenger waggons, and of the passenger carts to Du Toit's Pan, deserves specially grateful mention from me for the comfort, kind treatment, and good food I enjoyed there when ill. Mr. Jardine had everything of the very best: lost no opportunities of getting green peas, lettuces, and other luxuries, no matter what it cost to supply his table with them; and on "pudding days," which occurred twice a week, and were eagerly looked forward to, there was such a profusion of fruit puddings (made from bottled fruits), plum puddings, cabinet puddings, blanc manges, and custards, as would have done credit to any table in the colony, and used to cause hungry diggers to trifle airily with beef, mutton, and vegetables, and reserve themselves for the attack on these rare delicacies.—Mr. Jardine's cook tried his hand at jellies once, but they failed to solidify, and there appeared on the table wineglasses full of a lukewarm liquid, very pleasing to the taste, but still very far from the real, quivering, solid transparency which is so refreshing. It is true that the thermometer stood that morning at 100° in the shade; so how could the poor jellies be expected to turn from hot to cold, when men who had come out of the Vaal River cool soon found themselves melting?— There was another very grand thing at Jardine's, too, intensely appreciated by fellows from the dry diggings: he took measures to have a plentiful supply of milk, so that not only had we milk in our tea or coffee at breakfast—an unheard-of luxury at the "dry diggings"—but he also gave us milk soup, with rice, pearl-barley, sago, or something mild and nutritive of that kind, for tiffin. Comfortable bedrooms, large beds, plenty of washing apparatus, and an unlimited supply of water, combined with the above advantages to render Jardine's quite a little elysium to a convalescent from the horrible Colesberg Kopje; where though many of our enterprising hosts do their best, and spare no expense to give us wholesome food and occasional delicacies, they can only get fresh vegetables very occasionally, and milk not at all.

Small establishments for the retailing of liquors, not giving board and lodging, are called "canteens," and they are legion; for any man with fifty pounds in his pocket can start a canteen, if only on a very small scale, such as a small rough tent or canvas house, with only a bar, no chairs or tables. The number of these little places, of every possible shape and material, is fairly astonishing; still more astonishing is the fact that they all do a roaring trade. A canteen may be distinguished from afar, amongst other tents, by a flag of any nationality or pattern fluttering on a tall pole or bamboo. I have even seen a big red cotton pocket hankerchief doing duty as a flag. These places, in the outskirts of the camp especially, are very much frequented by Kafirs, Hottentots, and other natives, most of whom go in freely for Cape Smoke when their wages are paid, or when they get a present for the finding of a big diamond. The black fellows will either take a big drink of Cape Smoke at the bar, or will buy a bottle to take to the fire-place and discuss with their friends, and they are a very fertile source of income to the suburban canteen keeper.

General stores are very numerous on the Fields, in fact hardly anyone goes in for any special line of goods, but all deal miscellaneously in everything—diggers' tools, ready-made clothing, and preserved meats, fish, fruits, &c., being the staple commodities. The storekeepers also buy large stocks of every kind of produce on the markets, purchase eagerly all green vegetables, eggs, and other luxuries that may be offered, which they retail at a high profit; and as they all buy diamonds, and, almost without exception, sell liquors too, their aggregate profits must be very large. Storekeepers, hotel keepers, and auctioneers all pay a regular monthly license to Government. As the scale of licenses has just been altered in consequence of the annexation of the territory by the British Government, and I have not the necessary documents before me, I cannot give the license charges, but I know they are very modest in comparison with the large profits made.

Canteen keeping is much more simple, sure, and inexpensive for a novice to begin at than storekeeping, but it is open to many objections. "Difficulties" with drunken roughs are not pleasant for a gentleman—though as long as the host will supply the "rowdy" with liquor till he rolls dead-drunk on the floor, he is not likely to have any difficulty—it is only a refusal to let a man have more than is good for him which is likely to cause any awkwardness. Kafirs, too, will get drunk and annoying; it is best to keep a big, heavy stick behind the bar for them, and lay it on vigorously when they have had enough and ask for more. There is in many camps a regulation to the effect that no liquors shall be supplied to any native without a written permission from his master; but this seems to be universally evaded, or no notice at all taken of it, any more than of certain other provisions in the camp regulations, viz., that no hotel or canteen shall be kept open after 10 p.m., and no liquor sold on Sunday. The thirsty digger can get drink when and where he likes as long as he has small change, without which the canteen keeper will sometimes refuse to serve him. If he has nothing less than a banknote, his best plan is to call for his liquor and drink it off before he tenders payment, in which case the landlord is obliged either to change the note or give credit.

There are several auctioneers on the Fields, and those who are well known, and have the "gift of the gab," make very large profits; frequently selling in an afternoon a large number of waggons, carts, mules, and oxen, besides a vast assortment of miscellaneous property of different values, and, the general commission they charge being 10 per cent., it is a very paying thing.

Besides the waggons, carts, and cattle which they get from

parties arriving on the Fields, they have constant supplies of tents, tools, and furniture, from parties leaving or dying, and they also receive large consignments of miscellaneous goods of every kind, and often purchase large lots of cheap goods to re-sell. The Saturday afternoon sales are the principal amusement of the great mass of the diggers. No work being done after 12.30., from one till five p.m. rival auctioneers are trying their lungs to the utmost in commendation of the most heterogeneous lots of articles, from a bullock waggon to a bottle of pickles, or a box of paper collars, and very fair prices are generally realised.

Rothschild, one of the principal auctioneers at Du Toit's Pan, was most lavish in his use of the word "diamondiferous," which he would apply to any article without the slightest regard to its appropriateness. Thus, not only would he extol as diamondiferous a sieve, sorting-table, pick or shovel, but he would speak of a diamondiferous waggon, or a diamondiferous pair of trousers. Whenever he was selling any diggers' tools, the article he was selling was sure to be the "very identical sieve in which the 93 carat was found last week," or, "here's a nice little pick, a sweet little pick, a dear little pick, a diamondiferous little pick—it picked out a 40-carat stone two days ago, and is warranted to do the same again!" When he came to the last of any lot of articles, or the last but one or two (auctioneers' all the world over are far from particular in this respect), he would be sure to say "Now, gentlemen, this is the 'Last of the Mortimers!'"—Was he thinking of the "Last of the Mohicans?" No one ever knew.—But, with a constant flow of eloquence, half in rather indifferent English, and half in low Dutch, for the benefit of the numerous Boers who stood round, ready to buy anything that went cheap, our worthy auctioneer, refreshed now and then by a tall glass of beer from the neighbouring hotel, would keep the whole crowd of diggers amused for a whole afternoon in the scorching sun—"*faute de mieux,*" you know.

A capital trade is an auctioneer's on the Fields, especially because it requires *no* capital. (I didn't intend a pun when I began that sentence.)

Of course the auctioneer is also a diamond-buyer, and very often a canteen-keeper too, as only a bi-weekly afternoon is taken up with the public sale business. One or two sales of diamonds have already taken place, and it is probable that this most lucrative branch of the profession will soon be as extensively carried on in the different camps as it is in Cape Town.

I here subjoin advertisements of two wholesale and retail stores at Pniel, and at Du Toit's Pan, showing the principal articles of sale on the Fields.

J. B. EBDEN,
WHOLESALE AND RETAIL STORE, PNIEL,

Has just received, and has on hand—

Ale, in quarts.
Alum.
Ammonia.
Acid, Tartaric.
Augers.
Awls.
Arrowroot.
Alpaca, blk.
Biscuits.
Blacking.
Bathbricks.
Brooms.
Blue.
Brandy, Cape.
Do. French.
Bitters, Orange.
Bottle Baskets.
Barley, Pearl.
Bags, wool and flour.
Buckets, gal., 12, 13, 14in.
Boots, Men's E.S. and hobnail.
Braces and Bits.
Brushes, assorted.
Bowls.
Bedsteads.
Bolts, Tower.
Bolts and Nuts.
Blankets.
Bells.
Burning Fluid.
Belts for Diggers.
Breadpans.
Beeswax.
Butchers' Cleavers.
Boxes, Snuff.
Brass Butts.
Cinnamon.
Capers.
Candles.
Cement.
Cigars.

Chicory.
Cloves.
Chocolate.
Cocoa.
Coffee.
Camphor.
Curry-powder.
Confectionery, assorted.
Cream of Tartar.
Corks, Wine & Ginger Beer.
Coals for Smiths.
Campkettles.
Camphor.
Camp Ovens.
Canisters, rnd. & square.
Crowbars.
Candle Moulds.
Cooking Ladles.
Castor Oil.
Concertinas.
Champagne.
Cullenders.
Cider.
Chalk.
Cruet Stands.
Carbonate Soda.
Candle Cotton.
Chimneys, Lamp.
Carraway Seeds.
Coffee Urns.
Currycombs.
Cloth, Oil.
Deals, 1, 2, 3 & 5 cut.
Dry'rs.
Dates.
Dishes, Tin.
Demijohns.
Diamonds, Glaziers'.
Delivery Books.
Eau de Cologne.
Epsom Salts.
Earthenware, assorted.

Essences, assorted.
Envelopes.
Fruits, bottled.
Do. dried.
Files, Taper and Pitsaw.
Fusees.
Funnels.
Fish Hooks.
Flints, Gun.
Filters, Water.
Forks, Cooking.
Glass, Window, 7 × 9, 8 × 10, & 10 × 12.
Glue and Glue Pots.
Ginger.
Grease, A. E.
Gridirons, assorted.
Gimlets.
Gins, Rat.
Guttering, OG.
Guns.
Honey.
Hats.
Helmets, Pith.
Hammers.
Hoes.
Handles, Pick.
Hasps and Staples.
Huis Apotheeks.
Hatches.
Hinges, assorted.
Horse Brushes.
Hemp, Shoe.
Iron, rod and bar.
Iron Weights.
Do. Weaving.
Ink.
Knives, Pocket.
Knives and Forks.
Kettles.
Kits, Shoemakers'.
Lamps.
Lead, white and red.

Ladles, Melting.
Limejuice.
Lanterns.
Lightning Conductors.
Locks and Padlocks.
Lampblack.
Ladders, Amer. folding.
Lines, Fishing.
Lamp Wicks.
Latches (Norfolk).
Matches.
Maccaroni.
Maizena.
Marmalade.
Meal.
Mealies.
Mustard.
Medicines, Dutch.
Mirrors, Zinc.
Meats, Potted.
Mule Shoes.
Mattresses.
Mills, Coffee.
Machines, Sausage.
Magnesia, Citrate.
Nutmegs.
Nails, ½ to 5in.
Needles, Sail.
Nipples, Gun.
Oil, boiled and raw.
Oatmeal.
Oysters.
Oars.
Oil, Salad, half-pints.
Orange & Lemon Peel.
Pickles.
Pepper.
Pipes.
Pilot Bread.
Paints.
Pontac.
Pots, Iron.
Pimento.
Ploughs, Nos. 75 & 25.
Putty.
Pills, Holloway's.
Pans, Kneading.
  Do. Frying.
  Do. Bread.

Pan, Dust.
Peas, Split.
Planes.
Pincers.
Picks.
Plates.
Purses.
Pestles and Mortars.
Painters' Tools.
Pipe Covers.
Pipes, Wooden & Cutty.
Paper, Hanging.
  Do. Sand.
Pens.
Perforated Zinc.
Pencils.
Paper.
Penholders.
Pepper Pots.
Pit Saws.
Quinine, Sulphate of.
Raisins.
Ridging, galvanised.
Rules, 2 feet.
Roasters, Coffee.
Sheet Zinc.
Sherry, F. C. and Cape.
Seidlitz Powders.
Rakes.
Sugar.
Sauces.
Sardines.
Sago.
Salt.
Soap Pots, 16 & 18 gal.
Starch.
Saltpetre.
Salmon.
Spades.
Shovels.
Soda.
Squares, Masons'.
Saws, Hand.
Soups, Kidney.
Screwdrivers.
Sardine Knives.
Scales, Counter.
Spices.

Spoons.
Scoops, Tin.
Snuff Boxes.
Scales, Diamond.
Stationery, assorted.
Spirit Levels.
School Slates.
Sickles.
Saucepans.
Stools.
Sad-irons.
Steps, Carriage.
Steel, Octagon.
Sieves, Wire.
Sealing Wax.
Shoe Pegs.
Screws, Wood.
Stoves, Portable Camp.
Screwjacks.
Slippers, Men's Carpet.
Tea.
Turpentine.
Tobacco, Cavendish.
  Do. Golden Leaf.
  Do. Boer, packets.
Tar.
Twine.
Tinware.
Tumblers.
Teapots.
Taps, Brass.
Tobacco Pouches.
Tape Lines.
Tamarinds.
Traps, Mouse.
Tooth Brushes.
Tacks, Copper.
Trowels, Masons'.
Tin, IC, DC plates.
Thimbles.
Vermicelli.
Vinegar.
Varnish, Copal.
Vermillion.
Wrenches, Coach.
Rim Locks.
Whipsticks.
Wire Netting.

ALWAYS ON HAND,
A SUPPLY OF MEAL, MEALIES, AND KAFIR CORN.   FORAGE, FORAGE.

HOTEL-KEEPERS, STORE-KEEPERS, AND AUCTIONEERS. 135

Also for Sale and Inspection,

1 WOODEN HOUSE, 21 × 12.   1 WOODEN HOUSE, 23 × 16.

Fresh Supplies of Groceries, Oilman's Stores, Hardware, Wines and Spirits, &c daily expected.

Diamonds Bought.   Drafts on Port Elizabeth granted.

R. H. & J. STOCKDALE,
DU TOIT'S PAN,

Have just received further additions to their stock, consisting of—

- Scarlet Woollen Blankts.
- White do. do.
- Scarlet Flannel.
- White do.
- Cotton Bed Tick.
- Union do. do.
- Checked Ginghams.
- Derries.
- Shot Lustres.
- Blue and Orange Prints.
- Hoyles' Prints.
- White and Brown Baftas.
- Huis Linen.
- White Shirtings.
- Horrocks's Long Cloth.
- Printed Pilot Trouserings.
- Mens' Woollen Shirts.
- Do. Cotton do.
- Winseys, in variety.
- Gala Plaids.
- Gamboons.
- Coloured Coburgs.
- Coloured and Black Alpacas.
- Ladies Trimmed Hats.
- Cotton Blankets.
- Harvard Checks.
- Striped Jean.
- Buff Nankeen.
- Fancy Flannel.
- White Kid Gloves.
- Camlet Dresses.
- Challie do.
- Fancy do.
- Romal Handkerchiefs.
- Egyptian Edging.
- White & Blck. Voerchitz.
- Coloured do.
- Skirtings.
- Brown, Drab, and Black Corduroy.
- Brown, Drab, and Black Moleskins.
- Silk Handkerchiefs.
- Printed Coburgs.
- Turkey Towels, white and brown.
- Cotton do.
- Printed Cotton Handkerchiefs.
- Turkey Red Twill.
- Woollen Shawls.
- Men's Brown Cotton Half-Hose.
- Men's Fancy do.
- Do. Shetland do.
- Do. Striped do.
- Morley's W. W. Reels Sewing Cotton.
- Coloured Sewing Cotton.
- Rolled Jaconets.
- Cart Binding.
- India Tape.
- Steel Thimbles.
- Portmonnaies.
- Memorandum Books.
- Fancy Woollen Scarfs.
- Puggerahs.
- Women's Stays, white and coloured.
- White Moleskin Trousers.
- Woollen Bootees.
- Men's Felt Hats.
- Green Baize.
- White Swansdown.
- Diggers Boots.
- Men's Clothing, in variety.
- Mohair Braids.
- Wave do.
- Hbts. Coloured Kid Gloves.
- Ribbons.
- Ladies' Belts.
- Sealing Wax.
- Playing Cards.
- Mouth Harmonicas.
- Briarwood Pipes.
- Eau de Cologne.
- Rope.
- Brass Candlesticks.
- Lanterns.
- Liverpool Soap.
- Widnes do.
- Rimmel's Bar Soap.
- Tent Lines.
- Bass Brooms.
- Cooks Ladles.
- Iron do.
- Melting do.
- Garden Rakes.
- Wood Screws.
- Saw Files.
- Awl Blades.
- Tinned Iron Spoons.
- Coloured Flannel.
- Gridirons.
- Tailors' Scissors.
- Cambric Pocket Handkerchiefs.
- Men's do. do.
- Elastic Belts.
- Leather Belts.
- Embossed Table Covers.
- Coloured Damask.

Needles, in boxes.
Steel Pens.
Soup Ladles.
Dressing Combs.
Knives and Forks.
Carvers.
Cream of Tartar.
Black Pepper.
Carpenters' Saws.
Currants.
Scissors.
Galvanised Iron Buckets.
    do.   do. Baths.
Candles, Belmont.
Pick Handles.
Turpentine.
Paraffine Oil.
Paraffine Lamps.
Sago.
Confectionery, in ½lb. bottles.
Rice.
English Vinegar.
Green Paint.
Dates.
Window Glass, 8 × 10, 10 × 12.
Deal Boards, 1 × 9.
Do. Quartering, 3 × 3.
Assorted Crockeryware.
Cups and Saucers.
Bowls.
Dishes, Jugs.

Plates, &c.
Tar, in drums.
Iron Pots.
Snuff, in bottles.
Japanned Jugs & Basins.
Tin Funnels.
Hair Brushes.
Beer Corks.
Zinc Mirrors.
Copy-books.
Steel Spectacles.
German-silver Table Spoons.
German-silver Tea Spoons.
German-silver Table Forks.
Tea Pots, block tin.
Coffee Urns, superior quality.
Oblong Mirrors.
Corkscrews.
Padlocks.
Gimlets.
Knives and Sheaths.
Holloway's Ointment and Pills.
Cockle's Pills.
Dutch Medicines.
Fever Elixir.
Chlorodine.
Spalding's Glue.
Lemon Syrup.

Cut Tobacco.
Cue Tips and Cement.
Cut Deals.
Transvaal and Colonial Tobacco.
Mauritius Sugars.
Coffee.
Souchong Tea.
Curry Powder.
Fish, in tins.
Saddles, Bridles.
Sorby's Sheepshears.
Whitewash Brushes.
Horse Brushes.
Matches.
Steel Pens.
Writing Ink.
Blacking.
Shoe Brushes.
Slate Pencils.
B. Wove Note Paper.
    Letter do.
    Foolscap, plain and ruled.
Sausage Machines.
Salad Oil.
Castor Oil.
Blue Stone.
Starch.
Mustard.
Worcester Sauce.
Pickles, &c., &c.

TRANSVAAL AND BOER MEAL.

Shortly Expected: Europe Rope and a number of Blocks and Pulleys.

CHAPTER IV.

OUR COLOURED LABOURERS.

THE immense demand for labour, created by the rapid growth of the Diamond Diggings, and the splendid wages given, have attracted to our camps thousands of natives belonging to all the tribes around and a long way north of the Vaal River. Kafirs, Korannas, Hottentots, of every colour from pale sickly yellow to polished ebony, swarm at the Fields. Formerly the "up-country" Kafirs used to contract with the Boers and other farmers for a year's services, at the end of which time they considered themselves well rewarded with a cow, value 3*l*. or 4*l*.; now good "boys" are freely paid on the diggings 30*s*. per month, and fed well into the bargain. They are all indiscriminately spoken of as "nigger," and addressed as "boy," quite irrespective of age. The Kafirs are considered the best and most trustworthy labourers, and of the Kafirs the Zulus have the best reputation, and perhaps the Basutos next. Unfortunately Zulus and Basutos are in a chronic state of hereditary feud, so that a digger cannot employ two Zulus and two Basutos to work and live together. Three other tribes of Kafirs, known as Mahows, Maccatees, and Mankapaans are also extensively represented on the Fields. (I will not vouch for the correct spelling of these three words.)

Large parties of Kafirs are constantly coming up "on their own hook," and pervading the camp in search of a "baas" or master, which they are not long in finding, the demand for native labour being continually on the increase, Old colonists and traders frequently make money by going into the interior, bringing down lots of natives, and introducing them to masters, with whom they contract for three months' services, the trader charging 1*l*. per head for the accommodation; but anyone who has been long on the diggings will not have much difficulty in obtaining Kafirs. If he is a "good baas," his own "boys" will frequently bring to him relatives or friends who will offer their services.

A Kafir's notions of dress are primitive in the extreme; his only garment the ancient *mutya* or loin-cloth, with perchance huge plumes of gaudy feathers adorning his woolly head, and a necklace of tiger claws, shells, or beads; knowing probably no language but his own, or at the best but a few words of Boer Dutch; he arrives on the Fields as raw material, fit for any amount of hard work, and requiring the treatment of a big child, with no petting or spoiling, but plenty of scolding and occasional castigation if he is disobedient or lazy. It is well, on engaging a Kafir for any period of service, to take him to the magistrate's office and get him there to make his mark on a written contract, which formality makes a salutary impression on his untutored mind, and afterwards the master should, in the event of any disobedience or laziness, bring the culprit to the police-office, where he will probably receive a dozen lashes with the "cat." This is preferable to taking the law into one's own hands.

The raw, untutored, unclad Kafirs, fresh from their "kraals" up the mountains, are by far the best and most trustworthy workmen. The contact of civilisation seems to be almost invariably pernicious and demoralising to the peculiar organisation of our Kafir friends. Above all things, mistrust a Kafir who speaks English and wears trousers. They are very fond of assuming different articles of European garb; an old flannel shirt is a most acceptable present, or an old jacket; while, if you want to make your nigger supremely proud and happy, you have only to present him with an old military red coat; but let him keep to his *mutya*, and *don't* give him any trousers. I have seen a nigger walking about most complacently, dressed in a hat, an old paper collar, and a courier bag, not a rag else, barring the mutya. One of my "boys" once found one leg of a pair of trousers, and straightway put it on; but finding it inconvenient, frequently slipping down and hindering him in his work, to which I naturally objected, he finally converted it into a sort of turban, and wore it triumphantly on his head. Huge bunches of tall feathers and coloured handkerchiefs are much worn as headgear.

With regard to sleeping accommodation for the Kafirs, some generous diggers provide them with a rough tent; but if the "boys" are smart and active they will soon make a comfortable little hut for themselves with branches, bushes, &c., which they can go into the country to fetch on Saturday afternoons and Sundays. In any case one or two cotton blankets should be given them, for the nights are often very chilly, and they suffer much from cold. With regard to food, the digger must buy for them mealies (Indian corn or maize), crushed mealies, or mealie meal. If whole mealies are bought, they must be provided with a mill, rather larger than an ordinary coffee-mill, for grinding them. About 100lb., or half a muid, is a fair monthly allowance for each Kafir. Mealie meal fluctuates on the Fields from 25s. to 35s. per muid; crushed mealies and whole mealies are a good deal cheaper. A large iron cooking-pot should also be bought for the niggers. It is as well to give them a little coarse meat (sold cheaply as "Kafir meat") once or twice a week, and a glass of brandy (Cape Smoke) on Saturdays or Sundays. If the tent is anywhere near a slaughtering place, they will frequently provide themselves with an extra in the shape of offal, of which they will bring in huge quantities with immense glee, throw the filthy stuff on the fire without being very particular as to cleaning it, devour it with great satisfaction, but still have an appetite unimpaired for the discussion of their mealie porridge, or "pap" as they call it. Good "boys" should be encouraged with a small money present, say a shilling every time a diamond is found. The work that a Kafir is expected to perform at the claim is—picking, shovelling, hauling, and sifting. It is not desirable to let them *sort*, both because it is throwing too much temptation in their way, and because they are very slow sorters; in fact, it is always desirable that the eye of the master should be on the Kafir at work, not only because he *may* be inclined to yield to the temptation of concealing a large diamond he may see in the sieve, but because, if not looked after, he is very apt to "loaf," stand still, and stare about him.

One of our "boys" was very much given to these fits of laziness, and my partner or I, on turning round, would see him leaning on his spade or standing by the sieve, in a dignified attitude, calmly contemplating the busy scene around him. Our remedy on such occasions was to throw stones at his bare legs, which invariably recalled him to a sense of his duty.

Two Kafirs, if they understand the work, ought to be able to keep two white men constantly employed in sorting, and this is a very good division of labour for the hot weather, while in the winter the "baas" will often find it pleasant and warming to take a hand at pick, shovel, or sieve himself.

Two friends of mine brought up from the interior of Natal six of the best Zulus I ever saw. They were fine, tall, strong built young fellows, of rather prepossessing countenances and splendid figures, all clad in bright red coats, so that as they marched through the camp to or from the claim, singing their loud and not inharmonious songs, their appearance was most imposing.

Moreover they were thoroughly good "boys," hardworking, polite, good humoured, and lively. They used to go through grand performances at their "kraal," war songs and dances, pantomimes of hunting and other scenes, with great spirit and talent, causing large audiences to assemble to witness their barbaric sports. And they appeared to be thoroughly trustworthy, being sometimes left at the claim all by themselves, when they would not only keep on working steadily, but would bring to their masters any diamonds they might find. One of them, indeed, who had particularly sharp eyes, used frequently to find diamonds on the road, or among refuse stuff from other claims, and bring them to his masters.

The ordinary work performed by a Kafir at his master's tent and cooking-place, is simply to light the fire, boil water, fetch water from the wells, and wash up plates and dishes. They are in too filthy a state to be entrusted with the latter operation when they have been to the slaughtering places to fetch offal. The six above-mentioned Kafirs soon learned to perform some of the simpler operations of European cookery, to wash clothes, and otherwise "make themselves generally useful." A Kafir does not generally wash either his clothes (?) or himself, and if you give him an old flannel shirt he will probably never take it off again till it falls to pieces. One of my "boys" had a faint notion of cleanliness, however. He came to me one morning and said, "Baas, give little bit soap, head plenty full of —" (insects unmentionable to ears polite).

They are great smokers, but as Boer tobacco can be bought on the Fields for about 6d. per lb. (I have even bought it as low as 3d.), it does not cost much to keep them in the soothing weed. Two of my "boys" I never could induce to smoke pipes. They would moisten the ground in a certain raised spot, run a stick along it, to make a long hole, enlarge the orifice at one end, fill it with tobacco, put a bit of ember on to it, and, lying flat on their bellies on the ground, apply their mouths to the other end and draw out huge volumes of smoke—over which they invariably choked and expectorated freely, generally going through this performance within a foot or so of our tent while we were having dinner inside. They drink an immense quantity of water, and as much Cape Smoke as anyone will give them. It is also difficult to break them of the habit of keeping up big fires all the evening, round which they sit and smoke, and sing and talk with other Kafirs, who "just drop in," making a fearful hubbub till eight or nine o'clock, when they coil themselves up in their blankets or skins and sleep soundly till daybreak, when the rays of the rising sun, or more frequently the foot of the rising " baas" warns them to "opstaan, vuur maak " (get up, make fire).

I had once a "boy" who was rather of an intelligent and inquiring turn of mind, and he once astounded and horrified me by suggesting that "baas " should teach him to read ! Soon afterwards I showed him some pictures in an old *Illustrated London News*. He had never seen pictures before, and at first they conveyed no idea to his mind ; but soon it dawned upon him, and when he could lay his finger on the figure of a man and say " Baas ! " or " Seer ! " and point to the drawing of a woman and say " Mees ! " he was quite pleased and proud, for he thought he had learnt to read. He was rather a comical genius too, and used greatly to amuse us by the cheeky and fluent way in which he used to chaff his comrade, who was a good deal duller. They knew four English words between them, all very bad words. They were very proud of this little accomplishment, and would swear at one another for hours with this limited vocabulary. They were always singing and shouting at the claim, or yelling out barbaric " chaff " to neighbouring Kafirs. They were very weatherwise, could foretell storms and rains with wonderful prescience.

The natives have unfortunately been accustomed to very harsh, rough treatment from their Boer masters, and, generally speaking, an Englishman treats them with too much kindness and familiarity, which has a decidedly bad effect on them. They think that their "baas," if he treats them so kindly, must be very much in need of their services, they are evidently most valuable "boys" to him, and they consider it their duty to themselves to strike for higher wages. Or they lose all respect for their master, disobey him, become insolent, and finally run away, probably with some of his diamonds or other property. A nigger is all very well as long as he is kept in his proper place, that is " kept down ;" to treat him in the " man and a brother " style of the Exeter Hall philanthropists, is only to spoil him and injure yourself. New comers to the colonies find this difficult to realise, thinking that kind treatment *must* succeed, but they soon get woefully undeceived. Of course I don't mean you should ill-use Kafirs, but keep them in their places ; punish them when naughty, and never be familiar or laugh with them. I think it will not be out of place to quote here the following graphic portraiture of " Kafir exquisites," from the pen of my friend, Mr. Cowan, author of a book of very great interest on new African sport and travel, entitled, I believe, "Swazi Kafirs and Swazi Game."

The natives he alludes to in the following lines are town Kafirs, certainly, but they come from the same tribes and country as our "boys" on the diggings, so his appreciation of some of their most distinguishing characteristics possesses considerable value and interest for us.

To a new arrival, the spectacle of a darkey swell conveys only a laughable impression of negro vanity. He sees merely the repetition of the old fables of the raven in peacock's plumage—the ass in the lion's skin—and probably the prejudices of inherited civilisation would lead him to prefer the ludicrous appearance of the "tame" Kafir in civilised raiment to the sight of the *mutya*-clad Kafir "proper." "But," to use the pet phrase of one of our colonial Burkes, "he has yet to learn" that there is a physiological character in clothes, and that the fig-leaf, the first clothing on record, signalised the first lapse from original purity.

In order to trace the origin of our "Kafir exquisite," let us briefly follow the career of a rustic Kafir crossing the border in search of work. His legs are forthwith encased in those nether garments generally termed "unmentionables"—which are usually, in his case, curiously antique, containing more holes than material—a dilapidated hat, rather in the style of the Irish *caubeen*, and a patchwork shirt complete his costume. Now, no one would think of ridiculing the Kafir *pur et simple*. Nay, some indeed think that clothing him would be, like painting the lily, mere "wasteful and ridiculous excess." Caliban may be coarse, but surely he is not ridiculous or vulgar, on the principle that nothing real, genuine, or original can be. Imperfect as the dress of a "wild" Kafir is, and faint as are his conceptions of right and wrong, there are individuals so deluded as to prefer the comparative absence of clothing combined with the presence of good qualities, and with some dim idea of natural law, to the exaggeration of attire, combined with the destruction of those virtues, in his "civilised" brother. Our rustic Kafir does not at once become exotic; he has not yet turned his *assegai* into a jaunty cane, nor does he yet abandon the ancestral cow-horn pipe, his tiger-claw necklace, his bright bangles. At first everyone is stunned at his non-objection, nay, even willingness, to work. Nor can they credit their ears when, so far from being insolent and saucy, he is actually civil, and occasionally obliging —and they can scarcely believe that such an abnormal creature as a sober, steady, hard-working Kafir can exist in this our colonial Utopia. But soon, alas, "a change comes o'er the spirit" of our rustic Kafir. He begins to imitate the manners and fashions of his white acquaintances, and makes the grand discovery of the existence of a strong and inebriating fluid, generally termed (so we hear) *rum*, for which he acquires forthwith a violent predilection (probably because the transition from barbarism to breeches was so sudden that some stimulant became necessary to sustain the shock), and which he contrives to absorb into his system in quantities that render his removal to the "tronk" both a benevolent and a sanitary measure.

As soon as he can beg, borrow, steal, or—least probably—earn and save enough money, he proceeds to invest it in the purchase of a startling but limited outfit.

Like most tropical productions, he is partial to loud colours and strong contrasts. He obviously agrees with Shakespeare that "motley is the only wear," but not only for fools. A second-hand uniform, the more *vermilliony* the better, adorned with an incurable eruption of gleaming buttons is, in his opinion, the very *ultima thule* of the tailor's art. We presume that he must, therefore, have, in common with mad bulls and gushing young ladies (partial to *rouge* in any shape), an irresistible attraction to, and admiration of, those scarlet automatons, the military.

His next purchase is a painfully glossy and nappy hat, which, also *à la militaire*, he balances knowingly on the extreme tip of his left ear. He then buys a white shirt—white seems to him to imply the acme of respectability, if not of positive affluence, from the necessity, obvious to all who know his habits, of being constantly washed. He buys paper collars only when unable to pick up any that have been rejected by more fastidious owners; and finally completes his attire by the purchase of a pair of brilliant "unwhisperables." He has put off the old Adam, he has swept and garnished his lovely person, but we opine that the last state of that man is worse than the first. He becomes a public nuisance. There is now, in addition to the usual "perfumery" about him, an odour of *ingeniously* villainous rum, with which is mingled the scent of the execrable tobacco, puffed so complacently out of that brass-topped and coruscent pipe. He is, *now*, neither a fine type of animal man, nor even a passable fac-simile of educated man. A woolly head, full of emptiness or vice, a pair of somewhat yellow but drolly observant eyes, a brace of hands full of that commodity for which His Satanic Majesty so benevolently finds occupation, a couple of legs that with difficulty answer the locomotive purposes of their owner—in the entirety not at all the kind of biped intended to inhabit this planet. He assumes a *blasé* air, as indicating an exhaustive experience of civilisation, and a serenely self-confident look, as indicative of his approval of the *liberté, fraternité, et égalité* preached by those *braying* philanthropists with whom, if their theory be true, he has a natural chemical affinity. He has caught the present social epidemic, the wish to be genteel; and, aping the universal white deference to opinion and fashion, he unwittingly becomes, by exaggeration, a most trenchant satire, a biped homily on the follies of civilisation. He even, although probably a churchgoer, swears fashionably, and with remarkable volubility, displaying great fertility of fancy in variations on the too meagre—for him—catalogue of "white" oaths. Owing to his extraordinary powers of suction, to his very foggy ideas of *meum* and *tuum*, to prejudices in favour of miscellaneous polygamy, and to mormonising tendencies imbibed in the course of his social education; or owing, perhaps, merely to a civilised abhorrence of work, and a craving for novelty, he frequently changes his "wattle and daub" residence for that triumph of colonial architecture, popularly known as the "tronk," an abode for which his uncivilised brethren entertain an irrational and most unaccountable dislike. There are at present eighty-three Kafirs, we believe, in the Durban gaol. We are curious to know how many of these are miracles of civilisation, and how many are green Kafirs, *i.e.*, grossly ignorant of the manifold improvements of colonial life. To be finely feathered and dressed like a white man are to him ecstatic blisses "worn in their newest gloss," but blisses to which he is wedded by novelty, not familiarity. He is exalted from the comparatively pure air of native simplicity to an atmosphere of spurious gentility, in which he flutters with all the rapture of a new-born butterfly, just disenthralled from the chrysalis state. Mark the ludicrous affectation of his, what Albert Smith terms, "prancing gait;" he seems to be treading on air. His teeth, like the silver lining of a sable cloud, are ever and anon displayed in grins of ecstacy, as the reflection of his elegant person in the shop windows meets his eye. The whole pavement is too narrow for his strut; single ladies are unceremoniously driven off. He condescends to give the wall side to none but gentlemen armed with sjamboks. His unsophisticated admiration of his splendid self would be merely amusing were it not generally acknowledged "all is not gold that glitters," and that, so far from being sterling metal coined in civilisation's mint, he is merely a spurious and base coin, uttered by Exeter Hall optimists and their emissaries, and passed off as genuine on the strength of the breeches, or, perhaps, from his absurd similarity to his white brother Brummels. Surely they can be only visionary optimists who believe that they have thus civilised and Christianised our rustic Kafir. We assert that they have merely destroyed a Kafir without making a convert either to religion or civilisation. He is your real wild Kafir, degenerated by our accommodating him to the pleasure of corrupted tastes, whereas his unpolished brethren can lay claim to a few natural virtues, and have to deplore a lesser number of degrading and un-savage vices.

"All things," says Plato, "are produced by nature, by chance, or by art; the most beautiful by either of the two first, the least perfect by the last." Now we cannot regard our "Kafir exquisite" as a spontaneous production of mother earth, nor yet can we look upon him as a biped "fluke," a *lusus naturæ*—so he must necessarily be a creation of art—of tailors' art, and consequently inferior to, and less perfect than, his more scantily clad compatriots, those "images of God cut in ebony," as Fuller quaintly terms the black races, as deriving his would-be superiority from imitative powers common to monkeys and Frenchmen.

What can be more apparent than that a life of civilisation being unfavourable to the animal powers of men, animal men will necessarily suffer at first by the contact, and will continue to distil the easy vices rather than the difficult virtues from an existence so novel, so foreign to their very nature, until the continuity of their vice-distilling propensities be summarily checked by a more effective Kafir law than the colony at present possesses—or more gradually broken by ameliorating education. The true progress of refinement is to teach him to abandon all the mountebank drapery which, as being really barbarian still, he indulges in; and to get him to wear clothes, not for the purpose of display, but from some faint idea of general decency and social propriety. To judge from the various and constant notices appearing in our newspapers, it is absolutely dangerous for any European lady to indulge in the luxury of a promenade anywhere away from the immediate vicinity of Durban, or even then without male protection. A reign of terror is instituted by these scoundrels, under which neither the lives nor the honour of our mothers, sisters, daughters, wives, are for a moment safe. Over and over again instances of outrage and violation occur, which no means apparently can check. What does this prove? That the punishments inflicted on such scoundrels are not sufficiently terrorising, that the whole treatment of the Kafirs by the dominant race is radically wrong. To conclude, we are not inveighing against imitation, because, besides that quality being a prominent characteristic of the Kafir race, and deriving its evil from its model, it is in itself one of the chief causes of early civilisation; not so

much inveighing against Kafir affectation in particular, as against the general system, "which makes a dandy while it spoils a man."
So far from advocating a return to semi-nudity and pastoral simplicity, we wish, by ridiculing the opposite extreme, to point out the necessary medium; and finally, not so much condemning the vices and crimes which may be, perhaps, traced to this system of "regeneration," as the impotency and imbecility of laws, which are incapable of checking the results.

Well, our Kafirs in the camps are certainly not so far advanced in "civilisation" as the "exquisites" so graphically depicted by Mr. Cowan; still we have a few specimens now and then, very few and far between, I am happy to say. My two darkies were sitting by the camp fire one bright Sunday morning, when to them arrived two visitors, friends or relations I presume. One of them was dressed in an old suit of corduroy. That was bad enough. But the other! "Oh, ye gods and little fishes," to see a nigger with such breeches! Shiny black cloth ones, and a white waistcoat, *and* a coat, *and* a "deerstalker" hat, *and* a paper collar, *and* a flaming necktie! *My* "boys" had only flannel shirts and mutyas on, but they did not seem much impressed by the splendour of the new comers, and I, lying prone on certain buckskins in my tent, smoking a contemplative pipe, and dressed, I must say, in a costume which was in every point inferior to that of the "darkie swell," observed that the latter appeared to treat my "boy" with a good deal of respect, so I immediately flattered myself that I had the son of a chief in my employ.

Visitors were generally very frequent, both morning and evening, and my "boys" used to always exercise the duties of hospitality by helping them liberally to the mealie-meal "pap." I naturally objected to this, as I did not see that my "boys" ever went out and fed at other masters' expense; but whenever I remonstrated, on seeing how fast my mealie-meal was disappearing down the capacious throats of sundry shiny, half-naked black rascals, my "boy" would meet me with the argument that they were his "brothers," which he appeared to consider unanswerable. What a very large family the rascal had!

The niggers were, I must own, a very strong element of the picturesque in the appearance of the camp at night. Hundreds of dusky figures, in every variety of fantastic headgear, squatting round the bright camp fires, or perchance dancing their war dances, or singing barbaric songs. They are very happy as a rule: they may well be so, when they are getting such wages. Many of them will carefully save their money. The great ambition of every Kafir seems to be to buy a gun. When a Kafir has served long enough on the Fields to enable him to pay 5*l*. or 10*l*. for a gun or rifle, he shoulders his weapon, and turns his face towards the ancestral "kraals," a happy man.

He is then a mighty hunter, is sure of getting a good wife, and is ready to take an important part in any war that may arise between his and the neighbouring tribes—a very frequent occurrence. Some, it is true, are not so careful; they yield to the "white" vices of drinking, gambling, &c., are often to be found in "chokey" (prison), often changing masters, and never saving money.

Of Hottentots and Korannas I have had hardly any personal experience, and therefore cannot say much of them here. They are paler, more slightly built than the Kafirs: the Korannas, in particular, have emaciated looking frames and features, and a sickly yellow complexion. They work pretty well, but are not generally so good-humoured or willing as the Kafirs, being rather of a surly, morose disposition. Moreover, they pretend to more civilisation, being generally fully clothed. In spite of their appearance, they are very tough and strong. Nearly all of them speak Dutch fluently, and a few know a little English.

Women innumerable, black, brown, and yellow, are to be seen in our camps. Nevertheless, there are far more Korannas and Hottentots amongst them than Kafir women. They dress decently, with a natural preference for gaudy colours. They find ample and remunerative employment as washerwomen, household servants, &c. But it must be added that a great many of them are too lazy to work, and prefer to get money more quickly and easily, as is soon apparent, by their bolder and richer apparel, their constant promenading about the camp, and their impudent looks.

It is rather amusing to see a lot of "darkie swells," male and female, going out for a walk on Sundays—surely, in half a dozen of them, you shall see all the colours of the rainbow, and a dozen more, exemplified; but they are not so very much more *outré* in their notions of tasteful attire than the wives and daughters of the Boers, after all. I have seen both male and female niggers, Korannas especially, paint their cheeks with red ochre, which has a comically hideous effect. An album filled with good coloured sketches of the various types of natives round our camps, in their heterogeneous variety of costume, would be a source of endless amusement at home.

CHAPTER V.

TENT LIFE.

THE principal kinds of canvas dwellings patronised by the diggers are two, viz.: "bell tents" and "square tents." Round, or bell-tents, are not so much liked as the square tents; the disadvantages of the former being that they are not so convenient for the stowage of bedding, baggage, &c., inside, and also that they are peculiarly liable to the attacks of the wind. If a "young whirlwind" should chance to get inside a bell tent, away come pegs or fastenings, and up goes the canvas over the pole like a big umbrella turned inside out,—a ludicrous sight for the spectators, but a by no means pleasant sensation for the occupants. A square, or rather oblong tent, about twelve feet long by eight broad, is a very comfortable domicile for two persons. Such a tent can be bought ready made, or made to order by a tent-maker on the Fields, for 9*l.* or 10*l.*, or can be bought second-hand at the bi-weekly auction sales for somewhat less. It has an upright pole at each end, and a ridge pole: the bottom is fastened down by pegs, driven deeply into the ground, and the tent lines can either be attached to pegs, or, what is better still, to strong upright posts fixed in the ground two or three feet from, and of the same height as, the seam—generally about four feet from the ground—from which the lines are taken, and from which the canvas descends perpendicularly, which part is called the wall.

Care must be taken to sink the tent poles deeply into the ground, eighteen inches at least, more if possible. They are additionally secured by strong "guy ropes" stretched from the spikes at the top of the pole to a strong post in the ground four or five yards from each end of the tent.

The spikes are sometimes ornamented with a handsome knob or ball, but more often empty bottles are placed upon them, with a view to keep off the lightning, which often plays close round the tents with a "familiarity" which by no means "breeds contempt." At a short distance from the tent is the fire-place, simply a square hole a foot to two feet deep, protected from the

L 2

wind by a movable screen of bushes or other material. Outside the tent lie the diggers' tools, shovels, picks, sieves, buckets, and perchance a wheelbarrow, a very useful article; also a water-cask, a few rough cooking utensils, and sundries.

For a description of the interior of an ordinary digger's tent, I will refer to a private letter of mine, written soon after we (my partner and self) had settled down in our "canvas home."

On the left of the door (?) on entering, is my big box, whereon repose sundry books, my album, two small paraffin lamps, a few dishes, a lot of boxes of matches, and a joint of beef. In the corner, between the box and the side of the tent, are my old gun and fishing-rods, towered over by a Kafir walking-stick, 8ft. high, curiously carved with snakes. Going along the side you pass a couple of huge straw hats (useless in this winter weather and now used as receptacles for various small articles in daily requirement), a large roll of Boer tobacco, a keg of pickled fish, a wickered demijohn of Cape brandy, a large tin, holding 10lb. of coffee; and at my head, my fishing basket, with sundry rolled-up blankets. I am now writing, half-sitting, half-reclining, on the floor, which I have carpeted with the skins of many antelopes. Along the middle of the tent our two portmanteaus, lying lengthwise, separate my *apartment* from M.'s, and also serve as tables, writing desks, &c., &c. Furniture we neither have nor want; we have skins and blankets enough either to sit or lie comfortably. M.'s side of the house is similarly *furnished* to mine. We have also, stowed away in handy corners, some eighty pounds of sugar and seventy pounds of meal, a sack of potatoes outside the tent and some carrots in a bucket.

Now the above is the description of a tent as pitched and arranged by a couple of "new chums," and I need hardly say that our arrangements were very defective. No one ought to sleep on the ground, even with any amount of skins; after they have once got sodden with the chill winter rains it is very difficult to get them dry again, and they keep mouldy, damp, and unwholesome for a length of time. Everyone should sleep on a mattrass—we got capital straw mattrasses afterwards for 1*l.* each—raised from the ground, either on a "stretcher," made on purpose, of wood and canvas, or on two or three portmanteaus and boxes, which do just as well. We also found afterwards that it was far more comfortable to "sit at table" at our meals, instead of taking them in the old Roman reclining fashion; so my old box was converted into a dining-table, adorned with a bit of canvas as table-cloth, washed every Sunday, and the fish-keg and other small articles were used as seats.

In the beginning, moreover, we did not pitch the tent sufficiently firmly, nor take the necessary precautions of digging a deep trench all round it, and heaping up a little ridge of earth along the bottom of the tent, over pegs, &c., to give it additional security of holding. It is also a good plan to run a light skirting-board all round the tent, and to floor it with clean gravel from the claims. A few skins spread on the floor over this gravel give the tent a great air of barbaric luxury, and they are cheap enough.

As a natural sequence, almost immediately after the above description of a carelessly-pitched tent, follows a brief account of the miseries of a winter rain-storm. In a postscript to the same letter (26th June) I say:—

Since I wrote the foregoing, we have had three days and nights of very heavy rain; very detrimental and miserable, stopping all work at the claims, and flooding many of the tents, ours amongst the number. Fancy sleeping in a puddle! The first day we made a tiny fire just inside the tent, and managed to cook a little food; the second day too; but on the third morning we woke up, after a little damp sleep, to find not a bit of wood nor a single match dry, one side of the tent blown in, and water and mud mixing horribly with all our skins, rugs, stores, &c. You can hardly conceive how miserable, wet, and filthy everything looked. We managed to get some dry clothes and boots on (my sea boots had about a quart of water in each), and then fled from the place in disgust, and went to an iron hotel, where we breakfasted, dined, and at night slept on the table, very comfortable and *dry*. The hotels and canteens were all full of washed-out diggers.

One more extract from a letter of mine, dated Du Toit's Pan, 13th August:—

The weather has again shown us a few of the miseries of a digger's life. Last Friday week, hearing and feeling a tremendous gale, we had to get up several times in the middle of the night to make the tent more secure. In spite of our utmost efforts, I woke up early in the morning to find my half of the tent blown open from its fastenings, rain pouring in upon me, everything that I was lying on soaked, and a chill damp blast sweeping over me most unpleasantly. What could a fellow do? The gale was too strong to think of fastening the tent again, and it was evident that the whole frail structure must shortly come down. So I sat in the driest spot I could find, lit a pipe, and philosophically surveyed the scene of desolation. The lid of our big coffee tin had blown off, and coffee and mud mingled hideously with my clammy blankets; and the wind howled round us, and still the rain poured in through many openings, soaking and damaging our little stores. M. awoke, and began to groan. Then we both talked of Mark Tapley, and determined to be "jolly." Very creditable under the circumstances! Impossible to light a fire. I opened my portmanteau, put on the only comparatively dry garments I could find, and we fled to the "town," where we felt safe in a corrugated iron hotel, and made a very hearty breakfast.

Now all this trouble and expense may be spared by having

a strong waterproof tent, pitching it securely, flooring it with good dry gravel, sleeping on a mattrass well raised from the ground, and digging a deep trench all round the tent, which should be pitched on rather rising ground. A novice in these matters should, after selecting a location, ask some of his neighbours to give him their advice and assistance in pitching his tent. Diggers are always willing enough to help one another in these matters.

The tents of some of our richer diggers, round De Beer's and the Colesberg Kopje especially, are very comfortably arranged inside and out. They are not so thick together as at Du Toit's Pan and Bultfontein. A large well-furnished tent stands in the middle of a big enclosure, fenced in with thorn bushes, containing also a tent or "kraal" for the Kafirs, and little corral for horses, mules, or cattle. Any good-sized trees standing near the tent will generally be used as a larder, its branches tastefully hung with legs of mutton and other joints of meat, so that it looks like a very substantial Christmas Tree; and if the owner of the tent is a sportsman, a springbuck, with a hare and a brace of "knorhaans" or partridges, will often further adorn the family "leg-of-mutton tree," as some diggers call them.

It is very customary in summer to have a big "fly" or awning stretched over the tent, about a foot above it, which is found to be very promotive of coolness inside the tent. This object is also attained by having the tent lined inside with some suitable material—green baize, for instance. "Canvas houses," consisting of canvas closely stretched over a strong wooden framework, and houses made entirely of wood, are now becoming very numerous on the Fields. They are more comfortable and private than tents, as they may have a door and a lock, and perhaps even a window, but they are also more expensive, a small canvas house, say 12ft. by 8ft., costing at least 20*l*.

The following is the ordinary routine of tent life:—Up a little before daybreak, call the Kafirs to light fire, cook breakfast, then off to the claim; back to the tent at midday for half an hour's rest, and a "snack" of something cold; then back to work at the claim till five, cook and eat dinner; after which if the digger has really done an honest day's work, hotels, billiards, and other dissipations will have no charms for him, and he will be glad to lie down, amuse himself with a little light reading and the never-failing pipe, and "turn in" early, say nine or ten, to enjoy a thoroughly good night's rest. In the summer time, as people rise earlier and get through more work by midday, and as the heat is very intense between twelve and three, many diggers indulge in a couple of hours' *siesta* in the afternoon. Visiting is very frequent among the diggers; Sunday being of course the great day for going from tent to tent, from camp to camp, to see friends and compare luck during the past week.

CHAPTER VI.

FOOD, WATER, AND WOOD.

FOOD has been plentiful on the Fields from the first, especially at the large camps on the dry diggings. Beef and mutton can be bought at the different large butchers at 4*d.* per lb.; rumpsteaks have now risen to 5*d.* Veal and pork are rarities, very occasionally seen, and consequently fetching higher prices. Hams, bacon, and salt pork, are being brought on the market in large quantities by the Boers and other farmers, and find a ready sale at about 1*s.* 6*d.* per lb. Game is plentiful and cheap, consisting principally of springbuck, blesbuck, and wildebeest. Poultry is tolerably reasonable: fowls and ducks 2*s.* 6*d.* to 3*s.* 6*d.* each, eggs very dear, from 2*s.* 6*d.* to 4*s.* a dozen. Fresh fish not obtainable except on the Vaal River or the Modder, distant respectively twenty-five and eighteen miles; and as there are at present no professional fishermen, but only occasional amateurs, fresh fish never comes on the market. Something might be done in this line by an enterprising man with nets and a mule cart, for these rivers swarm with very good fish, which would command a high price on our markets. Vegetables are very dear as yet; but as the neighbouring Boers are daily becoming more alive to the fact of the great demand for these essentials to health, the cultivation and supply is increasing, and prices are falling. Still, such prices as half-a-crown for a cabbage, a couple of small lettuces, or a handful of onions, and five to seven shillings for a bucketful of potatoes, were freely given when I left the Fields.

With regard to bread stuffs, the staple article—Boer meal, has been fluctuating from 35*s.* to 50*s.* per muid (about 200lb.), while flour was retailed at 6*d.* per lb., and not procurable at every store even at that price. Rice 9*d.* per lb.; sugar, 8*d.* or 9*d.* Forage, for cattle, generally oat hay, 1*s.* to 2*s.* per bundle of about 5lb.

In addition to these staple articles of food in our camps, the well-to-do digger can procure an abundance of European luxuries in the shape of preserved and tinned meats, fish, vegetables, and fruits, of which nearly all the stores keep a good supply. Pickles 2*s.* 6*d.* per bottle. Fruits, bottled, for puddings, &c., 2*s.* 6*d.* Butter is scarce, and dear; fresh butter, 2*s.* 6*d.* to 5*s.* per lb., salt butter rather cheaper. Common Dutch cheese, 2*s.* 6*d.*

It is to be anticipated that soon, with the increased facilities for cheap and quick transport—notably viâ Algoa Bay—provisions and goods of all kinds will become much more reasonable in price on the Fields. Every digger who wishes to live economically, should attend the morning markets regularly once or twice a week, taking a nigger and a wheelbarrow or a sack for carrying home purchases, and should do all his own cooking. Those who have no idea of the latter should purchase a cheap cookery book, or get some of their fair friends to give them a lesson or two in elementary cuisine before going out. My partner and I used to live very fairly. I did all the cooking, of which previous Californian experience had given me a tolerable knowledge. Our general fare was as follows: Breakfast, something fried—chops, steaks, kidneys, or bacon, with coffee and bread; lunch—bread and cheese, or cold meat; dinner—roast joints, or good wholesome stews of various kinds, with plenty of vegetables in them. Pudding generally represented by boiled rice, with plenty of dried peaches, apricots, or quinces stewed. These dried fruits are very useful; they can be bought very cheaply on the markets, 3d. to 9d. per lb.; 1s. in the stores. Stewed for about an hour with a little sugar they plump out beautifully, regain a good deal of their original flavour, and form a very wholesome and succulent adjunct to a plain repast. On Sundays we generally had the luxury of a fruit pudding (bottled fruits), of which a lot can often be bought at auctions at 1s. 9d. or 2s. per bottle. With dinner, or directly after it, we took tea or coffee, and previously to "turning in," a "nightcap" of Cape brandy and water, hot or cold, according to the season. This had risen in price from 7s. 6d, to 12s. 6d. per gallon, but I expect it will now be cheaper again. I must not forget to mention a favourite food of the Boers—"beltongue" or jerked meat—the flesh of springbuck, blesbuck, wildebeest, and other large game, cut in thick strips, and dried in the sun by hunters who are too far from the markets to bring in the game fresh. Large quantities of it come in, and are sold pretty cheaply. High-dried "beltongue" is by no means bad eaten raw with bread, and it is excellent as an adjunct to soups and stews.

With regard to water, at Du Toit's Pan and Bultfontein, the committee sank wells, and charged 1s. per month "water right," for which the digger was entitled to two buckets per day, which he must fetch or send for, with his own buckets and ropes. The wells were nearly always crowded, and the water muddy. At a well sunk by private enterprise at Du Toit's Pan, there was a limited number of subscribers at 4s. per month. The water was very good, four buckets per day were allowed, and the well was secured by a cover and lock, and fitted with a windlass, rope, and bucket. This was a convenient and reasonable arrangement. Several other wells were being sunk when I left. At the Colesberg Kopje water was not paid for monthly, but was charged 3d. per bucket, and somewhat less in proportion for a hogshead, but it is better to get it fresh daily. The water of several of the wells was very bad. Here, too, many new wells are being sunk, and I do not anticipate that water will be either scarce or dear by this time. The need of a bath or thorough ablution is often much felt. A small bathing establishment has lately been opened at Du Toit's Pan. Charge for a bath, 2s. 6d. The new comer should be careful not to drink too much water at first, it is apt to give diarrhœa. A little—a very little—brandy in it is an improvement and a corrective in this respect. Cold tea is a good beverage to take to the claims in a bottle.

Wood is dear, and not likely to decrease in price, for there is no wood worth mentioning in the immediate vicinity of the dry diggings, and it is being cut to a rapidly-increasing distance from the different camps. The general price for good firewood was about 3l. per waggon load; 1l. per Scotch cartload. Persons having tents on the outside of the different camps may get it more cheaply, for a great many niggers go out far in the country on Saturday afternoons and Sundays to cut wood, and bring back large bundles of good-sized dry sticks, which they sell for ninepence or a shilling per bundle. I used almost always to catch one of these fellows on his return, as I was pretty well outside the camp, and the first customer he would call on. I found that one of these bundles would last, with care, about a week. Kafirs want a good deal of looking after, they are very much inclined to be extravagant with wood and water. They like to burn big fires all the evening, whether it be hot or cold weather, but no strict disciplinarian will allow them this expensive indulgence. Moreover, they are generally particularly averse to collecting dry bullock dung, or "mest" as it is called in Dutch, which makes most excellent fuel, and of which there is generally a good supply to be found on the neighbouring veldt. This objection is entirely owing to constitutional laziness, not to any motives of imaginary cleanliness—cleanliness, in fact, is a *very* imaginary quality in a Kafir. The digger should take care, both in winter and summer, no matter how fine and settled the weather may appear to be, to keep a little stock of wood securely dry in a snug corner of his tent, and to have a good stock of matches under cover, so that he may have materials for starting a fire when all is wet outside.

While on the subject of food, I ought to have mentioned the donkeys. Start not, reader, I don't mean to say that diggers eat donkeys—*au contraire*, the jackasses eat the diggers' potatoes and carrots. There were a great many donkeys round about the part of the camp where my tent was situated, and at night they would roam about at unholy hours, "seeking what they might devour." A sharp bark from the little watch-dog, and the tired digger awakes to hear heavy footsteps of felonious quadrupeds just outside his tent, and then, oh horror, a sound of munching, and he knows the brutes have discovered his little store of carrots, cabbages, or potatoes, which he picked up such a bargain on the market that morning, for *only* five or ten shillings a bucketful. So he steals cautiously out, and there stand three or four jackasses in the bright moonlight, busy at their wicked work. Boots, logs from the wood-pile, empty bottles, and any other missiles that come handy, are seized and hurled at the long-eared offenders, as they scamper off over the plain, but little impressed, alas—for African donkeys have tough hides—and soon to return and stamp and prowl, and nose round the tent again. Those donkeys were always coming to our tent. We got fearfully riled, and even asked a policeman if we were justified in shooting them if we caught them devouring our property. He said no, but we might take them to the pound, and charge the owner with the damage done. This was far too slow and complicated a process for us. Who was going to put on his clothes to drive asses to the pound at one or two a.m.? So we remained exposed to their inroads, continually disturbed in our needful rest by the well-known and hateful sound of their footsteps and their munching, and the aforesaid missiles were in constant requisition. At last I hit on a better plan. I kept a heavy iron crowbar close to my head When the donkeys came, I would steal very cautiously out, grasp the crowbar with both hands, get quietly close behind a donkey before he knew I was there, and then bring down the weapon with all my force on his stern or elsewhere. This seemed to impress them a little; anyhow their visits to my tent gradually became less frequent, and at last ceased, to my very great relief.

CHAPTER VII.

OUR POLICE.

DURING my stay on the Fields, we enjoyed the protecting services, at Klip Drift, of a corps of the F. A. M. P., or Frontier Armed and Mounted Police. These men, established in a pleasant little camp on the top of the "kopje," just outside the town of Klip Drift, were dressed in a serviceable uniform of dark brown corduroy with a peaked leather helmet. They were all well mounted, and carried revolvers. There were a good many scamps and "ne'er-do-weels" among them, and the force was also a refuge for many of those who had arrived on the Fields without capital, and spent all their little means before they had found anything remunerative, or before they had got sufficiently well-known in the camp to be entrusted with a half claim to work on shares, or with other responsible employment. Many too liked the idea of riding a good horse, wearing a revolver, and having generally very little to do, better than the hard, monotonous toil of digging. But it was upon the whole an effective and well-disciplined corps, and though a little latitude was allowed to the men in such minor peccadilloes as occasional drunkenness, &c., yet anything really criminal in the conduct of any of them was sure to be visited with condign punishment. I once saw two policemen, convicted of a trifling theft, tied up to a waggon-wheel to receive each four dozen lashes with the "cat," laid on vigorously by a black executioner—a most degrading and painful punishment, and I should think, a salutary caution.

But Mr. Truter's Free State Police were the most deplorable lot of seedy-looking ragamuffins that can well be conceived. Mr. Truter himself was an active magistrate, a conscientious man, and a courteous gentleman—as I believe all who knew him will testify. But the pay was so small, and other inducements so slight to enter this corps, which was on foot, and wore no uniform save a bit of gold lace round the cap of the inspector, that no workman or labourer of good character and steady habits felt any desire to enter it; and it was almost unavoidably recruited from the very lowest class of society on the diggings.

Drunken, dissipated, seedy-looking reprobates, in garments of every shade, cut, and pattern, but in dirt and dilapidation generally resembling those of the typical British scarecrow—such were the Free State Police. When they mustered outside the police-court it was impossible to look at the motley assemblage (about a score of them) without a mixture of pity and ridicule. They had a few swords and other weapons in the police-office, but didn't generally wear any arms, or indeed any distinctive sign of their honourable calling. Occasionally, when sent on a special or dangerous mission, they would take out swords, and the only time when they looked at all imposing would be when escorting some prisoner to the police-station with drawn swords flashing in the sun. The police-court was a little building of "wattle and daub," but a large wooden court-house, under the presidency of Mr. Truter, was opened a short time before I left Du Toit's Pan. The prison, called in colonial vernacular the "tronk" or "chokey," was a wretched, barn-like little place, the floor littered with dirty straw, on which were generally reposing one or two inebriated or felonious niggers, and now and then a dissipated white man. Fortunately the diggers generally were a peaceable, orderly, and honest lot; it would have fared ill with us indeed if it had been otherwise, and if we had had to rely on the Free State Police for order and protection. Perpetually loafing round the principal canteens, always very ready to drink at any one else's expense, thoroughly inefficient in the discharge of their duties, lazy and unintelligent, they were little more than utterly worthless as guardians of the public peace and order. Once indeed, when a fight had been announced to come off between an Englishman and a Dutchman, on the bank of a dam, the police went there in considerable force—not to *prevent* the fight, however, *à la* British Bobby, but to *keep the ring*, see fair play, and enjoy the spectacle.

Floggings were not frequent at Du Toit's Pan under the mild sway of Mr. Truter. There was a regular whipping-post close to the police-court certainly, but I never saw any but niggers flogged there, and the punishment was administered very much more mildly than at Klip Drift.

Mr. Truter certainly performed *his* duties well, and he had plenty to do—sometimes fining a lot of Boers for discharging firearms at night, or sentencing Kafirs or Hottentots to small doses of imprisonment or "cat" for drunkenness or theft, besides which he had plenty of civil cases to hear—disputes, breaches of contract, assaults, damages, &c., &c. The interpreter's berth at his court was no sinecure, owing to the immense number of different dialects and languages spoken by the various tribes of natives on the Fields.

Should any of the readers of this book arrive on the Fields, I think it is pretty certain that they will find by this time, under British Government, an efficient, well-organised, well-paid, and well-uniformed police force; and should they speak to any of the diggers of the very irregular state of things described in this chapter, they will be told, "Nous avons changé tout cela." And indeed the change, at which every right-thinking British digger or merchant must have rejoiced, did not come any too soon. There is only one thing to be dreaded under the new regulations—that the British Government may favour the natives too much, and possibly even allow Kafirs, Hottentots, and other "darkies" to dig "on their own hook"—a system which, I think, could never work well.

The subjoined letter from a resident on the Colesberg Kopje, which appeared in the *Times* of the 8th February, 1872, and was therefore, though it bears no date, probably written nearly two months after the annexation and the arrival of the British officials on the Fields, indicates, I fear, a most unsatisfactory state of things. It is sufficiently important to be given *in extenso* :—

A Growl from the Diamond Fields.

To the Editor of the Times.

SIR,—Under the Free State Government we complained absolutely of nothing but the inefficiency of the drunken blackguards composing their police force; and this was a small grievance, inasmuch as there was a tacit mutual-protection feeling among us which enabled us to ignore their existence. We knew best our own requirements, and elected our governing committee, whose acts were recognised and approved by the Free State Government.

When the British flag was hoisted, and Sir H. Barkly's proclamation was read, all British subjects, with their usual loyalty, cheered, but not because they expected better things. The result of British Government has been until now far worse than we could have anticipated. There is an everlasting growl among the diggers about being infinitely worse off than they were before. The Government have left undone those things that they ought to have done, and *vice versâ*. Among many grievances I will detail but a few.

This camp is now by far the largest, and numbers over 20,000 souls, and we have no magistrate. There is one, but his office is at Du Toit's Pan, the camp most distant (three miles). Besides, we all know that there is work enough for one on each of these three contiguous camps.

The Free State had post-offices here and at Du Toit's Pan, which were, of course, their own property. Our Government know this, and that they were to be abolished, and yet up to the present have made no effort to substitute equivalent offices. Last week the Free State structures disappeared, and the diggers have to wait the pleasure of the British Government as to postal arrangements.

We are taxed right and left, and are to be burdened still more by the most absurd impositions. The Free State "claim"—licenses improved upon, a labour tax on all employers of more than six natives, wood and water licenses are our present principal taxes; and they talk now of tent licences (akin to house tax) and sorting-table licences.

The diggers are cognisant of three good regulations as regards the natives—

1st. No native can legally have diamonds in his possession, *i.e.*, cannot hold them as personal property.

2nd. Any person buying diamonds from natives can be severely punished.

3rd. No liquor may be supplied to them.

The first of these is annulled by the fact that "niggers" are now actually working claims for themselves at Du Toit's Pan. Luckily for the peace of "officials," this fact is not generally known among the diggers.

A proof of the fracture of the second of these regulations was brought to light last week by the confession of a native. Yesterday a meeting of diggers was called by his master (a well known popular doctor from Natal); the native was produced and gave his confession, and a gentleman who witnessed the transaction proved the "case." The meeting, condemning the general torpidity of the Government, demanded that the nigger should lead the way and point out the canteen. In less than five minutes after, I saw it utterly demolished, the ruins in flames, and the owner narrowly escaping with his life. Five other suspected and well known offenders against the last two regulations were punished similarly during the afternoon.

I mention this incident to show you to what a climax the vexatious inaction of the British Government has brought its loyal subjects. It will be a severe lesson to them, and it will be rather difficult to allay the dangerous irritability that exists among us, especially as at least one-third of the digging community consists of educated and thinking men.

Let the British Government annex as much territory as they choose, but if they cannot properly govern their loyal subjects, let the loyal subjects govern themselves.

I am, Sir, your obedient servant,
E. W. B. B.

Colesberg Kopje, Diamond Fields, South Africa.

Much comment on this ably-written letter would be superfluous, yet I must try to point out to my readers the full bearing of some of the abuses complained of. That the most important, rich, and thickly-populated camp of the whole Fields should be without a magistrate is absurd.

As to the post-offices, surely measures will soon be taken to give us at least as much convenience as we had under the poor, feeble, old Free State. Increased taxation is of course a thing to grumble at; but if, as I hoped, it had been the means of giving us efficient sanitary, postal, and police arrangements, then no right-thinking digger, especially among the "fortune finders" of the Colesberg Kopje, would have objected to paying a few shillings more per month to secure these very desirable ends, especially the appointment of efficient sanitary inspectors, and thorough cleansing of the camps. I do not gather from E. W. B. B.'s letter whether this is so, and cannot therefore tell whether to join in his "growl" or not.

But if it is a fact that under the new government "niggers" are allowed to work for themselves, this is indeed a grave abuse, and one against which every digger, be he Boer, colonist, or Englishman, will join in protesting. Our only security against constant robbery by our servants, was the difficulty they found in disposing of the diamonds which they could not legally hold; and the fact that if some rascally little canteen keeper *was* unscrupulous enough to take a diamond offered to him by a native, he was generally also cunning and bold enough to obtain it for a mere trifle, or even to frighten the felonious darkey out of it for nothing. But if we are to have the utterly impracticable doctrine of black and white equality proclaimed, and if niggers can dig for themselves, and sell diamonds unquestioned, the employment of native labour becomes practically useless.

I have heard from other sources of the burning down of five canteens. This would not be for the very trivial offence of supplying drinks to niggers without written permits from their masters, for I think all the small canteens supplied any native unquestioned, and so did many of the big hotels too—facts of which the mass of the diggers were perfectly aware, but to which they were also perfectly indifferent. The cause of this summary proceeding—probably justified in some measure by the inaction of the police—must have lain entirely in the fact that the offending canteen keepers had been known to *buy diamonds from natives*—an offence against camp regulations, and against the general security of the digging community, which ought always to meet immediate and severe punishment.

Let us hope, however, that many of these complaints are owing to the new officials and their subordinates being as yet inexperienced in camp life and relations, and that, after thorough ventilation in our local and home papers, everything may be effectively set upon a right footing, and "all go merry as a marriage bell."

CHAPTER VIII.

AMUSEMENTS ON THE FIELDS.

DIAMOND diggers are now sufficiently numerous and civilised to require, appreciate, and have provided for them plenty of amusements, aye, and are able to pay handsomely for them too. First let us refer to things theatrical. Du Toit's Pan already boasts its Theatre Royal. This is a large wooden building, with a good-sized stage. It is all pit and stalls, there being no arrangement corresponding to boxes or gallery. Performances are frequently given there by the Harper-Lefller Company, a fairly-talented little band of actors and vocalists, making regular tours of the diggings, and finding large and appreciative audiences at our principal camps. Amateur theatrical parties also occasionally hire our Theatre Royal, and advertise at the different hotels and canteens, performances of comedies, farces, &c. It is not at all difficult to "fill a house" at the diggings, and not with paper either, all good sterling coin of the realm. The general price is 2s. 6d. and 3s. 6d., or 4s. for reserved seats. Concerts are also frequently given, and I have seen one or two spirited young gentlemen, amateurs, by giving an entertainment which would have been classed at home as a "Penny Reading"— that is, singing a few songs, and reading one or two comic pieces, such as "Mr. Bob Sawyer's Party," from Pickwick, &c.—fill a large room with a highly gratified audience at the above prices, aye, and there were beautiful young ladies in low dresses in the reserved seats!

A large circus was stationed for some time at Du Toit's Pan; and I shall never forget the comically gigantic appearance of the huge, circular tent, among the diminutive bell tents and square tents by which it was surrounded. My partner and I emerged from our tent one evening after dinner for a walk into the town. An extraordinary object met our astonished gaze. Towering high above surrounding tents glaring white in the moonlight, stood a huge round tent. We rubbed our eyes and looked again." What on earth can it be ?" asked M. " Looks uncommonly like a circus," said I. "Can't be!" "Must be, can't be anything else!" And

M

circus it was; and well it filled for many a night with merry diggers; many Boers, young and old, prowling round the outside, "prospecting" for furtive peeps through slight rents in the canvas.

Billiard tables are now numerous in every camp, and are very extensively patronised. Card-playing is also prevalent at many hotels and canteens; loo, "blind hookey," and similar sportive games, with the colonial "twenty-fives," and a very sweetly risky little game called sometimes "mamma," and sometimes another name which I have forgotten, being most often in the programme. It is desirable to exercise a good deal of caution in playing with comparative strangers, for some very sharp practitioners are to be found among the card-playing fraternity on the Fields. There are several alleys for skittles or American bowls, all doing a *roaring*—yes, a very noisy trade. Sometimes when there was a good gathering of diggers in the saloon of Benning and Martin's Hotel, at Du Toit's Pan, a pleasant element of harmony was introduced, and some capital songs volunteered. On such occasions, a young man named Rogers would come out very strong, having a capital voice and manner, and singing Christy Minstrel songs very creditably, accompanying himself on the banjo; the following song, which Rogers is believed to have composed, was extensively sung among the diggers, and also went the round of our local papers. It is more calculated to be appreciated by diamond diggers than by a general public, but I think my readers will understand the "diamondiferous technicalities" which are to be found in it.

DIGGER'S SONG.

Six months ago to the Fields I came,
  I was a heavy swell,
My clothes were brushed, my boots the same,
  My coat it fitted well;
I wore a collar then, of course,
  Alas! that day's gone past;
And stockings too my feet did grace,
  Oh dear! I've seen my last.

  Chorus—Rocking at the cradle, sifting all the day,
    That's the life we diggers lead.
    Rocking at the cradle, sifting all the day,
    That's the life for me!

I had some notions in me left
  I really thought were good,
But here there's no such thing as theft,
  Though "jumping" is understood.

Beware your morals, diggers dear,
  And don't let them decay;
If "jumping" 's winked at, soon you'll hear
  Your character's "jumped" away.

  Chorus—Rocking at the cradle, &c.

Now straying cattle and wayward "boys,"
  And diamonds never handy,
Have brought me down, and all my joys
  Are centred in Cape Brandy;
I wear a shirt and trousers now,
  And smoke a dirty clay;
My feet are cased just anyhow;
  This hat I "jumped" to-day.

  Chorus—Rocking at the cradle, &c.

Bad luck, however, cannot last,
  A turn must come some day,
A ninety-carat would change the past,
  And make the future gay.
May every digger's luck be this
  Who to these Fields has come,
And take back health, and wealth, and bliss,
  To those he's left at home.

  Chorus—Rocking at the cradle, sifting all the day,
    That's the life we diggers lead.
  Rocking at the cradle, sifting all the day,
    That's the life for me!

This song was composed on the riverside diggings, which will explain the allusions to "rocking the cradle," and "straying cattle," the old-fashioned "cradle" being used there instead of the plain sieve of the dry diggings, and cattle being necessary to cart "stuff" from the claim to the river, or *vice versâ*.

The principal outdoor amusement was cricket, which was sure to flourish where the British element was so strong. Many of the colonists are excellent cricketers, and matches are constantly coming off between Home and Colonial, Natal and Old Colony, De Beer's and Du Toit's Pan, and many other clubs or sets of cricketers. Rifle shooting matches, running and walking matches, and athletic sports, are also frequent in the neighbourhood of our camps, where there is abundant space for all of these. Shooting and fishing will of course enjoy a prominent place among the outdoor amusements of the British digger, and these, especially the former, are easily available, but I have treated specially of sport in a previous chapter. The different bi-weekly auction sales, also noticed in a separate chapter, afford much gratuitous amusement of a mild kind to the great mass of the diggers. With the increasing riches and populousness of our camps, we may expect a corresponding increase in the amount of amusements, and no one need be under any apprehension that he is coming out to a place where it is "all work and no play."

CHAPTER IX.

A BATTLE PREVENTED.

ZULUS and Basutos, as mentioned in a previous chapter, were always in a chronic state of feud, and lost no opportunities of showing their mutual hatred. At length, so much insulting, chaffing, and stone throwing had gone on that, in October last, the two tribes, or rather their numerous representatives on the Fields, determined to have a general settlement of their differences by means of a pitched battle. This intention soon leaked out, and was much talked of among both masters and servants all over the Colesberg Kopje camp, near which the fight was to take place on the following Sunday. We, the masters, of course objected strongly to the idea—it was not pleasant to think of one's niggers getting killed or spoiled at a time when the sun was hot and niggers were scarce ; so nearly every " baas " who had either Zulus or Basutos in his employ, cautioned his " boys " not to take any part in the hostilities, not even to go near the intended scene of the conflict, under pain of his severe displeasure and a probable dose of "cat." But, alas for poor human nature, I heard some diggers, whose "boys" did not belong to either of the hostile tribes, and who were consequently under no apprehension of loss or hindrance, express an opinion that it would be "a great lark to see the —— niggers knocking one another about a bit." And indeed, *par parenthèse*, let me remark that single combats of niggers were very freely encouraged among the miners, especially about lunch time, and whenever two darkies squared up to one another a ring was immediately formed, and each nigger found plenty of backers to stimulate him with shouts, yells, and perhaps an occasional " tot " of Cape Smoke. But to return to our belligerents ; as a matter of course, the Zulus and Basutos having been gradually getting more and more incensed against each other, and thirsting for each other's blood, naturally paid but little heed to the advice or command of their masters. So, on that hot Sunday morning in October, everyone, in hotel or canteen, in tent or wooden house, on the Colesberg Kopje and neighbouring camps, was asking his friends the question of the day, "Are you going to see the fight this afternoon? Will your niggers be in it?" Said C., a bold young Natalian, and very strict disciplinarian, "I've told *my* fellows not only not to fight but not to go near the place, and if I catch any of them even going to look on, I'll give them something to remember this Sunday, by ———."

I, myself, was lying in my tent, prostrate with burning fever, so I cannot give a very graphic account of this affair. I can only speak of it from the particulars I heard from eye-witnesses. It was evident enough, even to me, that there was something unusual among the niggers. In my occasional glances outside the tent I had seen numbers of tall strong Zulus, and the scarcely less well-formed Basutos, hurrying all in one direction, and, I even thought I saw here and there an *assegai* carried. Most of them had thick, hard sticks, or powerful bludgeons; many were armed with pick-handles, while those who had been unable to find anything suitable in the timber line, had collected large bagfuls of big rough stones. Not pleasant missiles at a short range, these latter! Most of the Kafirs who did not belong to the hostile tribes, like our "boys" for instance, were also moving out of the camp in the same direction; while a gay crowd of diggers, many of them in their "Sunday best," *i.e.*, a new felt hat with a clean ostrich feather in it, a clean flannel shirt, a paper collar, bright cord trousers, and shining boots, were following the swarm of natives, many simply to "see the fun," as they phrased it, but many to identify their "boys" for purposes of punishment. It must have been a grand sight when the two bodies of dusky savages, for they were little better, stood facing one another under that hot African sun, bathed in that wondrous glow of light which we, with our cold, damp, dark western skies, never even dream of, but which here flooded with its radiance the open veldt whereon they stood—a spot about a mile outside the Colesberg Kopje camp in the direction of Du Toit's Pan—a fine level piece of plain, where green grass was growing, pink and yellow flowers dotting it here and there, grasshoppers and locusts leaping, strange little birds singing, gemmed butterflies flitting all around. Up on yonder rising ground shine the white tents of the Colesberg Kopje; there, beyond, those confused white and grey heaps of gravel mark the rich claims where dozens of diamonds are found daily; down on this other side is Old De Beer's, with its thick "business quarter," its straggling tents, its numerous big shady trees; while behind yon farther ridge, but concealed by it from our view, lies the wondrous " City of the Pan."

But here are our niggers, many hundreds of them, drawn up in "battle array"—the Basutos and their allies apparently outnumbering the Zulus.

They have chosen temporary chiefs to lead them to the conflict, the barbed assegais are ready to be poised and hurled, pick-handles and bludgeons are grasped, stones are about to be thrown, the concentrated hereditary animosity of ages seems to gleam forth from the keen eyes and fiercely grinning teeth of these dusky warriors—not "boys" or servants now, but each transformed into a fierce brave warrior for the nonce.

Diggers are standing on the surrounding ridges, looking, some with eagerness, some with anxiety, for the approaching commencement of the fray.

But what is this little band of horsemen galloping so swiftly towards the combatants? Hurrah! Truter, the Landdrost, followed by his Inspector of Police and one or two mounted diggers. Brave Truter—come to preserve the public peace at all risks.

Clad in a neat dark uniform, with a gold laced cap, hotly spurring on a handsome horse, he rides impetuously, drawn sword in hand, into the very midst of the belligerents.

A few fierce indignant shouts and many low mutterings are heard, even some assegais are poised, and stones seem about to be hurled at the person of the interfering magistrate; but he, nothing daunted, lays lustily about him with the flat of his sabre on the woolly heads and bare shoulders of the ringleaders, Zulus and Basutos alike. The Inspector, and C., the Natalian, are there, with gleaming revolvers. Many of the spectators from the adjacent hillsides are hurrying up, animated by Truter's bravery, to place themselves on the side of law and order. So, at last, reluctantly enough, and with many a muttered curse, and threats that they *will* fight next Sunday, and no one shall prevent them, Zulus and Basutos retire slowly to their respective kraals, to gorge themselves with mealies or meat, and to indulge in wild war dances and yelling barbaric songs round the glowing camp fires in the evening.

C. rides swiftly back to his tents : his "boys" have all been there, contrary to his express command; so, as the disobedient niggers come slinking back to the kraal, C. vigorously administers to each a sound personal chastisement of a dozen lashes. His example is followed by many other diggers, most masters lecture their "boys" on the folly of the affair; moreover, the determined appearance and conduct of the Landdrost has made a powerful impression on them, so I don't think it likely, in spite of what some refractory darkeys say, that there *will* be another fight next Sunday.

CHAPTER X.

A DIAMOND DIGGER'S HOLIDAY AND SPORT ON THE MODDER.

It was Sunday morning at the diggings. The rising sun shone brightly over thousands of tents, whose occupants would on that morning indulge in a few hours' extra rest, and on thousands of claims from which would rise no clouds of dust, nor would on that day be heard the thud of the picks, the grating of the sieves, or the shouts and barbarous songs of our Kafir labourers. My friend D. and I stood at the entrance of my tent equipped for a sporting excursion.

Judge us not harshly, kind reader in the dear "old country." After a long series of weeks of hard, constant, unsuccessful toil, amid choking dust and turmoil, surrounded by an arid, flat expanse of "veldt," what wonder that we experienced a keen longing to look upon the fairer face of South African nature in her spring awakening; to pass some hours once more by the banks of running streams, beneath the cool, kindly shade of water-nourished trees, and to indulge yet again in the peaceful sport of the angler, dear to us both from early childhood?

I had brought out a stiff old sea rod and plenty of tackle for trying experiments in a river totally new to me. D. carried a gun. We were likely to find game which would afford us a savoury meal; but, to provide against any chance of hunger for that day, we took with us a few biscuits, a couple of very large sandwiches, a small piece of cold roast mutton, a couple of lemons, and a small flask of weak brandy and water.

D. had been informed by an old inhabitant of the Free State that a certain bend of the Modder or Mud River was not above eight miles distant from our camp at Du Toit's Pan; so, leaving tents and claims behind us with a sense of freedom and exultation, we marched gaily on towards a little knoll some six miles distant, two miles beyond which we expected to find the river.

The red-legged plovers shrieked shrilly around us, and passed by unharmed; the harsh cry of the knorhaan was heard on all sides as we passed over the broad "veldt," covered with hardy, stunted shrubs, and spangled here and there with yellow flowers. As we neared the little kopje, or knoll, a graceful springbok stood and gazed at us, at about a hundred yards, and then bounded away over the plain. We passed by the little hill and beheld an intervening flat, with more luxuriant growth of vegetation: a higher range of hills some miles distant, but no signs of the course of any river. We met a little negro boy herding cattle. I asked him in Dutch in what direction the Modder River lay; he pointed over the distant range of hills and said it was very far, but we might reach it by evening. Still we hoped he might be unaware of the existence of the nearer bend we had been told of, and we plodded on through long waving grass, already slightly incommoded by the heat, but hoping soon to be refreshed by the welcome sight and sound of running water. When we had nearly crossed the flat, and were approaching the high hills, we met a Kafir, who had just secured a speckled snake of a yellowish brown colour, which he was carrying hanging on a big stick, still alive and writhing, though sorely wounded about the head. He also told us the Modder River was "very far" (natives never seem to have any definite ideas of distances), and that the road to it lay between two big wooded hills, which he pointed out.

We left him, and soon passed by a congregation of vultures of different sizes and colours—black, brown, and light grey—busy over the putrescent carcass of a bullock. I picked up near here a huge feather, which I conjectured to have belonged to one of the largest species. The quill was quite as thick as the thickest part of my little finger. We next ascended a lovely gorge between the two high hills, all full of fragrant flowering shrubs, distantly reminding me of the fair English "May blossom." We reached a broad beaten road, ascended to the top of the hill, and another big plain lay before us. So we sat down beneath a large shrub to smoke and deliberate, for our confidence in the proximity of the river was shaken. To us there shortly came a kindly-spoken old Dutch farmer, on a good horse, and gave us friendly greeting. I asked him how far we were from the nearest point of the Modder River. He replied, "Two hours on horseback," and pointed out a hill close to which the river flowed. The said hill loomed a dull purple in the distant horizon! This was a severe blow. The heat of the day was coming on, we had walked at least ten miles, and there were full twelve more before us. But then the river, and the big trees, and the fish! No, we would *not* go back to be laughed at, and we steered a straight course across the next big "veldt" towards the hill on the river; not, however, before we had been still further disheartened by meeting a traveller just come from the stream, who told us it was very much farther than the old Boer had said, and that we should never get there before nightfall.

The sun, as noon drew near, scorched us and caused our weary steps to flag, and we were fain to halt often and take little tiny sucks at D.'s flask. Two hares started up close to us and scampered away unheeded; a "knorhaan" rose within range, yet D. did not fire, for his eyes were bent on that distant hill. Yet we could not help feeling enjoyment at the sight of numerous herds of lovely springbok, now peacefully grazing, now bounding away over the plain: at the slow flight of the huge blue-grey Kafir cranes, and the stately stalk of the magnificent "paauw," the big bustard of South Africa. Aye, and at the many new and beautiful flowers too, some of which I placed in the muslin "puggeree" of my broad straw hat. But as we at length in the afternoon approached a farmhouse, which seemed not far distant from our beacon-hill, our walk had become much slower, and our haltings much more frequent.

We reached the farmhouse. A Boer stood at the door. I asked him for water. He brought us each a small cupful, then said he was in a hurry to go and look after some cattle, and moved hastily away, evidently afraid lest we should ask him for food or a night's lodging. So we moved on to where a spring of moderately pure water flowed beneath the shade of a tall willow tree, and there we made a frugal meal. While there we beheld an illustration of the old nursery rhyme. "Hush-a-by, baby, on the tree-top," &c. There was a carrion crow's nest in the top of the big willow. The wind blew very hard just then, the cradle *did* rock, and out came tumbling three baby carrion crows, naked, yellow, and very unprepossessing. One fell into the water, two others at the foot of the tree. They all perished miserably, cut off in their earliest infancy, destined never to know the delights of a rotting bullock.

We walked on, rested and refreshed, and as we approached the beacon-hill the "veldt," evidently somewhat swampy here in wet weather, was clad with a gay luxuriance of crimson and pink flowers, something like daisies. The sun, almost setting, began to cast a mellow red light over green "veldt" and wooded hill, the great "paauws" came flying thickly overhead from their feeding grounds to their resting-places, and the face of nature, even in the fast-closing flowers, so clearly indicated approaching repose, that we began to speculate uneasily as to where our resting-place would be that night; for the nights were still very cold, and, expecting to return to our tents the same day, we had brought no blankets with us. But when, having fairly ascended our last hill, we could clearly distinguish the course of a river fringed by luxuriant trees, with a little farmhouse apparently close to its banks, the idea of seeing the water and "wetting a line" became predominant over everything—even fatigue.

Before it was quite dark, we scrambled down a sloping, bush-covered bank, to where the Modder River lay in broad, deep pools, with here and there a rocky rapid, overhung with huge old willows. And soon my line was in the water, with two strong hooks, baited, the one with raw beef, the other with paste. I got one bite, but missed him; and then the darkness and commencing chill warned us to find shelter if possible.

We went to the little farmhouse, but saw no light; knocked and called, but received no answer. The place was shut up, its Boer occupants probably being away at the diggings. This looked bad; but there was an outhouse. It had no door, so we entered, and lighted some paper. A bird rushed out in affright from the reed thatch. The place was empty, with the exception of one or two stiff, unbrayed ox hides and sheep skins; but there was a *fireplace* in it and a *chimney!* There was also an old cart-tilt, canvas on a light wooden frame. We at once took possession, or, in diggers' parlance, "jumped" the outhouse, which had probably been the cooking and sleeping place of the farmer's native servants, and proceeded to make ourselves snug. Collecting a goodly store of wood and dry bullock dung, by the aid of a scrap of the *Diamond News* and a lot of the dry thatch which strewed the floor, we speedily got up a blazing fire. Then we placed the old cart-tilt against the doorway to keep out the wind, sat by the hearth, smoked our pipes, and felt comfortable, both of us quite determined not to walk back to Du Toit's Pan, even if we had to wait a week for the passing of a bullock waggon or passenger cart.

We lay down to sleep with nothing between us and the hard uneven earth floor but a waterproof sheet of D.'s. Cold air and bright moonlight were freely admitted through many big gaps in the roof. The plovers shrieked around us, astonished at the unusual light; strange cries of night birds came up from the river; and fleas and other vermin helped the cold to keep us awake; so we only got short spells of restless sleep—often feeling a sudden chill, waking up to find the fire nearly out, and having to use much energy to rekindle it. Morning dawned at last, and soon after sunrise D. went out with the gun. I thought it was of no use for two to go out with one gun, and judged it too early and the air too cold for fishing; so stopped by the fire, which I amply replenished, and smoked a meditative pipe. But soon I heard the report of a gun; so I strolled down to the river, rejoicing much at the aspect of its cool deep pools, of the fine old willows, of the innumerable new and lovely flowers which studded its sloping banks, and of the many-plumaged birds which flitted among trees, shrubs, and flowers, and filled the morning air with joyous song.

Getting down to a "drift" or shallow ford, where waggons and carts cross the river, I came upon D. with a brace of magnificent guinea fowl—splendid, heavy, plump fellows, with much darker plumage than that of the tamed species, long necks, and little blue and red wattled heads. He was in pursuit of some more. I accompanied him among the thick scrub and bush that fringed the river in this place. He fired at another, and wounded it severely; but we lost it in the thick undergrowth.

Then I took the gun, and went a little lower down the river. Climbing up the bank, and emerging from the bushes on to the open "veldt," I beheld a sight equally gratifying to naturalist or sportsman. A hundred yards from me stood eight majestic "paauws," while around them clustered a flock of at least thirty guinea fowl. How I longed for a rifle! Seven of the paauws slowly took flight, the eighth let me approach to within eighty yards, but I would not fire, knowing that I could only slightly wound the grand bird with my shot gun. The guinea fowl separated into two bands, and scuttled away through the undergrowth with amazing rapidity, one lot running across the "veldt," the other flock making for the shelter of the bushes by the river, from which they rose before I could get within range, and crossed the stream.

I was not much chagrined at losing them, for I had come more for fishing than shooting; moreover, I was very hungry, so rejoining D., we went back to "our house" to eat our very scanty breakfast; but as it was getting pleasantly warm, and we were very anxious to begin fishing, we determined to breakfast by the riverside. Choosing a pleasant spot, and having found a few worms,

I cast a fine Thames roach line into this South African water, and landed a couple of very vigorous fish before I took my first mouthful of food. They were of the kind known here as "yellow fish," not very unlike a chub in shape, though having a small head and leathery mouth, something like that of our barbel, a large and rather deeply-forked tail, and a handsome golden tinge upon the scales, which are a little larger than those of the chub. My first two fish were only of $\frac{1}{4}$lb. and $\frac{1}{2}$lb., but they were the first I had caught for such a long time that I rejoiced exceedingly, and grudged myself the time I spent in eating my breakfast. Soon afterwards I caught one or two more small ones; we also saw several fine fish rising, apparently to a small fly. Then we had to seek more worms, and they were terribly scarce and difficult to get. How I wished for a few of that lot of "all sorts" which Mr. Francis Francis took down for his day's barbel fishing, and which, if I remember rightly, he did not want so badly after all, as the rain enabled the friend, in whose company he enjoyed such grand sport, to get a plentiful supply.

While we were hard at work digging with bits of wood, I heard a flapping of wings. Turning round, I saw a flock of ducks flying swiftly up stream towards us. Fortunately the gun was at hand, and as they passed us I gave them one barrel. Two dropped on the opposite bank, and I ran round by the ford and secured them. Then we got to fishing again. I tried a deeper pool, got another half-pounder, then hooked a big fellow, who dashed away to the opposite side like a salmon; and though I gave him line as quickly as I possibly could, the fine-drawn gut, which was old and rotten, gave way beneath one of his impetuous rushes, and he left me disconsolate. We fished quietly on, trying several likely-looking holes, till about four p.m. I took about a dozen yellow fish, the two largest being about $1\frac{1}{2}$lb.; my friend, having coarser tackle, was not quite so successful. Then we went in for a bathe, which refreshed us so much that, though we had vowed, when exhausted with fatigue and heat, that we would decidedly remain there at all hazards until some waggon or other conveyance passed for Du Toit's Pan, we now felt anxious to get back to our work, beginning to wonder whether our respective partners might not have turned out a diamond while we were fishing; and, after a short debate, determined to walk back through the night. Accordingly at about five we left the scene of a very pleasant day's sport, and marched away briskly till we reached the first Boer's farm, where the folks, though ready enough to ask us innumerable questions, totally refused to give or sell us either bread, milk, or brandy.

At the next farm, about half a mile further on. the Boer at first said he had nothing, but after a little conversation invited us to sit down on wooden stools outside the house door ; and one of the women-folk, after asking us many questions as to our success at the diggings, and expressing her astonishment at our having come all the way from England on so hazardous an enterprise, took compassion on us in consideration of the long night's walk which lay before us. and brought us each a bowl of milk and some sweet cakes, which were to us, hungry as we were. a delicious luxury. After about half an hour's rest here we started off in the dark, and a weary walk we had of it; for we had hardly any rest the night before, and had a good many things to carry, so that every time we sat down for a minute's rest one or the other of us would be certain to fall asleep instantaneously, only to be speedily awakened and urged onward by his comrade. By degrees our halts grew longer and our slumbers sounder, so that it was broad daylight when at length, from the brow of a sparsely-wooded hill, we were gladdened by the sight of the white tents of Du Toit's Pan, still some six miles distant. The remainder of the journey we performed at the same slow pace as three bullock waggons, heavily laden with goods for our storekeepers, and in two hours' time I was among the claims again, showing my birds and fish to excited diggers, many of whom immediately declared their intention to follow my example.

It was very tiring, but still very pleasurable, this trip to the Modder. A few days afterwards I made the same journey again, under more comfortable circumstances. Seven of us chartered a light covered ox waggon, and started off on Friday evening with guns, rifles, fishing tackle, half a sheep. bread and small sundry provisions, and plenty of blankets. Finding some time after starting that we had brought no cooking utensils except two kettles, we borrowed a large gridiron at Wessel's farm, five miles from Du Toit's Pan. About half way to the river we outspanned, cooked mutton, had supper and grog, sung songs, spun yarns, rolled ourselves in our blankets, and slept on the "veldt" beneath a big thorn bush till daybreak, when—I having occasionally replenished the fire during the night. so that it was still burning—we made coffee, and then "trekked" on merrily in the cool morning breeze over the plain, where the springboks were capering and the wary knorhaans rising at provokingly long ranges.

We reached the river about 10 a.m. on the Saturday morning, took possession of the whole of the empty farmhouse before mentioned, and enjoyed ourselves exceedingly till Monday evening. We went out shooting early and late, and fished during the day. In shooting we were not very lucky. I believe our total bag consisted of one springbok, two paauws, four Kafir cranes (*Anthropoides Stanleyana*, I think), a very large and handsome bluish-grey crane, with very long wing feathers, three ducks (species unknown to me, but somewhat resembling our teal, though larger), one knorhaan (*Otis afra*), and a few plovers, doves, &c. I found out some capital deep fishing places lower down the river, where I could sit beneath big shady trees and enjoy capital sport. I also found that by pulling up certain plants and grasses by the roots I could obtain worms in abundance. I caught an average of a dozen fish each day, some of the yellow fish being brilliant strong fellows of 3lb. each. I also captured a "barber" of 6lb. on a No. 11 hook on fine-drawn gut, after a very exciting play of fully ten minutes. The brute continually bored down towards the bottom, and made for weeds, stumps, and other dangerous obstructions. At length I got him fairly tired out, scrambled down the high bank on to a stump close to the water, and gaffed him with a big conger-eel hook which I held in my hand, having previously taken my rod to pieces so as to get him within reach by holding the top joint only. He was an ugly brute, with a huge flat cat-like head, small, sharp teeth, and very long barbs or feelers, more resembling the burbot than any English fish I know. The flesh is very like that of an eel, and moderate sized barbers are excellent eating, but big ones are coarse. They sometimes reach the weight of 100lb., and are frequently caught from 20lb. to 40lb. I think it is a species of *Silurus*. It is a voracious fish, feeding, however, best at night, and taking almost any bait, fish or flesh, offal, large worms, or big lumps of paste. One of our party set night lines for them, but found all his hooks and several of his lines carried away, having been either of insufficient strength or badly fastened. I also had a spare line, with a big float on, lying out for barber near my fishing-spot during the day time, but was unsuccessful, losing many baits and two hooks.

Hanging over the water, from a drooping spray of the willow tree beneath which I sat, was a beautiful bottle-shaped nest, woven of grass, round which flitted a lovely bright yellow bird with a black head, like a canary, taking no notice of my proximity, but carrying on an animated conversation, in melodious tones, with his mate inside. Numerous very large birds of the *Accipiter* tribe hovered over the wooded hollows by the river, and I often had opportunities during my fishing excursions which would have been very valuable to my companions with shot-gun and rifle.

What lots of game a fellow does see when he has no weapon with him! Paauws, Kafir cranes, and guinea fowl, all at easy ranges, were tantalising in the extreme. A leopard was seen twice in a thickly-wooded gully by the river, but the riflemen could not manage to get a shot at it.

I would advise any digger at Du Toit's Pan or the neighbouring camps, who cares for nature or sport, to imitate our trip —not the pedestrian one, for it is too fatiguing in the hot weather, but to go down with cart or waggon, taking bread, condiments, and a little brandy to qualify the water of the Modder river, which we believed gave several of us severe diarrhœa when indulged in freely, the intense heat causing us often to feel an irresistible longing to plunge our heads into the cool water and drink like horses.

The bathing we found intensely enjoyable, and we returned to Du Toit's Pan, which we reached at one p.m. on Tuesday, after a good breakfast *en route* at Wessel's, much delighted with our trip. Including hire of waggon, provisions, and liquor, it cost each of us 19s. 6d., giving as much fun and enjoyment for a small sum as any reasonable mortal could demand.

CHAPTER XI.

FISHING IN THE VAAL.

HERE is a little chapter for my brother anglers. The reader who despises the "gentle craft" is advised to skip it. The Vaal River swarms with fish, the principal kinds being "yellow-fish" and "barber." The "yellow-fish" much resembles the trout in its habits, and in the waters it frequents, being generally found in rocky streams, rapids, swirling eddies. It takes worm freely, but worms are far more difficult to find on the Vaal than on the Modder. A friend of mine, after half an hour's diligent bait-hunting, came back with two tiny frogs and two little reptiles which he thought were worms, but which I immediately pronounced to be leeches.

But the "yellow-fish" in the Vaal take a paste-bait very freely. I found plain stiff flour-and-water paste the best, on a small hook, stoutish gut, with a light float, and good long reel-line—for these fish, especially the smaller ones, are the most vigorous that I have ever met with. I have known a little quarter-pounder run a dozen yards or more of line straight out when hooked in a strong stream, before I knew what he was, and a pounder or two-pounder gives grand sport on fine tackle. The banks of the Vaal are very pleasant for fishing, especially a little wooded peninsula about a quarter of a mile above Pniel, where I have spent many a pleasant hour, either at a corner where there is a fine eddying stream abounding in fish, or, if the weather were very hot and sunny, under a big bastard willow a little higher up, fishing in some still water beyond the tail of a broad stream, comfortably shaded from the sun, with a bottle of Pontac lying amongst the cool dark water-weeds within easy reach.

I could generally catch from twenty to forty fish in a few hours' work. Looking over my diary I observe that on the 11th November last I killed about forty, and was also amused by the *insouciance* of three buxom Dutch girls, who came down to the opposite bank of the river (about eighty yards broad here) to bathe, and swam and splashed and otherwise disported themselves in the stream *in puris naturalibus*, while three young Boers sat smoking their pipes under a tree about thirty yards from them, chaffing these African sirens in a rough, *boorish* manner all the time.

I had not any good fly-tackle with me, but believe the yellow-fish will often rise freely to a fly, and would suggest lake-trout flies as the likeliest size for them. On this same day I hooked one splendid fellow, which I saw, and judged to be from ten to fifteen pounds. He broke my light and partially rotten gut when he had got about fifty yards away from me, though I was as gentle as possible with him. As the yellow-fish seem to swim pretty near the surface, and to frequent shallow rapids, a foot and a half to two feet of gut-line below the float, with a single shot, is about the best form of tackle for them. The gut should be stout, hook small, if for a paste-bait, a No. 10 Thames roach-hook, in very strong wire, is about the size; for worm-fishing about a No. 6 may be used with advantage. All tackle should be brought out from England, as only very coarse articles in the way of lines and hooks are obtainable at the Pniel and Klip Drift stores. A landing-net or gaff will often be needful; the latter is perhaps the most convenient, as it can easily be made by lashing a strong large conger-eel or hake hook to any suitable stick. The hook should have a very sharp point, as the skins of our Vaal fish are tough. The best time for fishing in the summer is from six to eight a.m., and from three to seven p.m. In the cooler months fish may be caught nearly all day long. I tried spinning-baits once or twice without success. I can rely thoroughly on the plain paste for the Vaal, and worms for the Modder.

I would advise a strong grilse-rod, not too heavy, fourteen or fifteen feet long. The best yellow-fish are often killed by making very long casts, or by wading into the middle of the stream, and letting the float go a long way down stream below you. If the angler wades barefoot as I often did, and keeps stationary any time, his feet will be considerably tickled by numerous fresh-water crabs of all sizes, which crawl about over one's feet in a familiar manner—but they never bit or hurt me. Good-sized fish may often be taken on the bottom, ledger-fashion, either with worm or paste-bait, the latter when used for bottom-fishing should have a little wool worked up in it to keep it on the hook.

In speaking of the voracious "barber," which may be taken of any size from half pound up to even one hundred pounds, I cannot say very much from personal experience, for I had no tackle strong enough to hold the big ones, the biggest I caught was a six-pounder, taken in the Modder (see preceding chapter). The "barber," a species of *Silurus*, takes freely almost any bait at the bottom, a large worm, a big paste bait, a small fish, a frog, or a piece of meat. A quarter pound yellow-fish is as good a bait as you can have. The barber feeds best at night, and is generally taken on night-lines. But the tackle must be very strong, especially near the hook, for this fish has terribly sharp teeth, and can bite through strong gimp. I set a line one Saturday night, and came down early the next morning. The line was there all right, apparently, yes, there was the big bung-float a few yards out, I hauled it in, and found the strong gimp had been bitten through near the hook; the barber had again been too many for me. A conger-eel hook on twisted brass-wire snooding would hold any barber, I should think. A night-line for these fish may be set in any deep hole, none the worse for being quite near the bank. Or the angler may obtain more real sport from these powerful fellows by having a short stiff rod, good easy reel full of strong line, and bung-float big enough to hold a bullet, and fish-bait. This he can throw into some convenient deep hole near any stream or eddy where he is going in for yellow-fishing; and while proceeding comfortably with his light corking, should give a frequent glance to the bung of his barber-line, and will probably be rewarded with a run every quarter of an hour or so. Ample time must be allowed the barber to pouch the bait. His play is vigorous and powerful, though of a somewhat sullen and deep-boring character, and he persistently makes for beds of weeds, trunks, and roots of trees, and other vantage grounds.

The early diggers on the Vaal, who had tents close to the river side, used often to have a strong barber-line out at night, attached to an elastic stick in or close to their tent. On this stick was fixed a bell, so that when the fish pulled the bell rang, and the digger would wake up and call one or two of his neighbours to help him to land a possible monster, with the promise of a bit of good fresh fish as a welcome addition to the morrow's breakfast.

I have seen a similar plan, viz., with a little bell fixed on a piece of whalebone, adopted by French fishermen when barbelling from the piers of the bridges over the Seine at Paris.

Besides the two species above mentioned, the Vaal also contains many small fish something like the yellow-fish, but with very small greyish scales. This little fellow, sometimes called white-fish, is excellent eating, and a capital bait for barber.

The angler on the Vaal will have abundant opportunity of making a collection of the beautiful river pebbles, and *may* even chance to stumble on a diamond. To anyone coming from the dry diggings the mere fact of being amongst leafy trees and by the side of cool running water, is so delightful, that I can imagine many a man turning angler who has never fished before : and I would advise everyone to bring out rods, reels, lines, hooks, and gut, as they make so slight an addition to general *impedimenta*, and are sure to be productive of much healthy and refreshing amusement.

Nearly all the streams to be crossed on the way up to the Fields contain fish ; but if the digger goes up by one of the preferable quick conveyances, he will hardly have time to fish any of them except sometimes for an hour or so if he has his tackle *very* handy.

CHAPTER XII.

A DINNER UNDER DIFFICULTIES AT MRS. BROWN'S.

"It is too late to cook dinner now," said my friend G., addressing a seedy-looking individual, gaunt, yellow, hollow-eyed, clad in canvas jacket, flannel shirt, yellow colonial trousers, and rough brown "veldt schoens," this wonderful *tout ensemble* surmounted and completed by a huge West Coast straw hat, with an Indian "puggeree" round it. The said seedy-looking party, kind reader, was your humble servant. I was tired of the monotony of my tent, where, between fever and diarrhœa, heat, wind, dust, and flies, I got no rest or peace, and little but misery, during that blessed month of October, 1871. So on this particular Sunday, feeling about as strong and lively as a fly in January (at home), and bethinking me of my kind friends G. and W., and of their big cool tents, with pleasant gravelly floors overspread with buckskins; bethinking me, too, of the hearty welcome, the kindly sympathy I was always sure of meeting at their hands. I had feebly invested myself in the wonderful garments above mentioned; and, leaning heavily on a big stick, had crawled along past rich claims, lying quiet in Sunday's repose—past canteens and restaurants, doing a roaring trade—past the waggons of the Boers and the rude "kraals" of the Kafirs, down to my friends' tent. And here I was in a state of dreamy, languid comfort, listening to pleasant chat, to happy reminiscences of the far-off home, whither my thoughts were beginning to turn so obstinately. It was a hot stifling day, scarce a breath of wind stirred the burning air; heaps of white limestone and gravel glared fiercely up through the quivering atmosphere; Kafirs, foregoing their usual "country walk," lay sleeping in their tents and huts; dogs lay panting, with lolling tongues, in the shadiest corners they could find; diggers were still and did nothing, or only talked slowly and languidly, and the general appearance of the simmering camp was lazy in the extreme. And thus it happened that G., finding that the usual dinner-hour was fast approaching, and that no preparation for that event was being made by anyone, said to me—"It is too late to cook dinner now. Let us go and feed at Mrs. Brown's."

"Agreed," said I, for I actually felt strong enough to walk as far as the well-known restaurant in question, and slightly hungry into the bargain ; so in a few minutes, with G., W., and another friend, I was tottering along the dusty road that led towards the "business part" of our camp at Colesberg Kopje.

A slight wind was now blowing, and two or three threatening-looking little clouds had already risen over the distant hills in the direction of the Vaal River ; and I looked at them nervously, for I knew they portended a thunderstorm, and I do not hesitate to own that I felt a wholesome dread of those terrific Diamond Fields storms ; besides, my tent was shaky and rotten, and I thought of the probable misery of returning to find it blown down and everything soaked with wet.

As we approached the spot where were situated the houses and tents of the principal hotel and restaurant keepers, Mrs. Brown's among the number, the aforesaid clouds, which had been coming rapidly up behind us, were beginning to spread themselves, black, lurid, and copper-edged, over the whole of the sky, and already we heard the distant growl of the thunder and saw the bright blue forks of lightning playing over the distant hills,

We entered the big marquee which was Mrs. Brown's dining-saloon. It was a big tent supported by three strong poles, the table, flanked by rude benches, and, of course, quite innocent of a table-cloth, was capable of seating at least fifty persons. A long row of tin plates with stout knives and forks adorned it on each side, while here and there a cruet stand, a salt-cellar, or a bottle of pickles, added ornament to the scene, and a promise of luxury to the dinner. It was early yet, only about half-past five, and Mrs. Brown's dinner-hour was six; still there were several diggers and merchants there, spruce in Sunday rig, the latter especially, all holding an animated conversation on the two pet subjects—diamonds and gold, with a slight reference now and then to fever and dysentery, quinine and chlorodyne, the sanitary condition of the camp, and the approaching annexation of the Fields. By way of a slight change my friends and I went into the adjoining tent, where was Mrs. Brown's bar, at which we "liquored," then returned to the dining-tent, thinking it was nearly time for dinner to be served.

But it had all the time been quickly growing darker, the thunder louder, and the lightning more vivid, and now the usual premonitory gale was upon us. In an instant we, the table, and everything inside the tent, were covered with a thick coating of red dust, not ornamental to us, but still less improving to the salt and pepper. Then came a tremendous blast, several of the tent-ropes gave way, and one of the big poles leaned over alarmingly. It was evident that if something were not done we should soon have the whole tent down upon us, and might very probably be suffocated; so, as nothing could be done outside in the midst of that fierce wind and impenetrable cloud of dust, several of the hungry diggers inside volunteered to stand by the poles. They leaped upon the strong tables, and three or four held stoutly to each wavering pole. There they had to remain, brave and patient caryatides, while the storm burst upon us in all its fury. The dust filled the inside of the tent so that one could not see across it. One little party of men were constantly employed in keeping the candles alight; all looked anxiously towards the windward side of the marquee, whose canvas flapped and whose poles creaked so ominously.

After the dust came a furious downpour of rain, much of which leaked through the seams and trickled down the sides of the tent, here and there pattering down and making mud of the red dust that covered the table. But especially did it pour upon and trickle down the necks of the brave men who were holding up the tent-poles, for in that part the wet canvas was flapping about them, and the rain leaked through, of course, far more than where it was still stretched taut. This rain lasted about half-an-hour. During the whole of the dust and rainstorm the crashes of thunder had been deafening, the lightning simply terrific in its vivid blaze. Many of the expectant diners were avowedly nervous. And where was the dinner all this time? Cooking in a very frail little kitchen outside the tent, which was probably blown down, and surely the most enthusiastic cook could not stand by the fire in such a storm as that?

Soon there came a lull, the wind fell considerably, the rain almost ceased In an instant all was activity. Mr. Brown and his assistants rushed out, hauled on guy-ropes, knocked in pegs, and soon, had poles and canvas all firm and taut again; while, inside the tent, a couple of men with buckets and huge cloths or swabs hastily washed down the long deal table and cleared it of dust. and performed the same kind office to the benches on which we were shortly to sit. Plates, knives, forks, all had to be washed, saltcellars, &c., to be replenished, but about half-an-hour after the original dinner time an excellent meal was served, the only really noticeable result of the storm being that the meat was a little over-done. So diggers and buyers, strong men and invalids, all forgot their late troubles, and chatted gaily as they did justice to the good dinner, at which figured plenty of roast joints, a curry, some pies, and a plum pudding. We inwardly congratulated ourselves, however, that the dinner had not been served before that horrid dust-storm came on, in which case everything would have been spoilt.

Soon after dinner, feeling thoroughly worn-out (I ought not really to have been out of bed), I walked back " slowly and sadly" through the drenched camp to my tent, which I scarcely dared hope to find standing; but to my great gratification it was erect, and though my bedding was rather wet, and there was more dust mixed both with it and with everything else than was desirable, it was in much better condition than I had seen it on some previous occasions.

I ascertained that our Kafirs, four very strong, willing "boys," had been holding on to the tent during the whole of the storm. Poor "boys!" *Their* little sleeping-arrangement was thoroughly drenched; but they did not seem to mind that, and I found them dodging among the neighbouring tents and waggons in the dark, searching minutely for sundry books and papers which had been blown out of my tent when the gale had lifted one of the sides up, and nearly all of which they recovered. And I lay in my wet bed, and fever and diarrhœa came on me again, and I was sorry I had yielded to the temptation of going out and eating; and I was lonely, and no one came near me but a very drunken mounted policeman, who rode half-way into my tent, to my great discomposure, to inquire the way to Klip Drift. Fancy, kind reader, lying ill on a wet bed on a chilly night and seeing suddenly half a horse and a big drunken man looming dimly upon you in the moonlight! I directed him to Klip Drift, then he wanted to light his pipe, for which purpose he got off his horse and made some ludicrous attempts to bring the bowl of his pipe in contact with my candle; finally, he having blown out my only candle, I gave him a light myself and he rode away. I hope he got safe back to the Police Camp at Klip Drift.

CHAPTER XIII.

CHURCHES AND HOSPITALS.

DIAMOND DIGGERS are by no means an irreligious community, Churches of different denominations are numerous on the Fields, and all well attended. The Church of England has regular chaplains on the Fields, and places of worship at Pniel, Klip Drift, Du Toit's Pan, De Beer's, and the Colesberg Kopje. The Wesleyan Methodist body is also well represented on the dry diggings. The insufficiency of accommodation afforded by tents, and the frequency of accidents caused by the high winds—a church tent being often rendered untenable, if not blown bodily away—have caused erections of brick and stone to be needed; for which purpose subscriptions have been collected among the diggers, and the appeal has been nobly responded to, so that by this time church-going diggers will find substantial structures everywhere.

Roman Catholic priests and places of worship are also to be found. The Dutch Reformed Church of course numbers a great many members among the Boers, and a large bazaar was held at Du Toit's Pan last year in aid of the funds of this church.

Hospitals have been much needed now and then by some of the poorer diggers, when suddenly struck down by illness and thrown out of work, many having neither friends nor relatives on the Fields. The Klip Drift Hospital was at first very defective in its arrangements and accommodation; but, public attention having been called to this state of things last year, subscriptions have been actively collected by an efficient Hospital Committee, and the institution is now flourishing, and deserving of increased support. There was a Catholic Hospital at Bultfontein, and a Diggers' Central Hospital at Du Toit's Pan. At a general meeting of the Central Hospital Committee, held on 31st October, 1871, steps were taken to have the hospital tent, which had been blown down in a late gale, re-erected and strengthened, and to provide proper accommodation for the attendants who were engaged to assist the superintendent and matron, and a collector was appointed for the Hospital, who was to receive a per centage on the sums subscribed. Father Hadien, President of the St. Mary's Society at Bultfontein, having volunteered to hand over to the Central Committee the St. Mary's Hospital tent and furniture, together with such funds as the Society might be able to spare, the offer was accepted, and the two hospitals are now amalgamated. Let us hope that hospitals may be increasingly well-supported on the Fields, but that, with improved sanitary arrangements we may have less sickness, and consequently fewer diggers in need of their benefits.

PART IV.

MY DIARY AT THE DRY DIGGINGS.

Du Toit's Pan, Diamond Diggings,
June 9.

I WAS rejoiced on Saturday last to find a batch of the *Field* waiting for me at the Klip Drift post office. I have been too hard at work ever since to read them, but promised myself that luxury tomorrow. As you will, doubtless, have many inquiries about the famous South African Diamond Fields, I will endeavour to put before your readers all the information in my power. Let me commence by advising any gentleman having a settled income at home, however small—provided that it be enough to live upon—by no means to come out here. To anyone not in receipt of any such regular sum, but possessed of a few hundreds he may think of investing in business, I would say, Come out here; start in business if you like, and you are sure to make money; or dig, and you *may* make more, but that is all a lottery.

We have a very big camp here—I should think not less than 6000 people, taking the two farmsteads of Du Toit's Pan and Bultfontein together. Of course we live in tents, and they are of every size and shape imaginable, and, with a few exceptions, pitched together all anyhow, or higgledy-piggledy; but the effect is far from unpicturesque. Many of the Dutch Boers live in their waggons, erecting cooking sheds and ovens close to them, and generally showing themselves keenly alive to comfort. Then we have large marquees, corrugated iron houses, and even brick erections are beginning to be made. There are stores, canteens, and billiard-rooms, and they all do a roaring trade. Claims are spreading in all directions, threatening to push away the tents and encroach upon the road. I need hardly say we have no gas, and on a dark night evening calls on friends in distant parts of the huge straggling camp are fraught with many dangers. One instant you narrowly escape falling into a 15-foot-deep claim; the next you are almost impaled on the horns of a bullock—and there are hundreds lying by the waggons at night: then you come upon huge rocks and boulders—and, just as you see the light glimmering in your friend's tent, you fall over a sleeping donkey.

Now, with regard to the mode of working here, and the probability of a good return. The soil seems to be principally limestone, intermixed with small pebbles, and here and there the diggers come upon big rocks; but, generally speaking, it is plain, straightforward pick and shovel work. The soil being taken out, and well beaten down with the shovel to break all clods of earth, is then sifted in one or two sieves, or a combination of coarse or top sieve and fine or bottom sieve. The sieves in general use here are strong oblong frames, holding about three feet by two of wire meshing or perforated zinc, the former being the best, but difficult to be obtained here. Two such sieves were sold on the auction market this afternoon, and fetched 24s. and 25s. My partner and I made one for ourselves; it cost us about 18s. When the stuff is properly sifted it is placed upon the sorting table, where the sorter rapidly spreads a portion of it over the table with a metal or wooden scraper, and, after a swift but careful inspection, sweeps it off the table on to the refuse heap. Two strong white men can work a claim advantageously, though of course, with plenty of capital, it would be well to employ black labour for the digging. Some even entrust sifting to their natives, but I think this imprudent, as a diamond of any size will very probably be seen in the sieve, and, if the master is not looking, it will equally probably find its way into the nigger's pocket, tobacco pouch, or mouth, instead of on to the sorting table. I admit that many instances of native honesty have been brilliantly shown: but then they have often been caught thieving, or "jumping," as the appropriation of another man's property is called here. A native servant found an 80-carat diamond under the roots of an old tree he was pulling up for firewood, and took the gem to his master. But here is an example on the other side. A gentleman, wishing to test the fidelity of two Kafirs he employed in sifting, cut two imitation diamonds out of alum, and slily put them into the heap from which the natives were just going to fill the sieve. He then went away for a short time. The stuff was placed on his table;

he sorted it, didn't find his sham diamonds, and asked the niggers if they had found anything. They replied, "No." Thereupon he insisted on searching them, and found his two bits of alum carefully concealed about their persons.

Children are profitable here. Some of the deepest holes are made, and the largest heaps of stuff thrown out, by Dutchmen with large families. It is a pleasant sight to see mother and daughter busily picking over a sorting table, while father and sons are all hard at work digging and sifting. In such cases "happy is the man who hath his quiver full."

Happy also is another man, whose hot lunch I see brought every day at one o'clock by a fair young wife; I envy that man. There is an Australian digger, too, working close to my claim—only he and his wife. She does all the sorting, and she has such a lucky hand for picking out diamonds that they have averaged 6l. 10s. per day since they started; and they are now going very deep, in confident hopes of finding a "big thing." Don't I envy that man! Almost everyone seems to find something, but there are a great many small surface diamonds; some large ones too, for one of 55 carats was found on the surface by a man walking in the veldt the other day. Many large ones, from 5 to 54 carats, have been turned out this week.

I must now give my own brief experience. Commenced working our claim Tuesday, June 5. Wednesday, the 6th, commenced sorting. Thursday, found our first diamond, a little thing of about ¼ carat. No more yet, but many have been found in claims immediately adjoining ours; and ours shows most promising indications. We have already found a great many garnets—the diggers call them rubies, and I fancy some of ours are real rubies —also some clear, bright, green stones like emeralds, and a great quantity of very hard, shining black substance, not unlike exceedingly hard bright coal. It only occurs in very small lumps indeed, and is called here carbon. I don't know exactly what it is; it certainly has some value. Some say it is worth 20s. per ounce, some say 10s.; but there is a man here who will give 5s. for any amount for it. So it is worth collecting even at that, and we have a couple of ounces already; but I won't sell it till I know what it is worth in London. Can you tell me from the description? I won't send a specimen, for fear some one should take it for a diamond and purloin the letter. It shines very brightly; the smallest bit of it is instantly seen amongst the gravel. Another party who came up in the waggon with us have found to-day a nice diamond of ½ carat, so we have all got some encouragement to start with.

Claims are 10s. per month here, and new comers pay 1s. registration fee. This place is in the Free State, the authorities of which have decided that all diamondiferous lands, private property or otherwise, be thrown open to diggers under the licensing system, half the licence going to the proprietors of the land, half to the Government. This measure is very satisfactory to the diggers. There is a mass meeting of diggers called this afternoon to take steps for the formation of a Diggers' Mutual Protection Society. My partner has gone; I have stayed in the tent to write this, as the mail goes out early to-morrow. Free State postage has to be paid here, so that letters to England are charged 1s. 6d. instead of 1s., and newspapers 3d. I believe Klip Drift, on the Vaal River, being now under British Government, English postage suffices—1s. letters, 1d. ordinary papers.

Now about expense of living out here. First you must have a tent, which can be brought out from England, or bought here reasonably. I bought a very well-made strong tent, 10ft. long, 7ft. wide, 9ft. high. for 8l. 10s. It affords ample accommodation for two people. Meat is cheap; there are several butchers' shops, and beef and mutton are always 3d. per pound, except rump-steaks, which are 4d. Flour and meal rather dear. Bread 1s. per loaf of 3lb. or 4lb. English beer, 2s. 6d. reputed quart bottle. Draught ale, 6d. per glass. Drinks at hotels and liquor-bars, 6d. upwards. Cape brandy 8s. to 9s. per gallon. Wood very scarce and dear. 2l. to 3l., or more, per waggon load; 15s. per Scotch cartful. We make most of our fires of bullock dung. It is amusing to see those whose turn it is to cook sallying forth over the veldt with sacks and buckets in search of dry dung. It makes capital fires, and we are all pretty good cooks. We are not satisfied with plain roast and fried meat, but go in for elaborate stews, curries, puddings, and cakes. To-morrow I am going in for a big bread-baking. Very wrong to bake on Sunday; but then I have no time in the week. Many of the diggers spend Sunday in prospecting about the country, diamonds being frequently picked up, even by children playing round the camp. And let me tell you there is scarcely a child here over five years old on whom you could pass a crystal or artfully broken bit of glass for a diamond. The want of water is keenly felt here. We have two dams or artificial rain-water holes, but they are barely fit for washing clothes in. Several wells, always besieged by a crowd of male and female natives, in every variety of costume—from native innocence to a suit of "store clothes." From said wells muddy water may be extracted at the rate of about half a tumblerful per minute, and they are half a mile from my tent. There is a Dutchman here who sometimes has clear, good water to sell at 3*d*. for two bucketfuls; but sometimes he has none to spare.

Fortunately for us, a member of the committee here—a most excellent and kindly old gentleman—sends a waggon some six miles weekly for a large supply of water, and allows us to put a little cask on his waggon; so we have enough for all purposes with economy, and are thankful accordingly. Generally speaking, the Du Toit's Pan diggers are dirty perforce. Washing of the hands and face is a luxury not to be indulged in every day. For the delights of a bath, many of our diggers will from time to time travel by passenger cart or otherwise to the Vaal River, twenty-five miles distant. It is related of one of them that, while bathing at Klip Drift a few days back, he found on his feet the remains of a pair of socks which he thought he had lost a month previously!

We are not without amusements in this camp. From many a tent may be heard at night sounds of music and of song; while travelling concert companies and amateur Christys frequently honour us with their presence. Nor do they go away empty, for diggers are an openhanded race. As evidences of civilisation, I may mention that a butcher's cart calls at our tent, a Dutch boy brings round some excellent sausages made by the good old "vrouw" his mother, and the *Diamond News* is brought round weekly. Our crier, with his loud tinkling bell, summons us in the morning to market, and on Saturday afternoons to sales, meetings, &c.—for we diggers take our Saturday half-holiday like the clerks and counter-jumpers in dear old London; and don't we deserve and enjoy it! There is one thing the new comers grumble at, and that is the weather. They say they came out to South Africa expecting to be "frizzled," but they didn't bargain for being frozen. Now we have had certainly some very keen frosts lately, even to finding water frozen inside our tents of a morning; and fancy getting up and lighting a fire at daybreak then, with the bullock dung all over hoar frost and refusing to be lighted, while the unhappy digger stamps about with icy feet and blue fingers. But in a couple of hours what a change! Such is the clearness of the sky and power of the sun, that by nine o'clock all is warm and glowing; and I can sit on my little heap and sort with a light canvas jacket on, and no collar or necktie. Collars are a good deal worn on Sundays.

We have many types of diggers here: your working man who is disgusted to see how soon gentlemen learn to handle pick and shovel, speaks to them with surly insolence, and tries to pick quarrels; your other sort of working man—nature's gentleman—honest, intelligent, kindly, and civil: the latter type, I am happy to say, by far the most plentiful. Your bar-room loafer, who spends all his time, as long as he has money, in the tents where are grog and billiards, and is great at imparting "colonial information" to "new chums." He will take a fit now and then, and work for an hour or two, but soon you shall see him back for another "tot" of "Cape smoke" or "Hennessy's French." Your swell, in polished top-boots, spotless breeches, trim-fitting jacket, and shapely felt hat with feather in it. Your old Australian or Californian, looking the very typical digger, with broad-leaved hat, thick loose flannel shirt, red sash, cord trousers, and huge waterproof sea boots; and your digger who dresses in a colonial suit of plain brown corduroy, and works hard, and is brown as to his hands and face and tattered as to his clothes, but yet whom no one can possibly take for anything but a gentleman. Your Dutch Boers, an industrious though somewhat sluggish race—reconcile that paradox if you can—affectionate to one another, kindly, courteous, and helpful to strangers, especially to such as speak their language, keenly sensitive to ridicule or ill-treatment of any kind, and often imposed upon by keen colonial traders. A Jew made much money once by travelling round through a farming country and selling pinchbeck watches to the Boers for gold. I don't think he would dare to show his face there again. As to the natives here, you have them of all tribes and all colours, from sickly yellow to jetty black; Kafirs and Hottentots, Korannas, Griquas, Fingoes, and many more are here, helping the all-powerful white man to turn up the bright gems which so long lay hidden in the soil. Not a little do they contribute to the picturesqueness of the scene, though truth compels me to say they are sometimes more picturesque than decent. Some of the women have good features, and many of the younger ones have splendid forms. They are a noisy lot, singing and shouting over their work, and specially glad when a diamond found and proclaimed gives the signal for a loud "Hurrah!" from all the neighbouring claims, or when the mule cart for Pniel dashes by with its six fine mules at full gallop—or at any other excuse for a shout or a yell.

There is a plenty of game here; plovers often come quite near the tent, so that I can shoot one or two for a meal. A few miles further, bigger game may be found. Now I must draw this to a close, and tell you more about this and other diggings in another paper.

Just a few more words of advice to intending emigrants. Don't come out without some capital—at least 200*l*. If you know any trade, you may combine business and digging with a partner. Blacksmiths and carpenters are very well paid. If you don't know any trade, you can start a canteen or set up as auctioneer, or you can just work hard at digging and nothing else, as I am doing. If you mean coming up by passenger cart, you must bring out hardly any luggage, but buy here at an increased price. Or you might let your luggage come after you by waggon, in which case it would reach you a month or six weeks later. In summer time (English winter) bring plenty of protection against *wet*. In winter (English summer) be prepared for severe cold.

The climate is very healthy; diarrhœa and dysentery rather prevalent at the diggings, from bad water. Filters are almost indispensable. I have found Dr. Collis Browne's chlorodyne a capital cure for the above complaints. Quinine should be brought too.

A fact or two come into my head at the last moment. A Dutchman bought an old claim last week for 10*s*. Before dinner time he had found in it a 14-carat diamond. Another Dutchman worked for about three weeks, never said what he found, but at the three weeks' end inspanned his oxen and rode away in his waggon, his servants firing off many guns. It afterwards came out that he had made over 14,000*l*. I know for a fact that a gentleman who has been digging at Pniel, and is now going to work here, has in his possession a bag containing 255 diamonds! So there is plenty of encouragement. On the other hand, four English gentlemen lately set off to tramp down to the seacoast with the intention of working their passage back to England. Hard lines! and there are plenty of broken-down loafers about this camp. But then of course it is all a lottery; so says every one. I will try to send you a livelier article by next mail.

Du Toit's Pan, Orange Free State,
June 18, 1871.

I will now give you a few of the incidents that have enlivened this busy camp during the past week. On Monday I heard of the sale of a claim at De Beer's Farm a few days ago for 110*l*. The lucky purchaser made 150*l*. by diamonds found in the said claim within three days after. In the afternoon we had a bright sample of "advertising at the diggings." A grinning nigger boy perambulated the claims, bearing a board, on which was very roughly written an announcement that a good band would play that evening at Turner's Billiard Rooms, coupled with the great attractions of "Marionettes and Punch," and "Rogers, the Ballad Artiste." The little darkey called the attention of the busy miners to his progress amongst them by a very loud drumming on an old biscuit tin. On the 13th we were gratified by finding our second diamond, though only a small gem, ¾ carat, and of bad shape. It never reached the sorting table, for it shone so as to attract the notice of my partner as he was sifting a lot of stuff in the sieve. In the afternoon we were visited by three curious little birds, which I have seen several times before and since. They are a little larger than a linnet, and of a dusky black colour, with the exception of a few half-white feathers in the wings, and they sing very beautifully. Their tameness is remarkable; they fly right into the midst of the dust and turmoil of the diggers, and settle within a few feet of us on a heap of "stuff" or on our sieve props, from which perch they indulge us with sweet melody for a quarter of an hour or so, accompanying the same with a most comical swift raising and dropping of the tail. I saw many of the diggers pause to look and listen. They are welcome visitors, and of course never molested.

The evenings in camp are pleasant enough. I hardly ever feel inclined to stir out, but lie on many buckskins and rugs, and spend the time between dinner and ten p.m. in reading. But others are not so quiet; there are plenty of amateur bands frequently promenading or playing in neighbouring tents, so I get plenty of music. At ten a bugle sounds, which is the signal for all natives to retire to their respective locations. Any unfortunate darkey found in the "streets" after that hour is taken to "chokey," the slang name for our little prison, and receives fifteen lashes.

On the 14th two good diamonds were found under somewhat singular circumstances. An English gentleman, having worked a claim for six months and found nothing, went home disgusted, giving away his claim. The man who got it found on the 14th a fine diamond of 29½ carats before he had gone six inches deeper than his predecessor. I believe he was offered 2500*l*. for it. Pleasant news for the other! Another digger found a beautiful 10-carat stone—which I saw directly it was found—in another old claim, under similar circumstances,

The variety of dress among the different tribes and classes of natives is somewhat striking. Many wear merely a parti-coloured bunch of rags before and behind, barely sufficient for purposes of decency. One will strut about with nothing on but a hat and a loin-cloth; another with an old shako and red coat, formerly the property of a private in the 20th; another with hat, jacket, and shirt, but both totally innocent of trousers. Many have coloured handkerchiefs twisted round their heads, and feathers are still affected. These semi-barbarian, half-naked negroes are said to be the most honest and best workers. Educated, and consequently fully-clad, natives are looked upon with distrust. The bare-legged fellows go about singing weird native songs, of strange tone and wonderful discord. On this day, the 14th, many large diamonds were found—one of 93 carats, and many between 50 and 10. The 93 was found by a Dutchman, and in the evening he and his friends held a great merry-making, firing off also many guns, crackers, &c., so that the camp was very noisy. I had an idea that they fired off a shot for each carat of the diamond, but was too lazy to count.

On the 15th I went with a party on a bullock waggon with many large casks to fetch our week's supply of water from a spring on a farm six miles distant. It was a very pleasant trip. The farm, a large one, did not show any signs of grain or vegetables, except prickly pears, but seemed to be devoted to the raising of sheep and cattle. At a dam close to our spring negro women were washing clothes, brought from Du Toit's Pan; while the scene was continually enlivened by huge herds of cattle, mules, and horses, and large flocks of sheep, coming down to the dam to drink. Many of these herds and flocks were driven over from our camp to this water, as our dams are nearly dry. I heard from one of my companions on this excursion an incident which well illustrates the uncertainty of diamond digging. An old man, who has long worked a claim most perseveringly—even working quite late at night—at last got hard up, and left, selling his claim for 10*s*. The next day the purchaser got out of that claim a diamond of 12½ carats and two smaller ones. The Dutchman who found the 93-carat stone yesterday has left; he had only been a fortnight at the "Fields." A 94 and several other large gems were found to-day.

There is plenty of game within a short distance of the camp —red-legged plovers (very good eating), doves, the "courant" before alluded to, a few springbuck, &c., and a short journey will bring a well-mounted sportsman among abundance of large game.

A doctor here found a native in his tent last week; he put a "rheim"—a stripe of hide universally used as rope—round his neck and took him to the police station, where the thievish nigger received twenty-five lashes.

On the 17th I attended the morning and afternoon markets. Wood, potatoes, "beltongue" or dried meat, "mealies" or Indian corn, tobacco, butter, honey, &c., were brought in by the farmers and sold very quickly by auction. A few small lots of potatoes and pumpkins went very dear. The wholesale price of potatoes is 2l. to 2l. 10s. per bag of about 1cwt.—and I could have brought any quantity at from 2s. 6d. to 5s. at Queenstown! Tobacco is 9d. to 1s. per lb., flour retail 6d. per lb., cabbages, 1s. 6d. to 4s. each, according to size. In the afternoon there were auctions of miscellaneous goods, mining implements, drapery, guns, &c. Everything fetched high prices, sometimes absurdly high. The only articles for which there were hardly any bidders were revolvers; and indeed they are of very little use here, for we are a quiet and peacable community, with the exception of a few wild spirits who will go in for a "big drink" on Saturday night, and occasionally wake up to find themselves lying on straw in "chokey" on Sunday morning, in the pleasant companionship of sundry strong-smelling aborigines.

A very stormy meeting was held yesterday afternoon on the market square here for the purpose of inducing or compelling the committee to make certain sanitary arrangements highly necesssary for the health, cleanliness, and comfort of a camp which contains now some 10,000 people. The greatest disorder prevailed, and no definite conclusions were come to, though many diggers were in favour of turning out the present and appointing a new committee. A 90-carat diamond was found yesterday morning by another Dutchman, supposed by certain connoisseurs to be only the half of an immense stone. He was offered 10,000l. cash for it. He sold his claim shortly after for 40l. Our claim continues to show very favourable indications—plenty of "carbon," "rubies," and a few of the bright green emerald-like stones which the diggers love to see.

I cull the following from the *Diamond Field*, a paper published at Klip Drift in opposition to the original *Diamond News* of Pniel: "A native man, while chopping wood near Mr. Jardine's, on Saturday last, picked up a very beautiful diamond of 87 carats."

The next "item" is one which is likely to increase the number of church-going diggers: "Master Kidd picked up a diamond in church during prayer-time on Sunday last." The English reader must bear in mind that many buildings, both public and private, are floored with gravel from the claims.

"Mr. Unger, the great diamond merchant, is making experiments with a view to ascertain whether diamonds are to be obtained by diving in the Vaal river."

"Mr. Wilhelm Schultz, merchant of Klip Drift, found a 2-carat diamond in the ground he is excavating at the back of his stores. Mr. Schultz is digging away a bank for the purpose of making a yard, and, like a sensible man as he is, he washes out all the gravel before removing it. Mr. Schultz lives about thirty yards from Mr. Pincus, who also washed out all the gravel he excavated when making his court-yard; and he also found a diamond. There is no doubt that the whole of Klip Drift, town property and all, is diamondiferous."

The next is headed "Hail, Columbia!—A veritable Forty-five. —Mr. Hopkins, an undoubted Columbian of the first water, has just brought into Klip Drift a beautiful diamond of 45 carats, which he found at Du Toit's Pan on Tuesday. He tells his tale of great good luck as follows: 'I was not thinking of diamonds, I was looking for garnets and agates, and I had a bit of hoop iron of about four inches long that I scraped about the earth with. I had picked up some very pretty stones, and had put them in my waistcoat pocket. I then scraped a little wider scope, and a bit deeper, when the corner of this blessed thing (the diamond) showed up above the earth.' Upon Mr. Babe's authority, we state that Mr. Hopkins was paralysed for the moment, and was so weak that anyone might have taken the gem from him. However, that may be, he would like to see anyone try it on now. Mr. Hopkins was not long, we fancy, in recovering himself. He has the precious stone, and he looks as if he means to keep it."

And now, being rather tired, I will draw this rambling letter to a close. Let me add as another reason that it is time for me to cook our Sunday dinner, consisting of roast beef, potatoes, and a rice pudding, with stewed apricots. These fruit, with peaches, apples, &c., are dried in thin slices, and make, when well stewed, capital adjuncts to a plain pudding.

June 20.

Little of moment has occurred at this camp since I wrote you a week ago. The camp is daily becoming larger; it is estimated that not far from 20,000 people are here now; new stores and hotels springing up with mushroom-like rapidity, all doing a roaring trade. This is now becoming the principal market of the Diamond Field district, and, in spite of the immense quantities of produce daily brought in by farmers from all parts, prices, especially of such luxuries as vegetables, still rule very high. The Dutchman who found the 93-carat diamond yesterday week found a 43 and a $2\frac{1}{2}$ the same day. The 43 is supposed by connoisseurs to be a fragment of the same stone as the 93. The 93-carat stone was sold the same day for 10,000*l.*—a low price. The fortunate man gave a great banquet to all his friends the next day (last Sunday); much champagne was drunk, and the fun kept up fast and furious till 5 a.m. on Monday. I imagine a few of the guests would not care much for handling pick and shovel that day.

On the 19th a fine gem of 50 carats was found at Bultfontein, and one of 7 carats was picked up on the surface at the same farm.

On the 20th a 105-carat diamond was reported to have been found here, also a $27\frac{1}{2}$ and a 47.

There is great fun whenever a bullock waggon passes along the narrow little road left among the claims. All the niggers who are digging near shout and yell at the oxen in the most contradictory and confusing manner, some shouting "Yek!" "Trek!" the stimulus to increased speed; others "Ah now!" and the apparently cosmopolitan "Wo!"—the signals to stop. The effect of these, all yelled at once by some dozens of strong-lunged Kafirs, is to put the oxen into a fearful state of bewilderment, and their drivers into a considerable rage. The other day four bullocks, confused and terrified, started off up hill at full gallop, and a lot of boxes, somewhat loosely packed in expectation of uniform slow progress, were precipitated into the road. How all the niggers, aye, and diggers too, laughed, and how the old Dutchman swore at them!

On the 21st we had a bitter cold day—keen frost in the morning; very uncomfortable working, especially lying on the ground by the sorting table. On the 22nd it was colder, and for once the sun was obscured by dull leaden clouds all the morning. There was a strong wind too, and snow was looked forward to with dread by many; but neither snow nor rain came. It was particularly trying work for the lady sorters, and artful little arrangements of rugs and blankets spread on poles were in most cases erected to keep off wind, dust, and cold.

On the 23rd it was still windy and dusty, but not so cold. A neighbour of ours had given up his claim. A Dutchman began to work it, and before he had got a foot down he found a beautiful diamond of $7\frac{1}{2}$ carats. When I congratulated him, he replied, "Well, I think I deserve a bit of luck like this, for only last week I sold half a claim to a man and he turned out a $13\frac{1}{2}$ the next day!" On this same day, the 23rd, my partner and I found our third diamond—a poor little thing, scarcely half a carat. But we must not "despise the day of small things," and we still indulge bright hopes of some big things deeper down. We have found a great deal of "carbon" and "rubies" this week.

Yesterday being Saturday, I attended the market, and an immense market it was. There were the carcasses of the huge brown, shaggy-maned wildebeest; of the graceful brown and white springbok, and other antelopes; there was "beltongue," or jerked meat, by the ton; huge waggons laden with wool, meal, hides, &c.; while such luxuries as potatoes, cabbages, onions, beetroot, and carrots suggested savoury stews; turkeys gobbled and ducks quacked loud invitations to buy, kill, and eat them. Everything was sold by auction, and it is really astonishing what an enormous amount of produce, in large and small lots, the market master cleared off in the space of two hours and a half. The attendance of diggers, as well as keepers of hotels and stores, was very large. The provisions, with a few exceptions, fetched such high prices as fairly horrified a few new arrivals by the last mail steamer whom I noticed in the crowd. There was a good quantity of fine oranges and lemons, refreshing and healthful, and they went pretty cheap—10s. per 100; ducks, 4s. or 5s. each; little shrivelled cabbages, 1s. each; good-sized onions, about 6d. Sheep and oxen were to be had cheap enough, the former selling at 3s. 6d. and 4s. each. I have managed to lay in a stock of potatoes and meal at reasonable prices, and I think I may venture to affirm that, if a man keeps aloof from dissipation and eschews luxuries, he may live here for about 10s. per week comfortably. We had three or four large auction sales of tents, tools, fancy goods, and general merchandise in the afternoon. I had the pleasure of meeting a gentleman who was among the very earliest diamond diggers soon after the first discoveries. He is digging here now, believing, with most persons I have met, that Du Toit's Pan is about the best place on the Fields. He has found from first to last, at different diggings, no less than 730 diamonds, a 54-carat and many large stones being among the number! Of course he has made his fortune. Several of our fellow-passengers have already been tolerably lucky. One who called here half an hour ago has four already, the largest a beautifully-shaped gem of 10 carats, pure water. Another got his first diamond yesterday—16 carats. I hope we shall lay hold of a big one before long. The 7½-carat found near us on Friday was sold for 140l., a very good price. We had a thunderstorm and heavy rain during last night, and this day (Sunday) has been cold and windy, with occasional rain—a very bad day for cooking in the open; nevertheless, I have managed to bake four loaves and three plum cakes, and to cook a very good stew, followed by dumplings! This is the day on which we indulge in the luxury of a thorough ablution, and a very great luxury it is. To-morrow we shall see how our "stuff" is affected by the wet. I fear it will be very bad to sift and sort.

Very well pleased with the life here, so far. It is a hard-working, quiet, peaceful life. How enjoyable are the evening's rest and the night's sound sleep!

A club is being formed here, and musical and other entertainments are getting more frequent; but I do not think anything will tempt me out of my snug little tent. I hope it won't get much colder, though. I hope to be in a position shortly to give you a list of all the "finds" publicly reported here, but there is a great tendency to keep things quiet among many of our diggers, in consequence of the camp being so very full already. The list of "finds" and names published in the *Diamond News* of the 17th inst. shows for Du Toit's Pan alone 118 diamonds, among which figure gems of 99, 64, 59, 33, 32, and many other large stones, besides very encouraging lists from the adjoining farms—De Beer's and Bultfontein. A few finds are reported from Pniel and Klip Drift, and the lists from Robinson's, Liversage's, Spence's, and Hebron are all pretty good; but I am happy to say that "Toit's Pan" bears the palm. There is a "new rush" close by here, between this and De Beer's, on the Bultfontein land. I believe it is turning out well, though the diggers are trying to keep their finds quiet.

Mr. Tobin, of the Polytechnic, London, is here, and is writing in the *Diamond News* a series of articles "On the Matrix of the Diamond," eagerly read by the diggers. He speaks very highly in favour of this place, and says, "Daily experience at Du Toit's Pan seems to point to the fact of the trap rock being the source of the diamond."

At Klip Drift the acting British magistrate is inflicting pretty severe sentences on all offenders convicted of theft, &c. A man has just been sentenced to seventy-five lashes and one year's imprisonment for receiving stolen goods, the proceeds of a burglary from one of the principal stores. I saw five white men and a nigger flogged the day I was at Klip Drift. Two of the white men belonged to the mounted police, and received "three dozen" each for stealing a bottle of wine and some meat from an hotel. Two other white men (Irish) received "four dozen" for swindling an old Dutchman. The culprit is tied up to a waggon wheel, and a black executioner inflicts the degrading punishment with a very powerful "cat."

July 2.

I now sit down to chronicle the events of another week. Monday was a very cold and windy day, and the "stuff," being damp from Sunday's rain, was very difficult to sort. A young American found an 8-carat diamond in the next claim to ours on the previous Saturday.

On Tuesday, after heavy rains during the night, and finding it still showery and the stuff too wet to sift, we walked over to the New Rush, near De Beer's. We found many diggers and promising-looking stuff. Only one confessed to having found anything; he had a large hole 17ft. deep, and had found two diamonds, the largest $7\frac{1}{2}$. We had a terrific thunderstorm and very heavy rain in the evening.

Wednesday was cloudy, but it did not rain. A diamond of a carat and a half found near us. We were offered £5 for half our claim. Would not sell.

On Thursday incessant pouring rain not only rendered work impossible, but flooded most of the tents.

On Friday awoke from my second night of sleeping in a

puddle, to find that one side of the tent had blown in, and our rugs, blankets, provisions, &c., were all soaking with water and mud ; and, as we had not a bit of dry wood or even a dry match, we fled from the miserable scene in disgust, and betook ourselves to Benning and Martin's hotel, which we found crowded with "washed-out diggers."

We breakfasted and dined there, and slept upon the table. Everybody being damp and cold, and having no work to do, there was, of course, a good deal of hard drinking, and in the evening there was any amount of singing, music, and general fun and jollity. I am happy to say that, although I saw many who had taken too much Cape Smoke, there was no fighting, only a little rough horse-play now and then, and one or two attempts at rows.

On Saturday it was fine again, but hardly any of the claims could be worked, except by washing, and most of our diggers are unprovided with cradles for the wet work, dry-sifting being the regular thing at Du Toit's Pan. In the morning I attended the police court, presided over by Mr. O. J. Truter, Landdrost. The cases were mostly of trifling importance. A lot of Dutchmen were charged with firing guns and rifles in the camp after sundown. It appeared that they were celebrating in this their favourite manner the finding of a large diamond by one of their friends ; in some instances there were bullets in the rifles. The police came down upon them and took eleven guns, summoning the owners to appear the next morning at the police court, where they were severely reprimanded and fined 2s. 6d. each.

Two Hottentots, who had stolen some sheepskins and offered them for sale to the very man they had stolen them from, were sentenced to fifteen lashes with the "cat." Another was fined 5s. for being drunk and beating his wife. Two Kafirs were fined 2s. 6d. for being out after hours. A charge of assault, brought by a Kafir against a Hottentot, was dismissed. A white man, found at night in another man's tent, and pleading drunkenness and a mistake, was fined 1l. or twelve hours' imprisonment.

After the court rose, the two Hottentots and two other prisoners were conducted to the whipping-post, and received their lashes with great equanimity. It is apparently a much lighter "cat" here than at Klip Drift, and I think the executioner is either less vigorous or more merciful. I hear on good authority that a *white woman* lately received twenty lashes at Klip Drift.

Saturday afternoon brought us the usual amount of sales.

during which the waggons of another successful Dutchman were seen slowly "trekking" away from the camp amid the firing of many guns. The weather is bright and sunny again now, so we are gradually getting dry again. Very little work has been done this week, and I have not heard of many finds.

Du Toit's Pan, Orange Free State,
July 8.

There is very little news in camp this week. We have had bright, warm days since I last wrote, but the ground was so wet after last week's heavy rains that very little work could be done in the beginning of the week. On Monday, finding work impossible owing to this cause, I took my gun and went for a walk in the direction of some hills about fifteen miles off. I saw nothing except vultures (which are very numerous round the camp), red-legged plovers, and some little beasts called meerkats, which live in colonies in holes like large rat-holes. They are pretty little creatures, something like weasels, generally grey with blackish stripes, and have long and rather bushy tails. In returning I passed by the cemetery, the sight of which is only indicated by a black flag floating over one of the numerous large ant hills. I counted thirteen graves, mere rough mounds of earth and gravel, generally with a big rough stone at the head, but no inscription.

On Tuesday afternoon, hearing the cry of "Hurrah" from a neighbouring sorting table, I hurried to it and saw a beautiful stone of over 20 carats, which had just been found by a lucky Englishman—one of the most beautiful diamonds I ever saw, a perfect dodecahedron, of pure water, without speck or flaw. Went back to work with renewed courage, but we have found nothing for the last fortnight.

On Wednesday, hearing that diamonds had been picked up on the surface at a "pan" six miles off—eight being found by a Kafir, and three by a neighbour of mine—and a 10-carat stone being rumoured to have been picked up, I and three others determined to go and "prospect," so started off early in the morning with pick, shovels, and sieves.

We had a pleasant walk across a big, dry flat, with a stunted bush here and there, till we came to the pan, a hollow, similar in character to the one from which this camp takes its name, but much smaller, and surrounded by willows and thorn trees. We searched carefully on the surface in and around the pan; found no diamonds, but a few small crystals. A few natives were similarly employed. We then dug, sifted, and sorted, at different points of the ridge surrounding the pan; found white limestone in abundance, but no signs of diamonds, no garnets or carbon. Still, from the fact of diamonds having been found on the surface, it is very probable that this place would repay working, and I hear to-day that several diggers have gone over to give it a more thorough trial.

We saw no buck or large game of any kind, only a few plovers and doves. In the evening I took a walk round the "town" of Du Toit's Pan. Besides numerous hotels and billiard rooms, the camp now boasts a well-conducted club, where gentlemen may see all the latest home and colonial papers, or select a novel from a small but rapidly increasing library.

With these attractions, combined with the pleasant society one is sure to meet there, anyone may be sure of passing a comfortable, home-like evening at the Zingari Club. An enterprising hotel keeper has also opened a large American bowling alley, which is very much frequented.

I have just seen a friend who is digging at the adjoining farm of Bultfontein. He reports gems of 98, 77, 53, and two of 42 carats among the principal finds this week; also that twenty were found in one day between the weights of 10 and 20 carats. I can rely upon the truthfulness of my informant.

It is currently reported that a diamond mine will shortly be opened on the farm of a Mr. Jan Steyn, close to the village of Cronstad. Seven beautiful gems have been picked up on the surface. Parties are begining to go thither at once. This "new rush," being situated over 100 miles from the centre of the locality hitherto recognised as diamondiferous, would seem to indicate that we have considerably under-estimated the vast extent of land on which diamonds may be found. Many are now bold enough to affirm their conviction that the whole of the Orange Free State is diamondiferous.

Diamondiferous! What a favourite word that is in these regions. Our principal auctioneer has it for ever on his lips, and at our Saturday afternoon sales you may hear him eloquently praising not only "a most diamondiferous pick," "a highly diamondiferous sieve," "a diamondiferous sorting-table," but even applying the same sonorous and rich-sounding epithet to a bedstead, a waggon, an ox—aye, even a coat or pair of trousers. Talking of sales, I am happy to say that there is a slight fall in the prices of meal, potatoes, and wood.

I now give you a summary of diamonds reported at the different camps during the past week, premising that these form a very small proportion of the actual finds:

At Pniel 13, largest $3\frac{1}{4}$ carats; at Du Toit's Pan 62, largest 40, two of 23, 15, 11, $10\frac{1}{4}$, 10 carats; at De Beer's 9, largest 50, 21, 10, 9 carats; at Bultfontein 27, largest 33, 22, 15, 8 carats; at Moonlight Rush 13, largest 18 carats; at Winter's Rush 3; at Esterville, 1, $5\frac{7}{8}$ carats; at Hebron 63, largest $42\frac{1}{4}$, $10\frac{1}{4}$ carats.

It will be seen from this that our neighbourhood is still doing well. Some enterprising Americans have brought up a large steam engine, with an ingenious apparatus for sifting. They say they can sift out thirty cartloads of stuff in a day, and work a claim of thirty square feet in three weeks or a month to the uniform depth of 18ft. Of course they must employ many workmen, but native labour is cheap. There will also be a great deal of sorting to do, but they have provided for this; and if the machine can really do anything approaching the above work, the proprietors of it ought to realise rapid fortunes. But how will the rest of us humble diggers, who do everything by hand, like seeing the work done by machinery about fifty times quicker than we can do it? That seems rather a knotty question; but that these wonderfully rich fields will have eventually to be worked on a large scale seems pretty certain.

I have before me the prospectus of the Klip Drift Mining Company (Limited), just in process of formation at Klip Drift, for the purpose of working that and other diamondiferous localities on a large scale. The capital is modest—5000l. in 1000 shares of 5l. each. The names of the provisional committee and officers are well-known and good names, and I fully believe the enterprise will succeed. I yesterday received the *Field* of April 29, May 6, and May 20; that of May 13 missing. Mails have been very irregular lately, the rivers being flooded by the extraordinary rains. Part of the mails are reported to be actually lost in Riet River.

The swollen state of the rivers has been productive of many other annoyances. Mr. Sonnenberg, merchant of Jacobsdal, offered a Fourth of July banquet last Tuesday to all Americans on the Fields. Many Americans from this camp started from Jacobsdal, but, owing to the Modder or Mud River being flooded, they could not cross, and were compelled to return. Then, again, the Inland Transport Company's waggon did not arrive at Pniel as usual last Saturday. On Tuesday intelligence was received that it was detained at Riet River, impassable owing to the rains. One of the Pniel "big-wigs," being among the passengers, sent a note to the agent requesting that a boat and some carts might be sent down, the former to ferry the passengers across, the latter to convey them to Pniel. This was done on the Wednesday, and the passengers arrived in Pniel safe and sound late on Thursday evening. The British commissioner. Mr. Campbell, has taken his seat again on the bench at Klip Drift. His representative, Mr. Jackson, who officiated during Mr. Campbell's absence as acting special magistrate, was somewhat disliked in the camp for his over free use of the lash. This Du Toit's Pan is a very quiet and orderly camp, although we have at present only six of the Free State police to keep order in an assemblage of about twenty thousand people.

July 17.

As the mail cart leaves in two hours, I must hasten to close this letter. Of news since I last wrote there is very little. Here is the list of finds reported last week:

At Pniel 8 diamonds, largest $9\frac{1}{2}$, 8 carats; at Du Toit's Pan, 24 diamonds, largest 40, 40, 39, $19\frac{1}{2}$; at Bultfontein, 36 diamonds, largest 12 carats; at De Beer's 14 diamonds, largest $16\frac{2}{3}$, $11\frac{1}{2}$ carats; at Spencer's, 24 diamonds, largest $36\frac{1}{2}$, $9\frac{3}{4}$ carats; at Hebron, 23 diamonds, largest $14\frac{1}{2}$, $8\frac{3}{8}$ carats.

This seems rather a meagre list, especially for Du Toit's Pan, but I know that many more diamonds have been found than are here reported. We have not found lately, but several good stones have been picked up in adjoining claims. A friend of mine at De Beer's made a good beginning last week, finding in the course of the week five diamonds averaging $7\frac{1}{2}$ carats each. A 93-carat stone, found at Bultfontein, has been sold for 2000*l*. only. It was flawed and off-colour.

We hear that the Governor, Sir H. Barkly, has received full power to annex the Diamond Fields, with the consent of the Colonial Legislature. A party working at Moonlight Rush has found in seven weeks forty diamonds, weighing in all 164 carats.

We have had tolerable weather lately, with the exception of one night's heavy rain, a day of almost intolerable wind and dust, and several sharp frosts. The Americans are hard at work with their steam engine. It seems to answer well. It works, by means of endless bands, a huge revolving cylinder of fine wire meshing. The native workmen of the American party pour the stuff to be sifted in at one end of this cylinder. It passes quickly through it, revolving very rapidly, and falls on to a sorting table at the other end, freed from all dust, earth, &c. From three to six white men are kept fully employed at the sorting table. The machine is constantly surrounded by an admiring crowd. It is great fun to see the natives, and even many of the Boers, rush away in terror when the whistle is sounded or steam blown off.

And now let me say a few words to intending emigrants, as there are many such doubtless among the readers of the *Field*. The diamond fields of South Africa are no myth, but a great fact and a brilliant success. It will be years before they are worked out. I was inclined to say at first that no one should come out without enough money to keep him independent for a year. Now I must considerably modify that advice. Men of good character and sobriety will find work and good pay here. There is a great demand for carpenters, and they can make 2*l.* per day, or more, at sieve making, &c. Blacksmiths, too, will find remunerative employment. Engineers can make large sums of money by well-sinking. A well, just sunk by a private gentleman on part of his claim, is being subscribed for by two hundred members at 4*s.* each per month, each member being limited to four buckets of water daily. Wells are becoming numerous, and water consequently plentiful, so that we can now indulge freely and frequently in copious ablutions. There is always work at actual digging, too, for industrious and sober men. A good man will have no difficulty in obtaining a fair weekly wage, board and lodging, and a good percentage on all finds. I even heard, the other day, of a man getting board and lodging and half all finds; but that is an exceptionally good case. The camp continues to be most peaceful and orderly; nowhere could person and property be more secure. Store keepers and hotel keepers, doctors, dentists, chemists, jewellers, are all reaping rich harvests, most of them working claims in addition to their ordinary business. Money is very plentiful in the camp. Large raffles— for instance, a hundred or more members at 10*s.*—are got up frequently at one or two days' notice. Du Toit's Pan is eminently prosperous.

Du Toit's Pan, Orange Free State,
July 22.

This has been an exciting week at Du Toit's Pan, the number of finds and size of diamonds being remarkable. A friend of mine at De Beer's found last week five diamonds; total weight, 30 carats. There is a "new rush," four miles beyond De Beer's, reported to be very good. On Monday afternoon a diamond of 124 carats was found, two claims from mine. Crowds flocked up from all parts of the camp as the news of this monster spread, and the lucky finder had to hold it up for nearly half an hour to satisfy the admiring and constantly changing crowd. I had a very good view of the stone; it is of irregular shape, yellowish colour, and marked with many small black spots. I hear it was sold for 2000*l*. Had it been a perfect stone, of good water, it would have been worth at least ten times that amount.

On the same day a stone of 120 was reported, but I have not heard this confirmed. The 124 was found in an outside claim, and in a few minutes there was a rush of excited diggers busily marking out new claims beyond it, on ground partly occupied by the tents and waggons of some Dutch families, who all received notice to quit. An hour afterwards the surveyor of the committee was on the ground, measuring and numbering the new claims.

A party at De Beer's found last week eleven diamonds; the smallest 6 carats, largest 27. On the 19th a 104-carat stone was found in the next claim to the one from which the 124 was taken, by a man who had found a 55-carat stone 10 days before. I was on the market that morning. There was, among a great variety of stock, goods, &c., a big waggon load of wildebeest, blesbok and springbok, at least five dozen animals in all. They were all killed by two guns on Monday, proving that game is still plentiful not very far from this camp. I bought a good springbok for 3*s*. 3*d*. The "courants" I mentioned before are, I believe, properly called "knorhaans." They are difficult to approach, except by patient stalking on hands and knees or *à plat ventre*, according to the height of the covert. I shot one yesterday. On the 21st a beautiful perfect gem of good water (12 carats) was turned out of the next claim to mine. I hope my turn will come soon.

Claims are rising in price at Du Toit's Pan, 10*l*. to 20*l*. being freely given for claims in good positions; but at De Beer's, where the diggers are mostly men of capital, employing large parties of natives, and consequently getting through much more work than we can, 100*l.* is considered quite a moderate price for a good claim.

This morning I hear on the best authority that a diamond of 170 carats has been found at Du Toit's Pan. A 51-carat was also found this morning not far from my claim.

New diggers are constantly arriving, but new locations are being "prospected" with proportionate frequency, and the camps round here are flourishing in the extreme.

Ladies, I am happy to say, are adding to our civilisation by their graceful presence; and it is no uncommon thing to see faces—aye, and costumes too—walking and riding through the camp that would do no discredit to Kensington Gardens or "The Row." I am sorry to have to record a case of crime this week— a blot on the fair fame of Du Toit's Pan for peace and order. An Australian digger, rather a lucky finder, being very drunk yesterday at midday, violently assaulted his wife, a frail little woman, knocking her down and kicking her furiously, inflicting very severe injuries. The cowardly brute was promptly marched off to the police station between two constables with drawn swords, and I heard the wish expressed by many of the indignant diggers that he might get at least "four dozen lashes and six months."

We have been favoured with beautiful weather this week, so that all, except loafers and invalids, have been at full work. There was a big market this morning. Wood is still very high. Meal about 2*l.* 10*s.* per 200lb.; potatoes down to about 25*s.* per 200lb. There was a waggon-load of cauliflowers, which were eagerly bought up; but I managed to secure a nice lot of five for 2*s.* 9*d.*—a very good bargain. A lottery is coming off shortly for money prizes, 300*l.*, 150*l.*, and 50*l.*, by 1050 tickets at 10*s.* 6*d.* each.

July 31.

I have several more interesting incidents to report. We have a "new rush" only about a mile from De Beer's, where the precious gems seem to be wonderfully plentiful, it being no uncommon thing for one party to find from two to six good stones in a day. I believe the largest yet found there is 45 carats. Claims taken out there at the beginning of the rush are now worth over 100*l.* each. A friend of mine saw last Tuesday a 20, a 10, and a 5 carat (about) turned out on one sorting table in half an hour. One man found seven diamonds there last Saturday.

The report is now confirmed that a diamond of 175 carats was found about ten days ago—that 33,000*l.* has been offered for it, and that the lucky finder is a poor Englishman, who never had 20*l.* of his own. Here is another amusing incident: A man possessing a waggon and oxen, a tent most luxuriously furnished, and good stores of provisions, &c., came up to his tent one afternoon, and, having collected all his neighbours, said, " Here, you can take all these things, I don't want to see a single one of them any more. I have made my lot, and I'm off." And he stood calmly by, hands in pockets and pipe in mouth. while his waggon, tent, and stores were rapidly vanishing. What is the " lot " which he has found has not been divulged, but it must be a " big thing."

On the 26th I started by passenger cart for Pniel and Klip Drift, hoping there to obtain one or two natives, as I was not satisfied with the amount of work my partner and I could get through unaided. Stopping for a few moments at De Beer's, I was shown a beautiful 7-carat diamond just found half an hour previously by a young German who has only been two months on the Fields. and has already found a 9, a 4, a 3, the 7 just alluded to, and many small stones. One of my fellow passengers showed me the results of three weeks' work—about a dozen and a half of diamonds in a small box, two of about 10-carats, the rest rather small. As our six mules careered rapidly over the veldt, the talk of all in the cart was " diamondiferous," one man even asserting his belief that there are diamonds "all over the colony." There are certainly many spots between Du Toit's Pan and Pniel where I will venture to predict that diamond digging will be successfully carried on within three months from this time, especially round a " pan " by the Halfway House. where we got an excellent luncheon for 1*s.* 6*d.* Farther on, about five miles outside Pniel, is the Digger's Joy, a little refreshment shanty. the proprietor of which has made a fine collection of crystals, garnets, &c., and I expect diamonds will be found in that neighbourhood. At Pniel and Klip Drift, though they look very quiet and deserted in comparison with Du Toit's Pan and De Beer's, there is still a good deal of work going on, and new claims being opened. The work is very hard, every claim being full of immense rocks and boulders, so that it takes a long time to get out a cartful of stuff for sifting.

I remained at Klip Drift from Wednesday to Saturday last in the vain search for natives, the few whom I found disengaged refusing to go to Du Toit's Pan. This place has a bad name amongst them, as being very cold, and wood and water scarce. Just as I was on the point of returning unsuccessful yesterday I met a Pniel digger, whom I persuaded to part with two young Zulus, not strong enough for the heavy work among the boulders. Having effected the transfer, they were told they must follow me, but when they learnt whither I was bound we had to use much alternate coaxing and threatening. At last they sulkily picked up their sheepskins, and trudged unwillingly after me. The present of a little tobacco and a biscuit each improved their spirits. I would not trust them to come down by themselves, so set off to walk with them. About eight miles out of Pniel I got a "lift" on a cart drawn by four oxen, driven by a very drunken Koranna, who frequently lashed the beasts into a full gallop, and never "outspanned" till we got to De Beer's, where we arrived about nine p.m., my driver having fallen off the front of the waggon twice. The second time he fell close to the hoofs of the hinder oxen, and the wheel of the cart went right over his chest; but he didn't seem to mind it much, though the cart was prettily heavily laden. When we arrived at De Beer's, of course we found we had left my "boys" and one of his a very long way behind; and, the camp being large, and many roads leading to it, I was much afraid of losing them, so walked back two miles, and presently saw three dark figures advancing over the veldt in the moonlight. I shouted "Abraham," "Frans!" and heard the former exclaim, "Daar is meen baas!" (there is my master). I sent the other "boy" to his master's tent, and guided my two youths from De Beer's to Du Toit's Pan, where they speedily slept soundly after their twenty-five miles walk, lying at the door of my tent wrapped up in a big springbok "kaross" and a couple of blankets.

This morning they seem quite happy, and very willing and active. They will cost me 15$s.$ per month, and their food, consisting principally of "mealies" and "mealie meal" (Indian corn). The wages of a fullgrown native are about 30$s.$ per month and food, or 2$s.$ per working day, finding himself.

I now give you last week's list of finds, authenticated. Those of the previous week I am unable to obtain at this moment.

Pniel, 6 diamonds, largest $5\frac{1}{2}$ carats.
Moonlight Rush, 5 diamonds, largest 25 carats.
Sixpenny Rush, 1 diamond, largest $21\frac{1}{2}$ carats.
Du Toit's Pan, 119 diamonds, largest 175, 103, 66, 57, 55, 54, 40, $36\frac{1}{4}$, 33, 30, 20, 19, 16, 13, $12\frac{1}{2}$, 12 carats.

Bultfontein, 27 diamonds, largest 4½ carats.
De Beer's, 39 diamonds, largest 18, 15, 9, 7, 6 carats.
New Rush (De Beer's), 14 diamonds, largest 12, 9½ carats.
Hebron, 27 diamonds, largest 27, 13½, 12⅞, 10 carats.
Spence's, 4 diamonds, largest 13½ carats.

I extract from the *Diamond News* two characteristic advertisements :

Cremorne Gardens—between Union Kopje and the New Rush, Gong-Gong—Good Digging, Fishing, Shooting, Boating, Quoits, &c.

Notice.—The individual who took an ostrich feather from the hat of a gentleman in Jardine's dining-room on Wednesday evening last is hereby requested to return the same forthwith to Mr. Jardine, or to the office of this paper.

Observe the nice distinction between the "individual" and the "gentleman." What will the ladies at home say to the alarming fact of "male individuals" wearing ostrich feathers in their hats? We do, though, nearly all wear them. I have one in mine. Are not the heterogeneous attractions of "Cremorne Gardens" irresistible? I should think many of the *habitués* of the famed gardens by the banks of the Thames will be attracted thereby to the banks of the Vaal.

Du Toit's Pan. Orange Free State,
August 20, 1871.

In giving you a brief account of the incidents of the past three weeks, I must first notice the astounding wealth which is being developed at the New Rush beyond De Beer's. Though it has as yet scarcely been worked a month, fortunes have already been made there. I will give you a few instances of luck which have come under my own knowledge.

A friend of mine, having-secured a claim there, sold half of it for 50*l*. The buyer has found over fifty diamonds, two of them over 40 carats, and many of them large stones: my friend has found nothing in his half. Many men at the new rush are turning out from three to six diamonds per day.

A gentleman of my acquaintance found no less than twelve diamonds in one day, Friday last. As may be imagined, claims in good positions command enormous prices. Half a claim was sold there a few days ago on the following terms : 47*l*. to be paid down, and 20 per cent. of all diamonds found in the claim afterwards. The old diggings at Du Toit's Pan and De Beer's are still turning out well; but the wonderful finds of the privileged few who secured good claims at the new rush naturally excite great envy, especially among those who, like myself, have worked hard for months and found hardly anything.

We had some very trying weather in the beginning of this month; it commenced with a furious gale of wind late one night. One corner of our tent was torn from its fastenings; in rushed the wind with a cloud of dust, away flew the lid of our coffee tin, and dust and coffee, hideously commingled, were thickly spread over and amongst our blankets. We both had to get up many times that night, and rush out to fix extra fastenings. About three a.m. there was a thunderstorm, followed by a copious downfall of rain. Part the tent collapsed, and I woke in the early dawn to find myself lying in three puddles, rain pouring in upon me, a chill blast driving over my face, and my blankets soaked through with rain and smeared with mud, the results of the aforesaid mixture of dust and ground coffee. I sat up shivering in the dryest part of the tent that I could find, and my partner awoke and groaned dismally. Then we thought of Mark Tapley, and endeavoured to be jolly. but it was rather a failure. Still the wind howled, and the rain poured down in torrents. We opened portmanteaus, got out dry clothes—for we were wet to the skin—and fled from the scene of desolation. We found refuge in a corrugated iron hotel, where we did ample justice to a very substantial breakfast. Soon after, the rain abating a little, we went back to view the tent. We found it half down. Our newspapers and other light articles were flying all over the camp, and the whole interior of our tent, with a miscellaneous and muddy chaos of most heterogeneous articles, was exposed to the public gaze. Putting the tent up again in that gale being out of the question, we covered the things over with the loose canvas as well as we could, and took a precipitate departure from our desolate Lares and Penates, resolved to dwell in something more solid until fine weather returned. Many other tents were down, including the big church tent, and the hotels were all full of "washed-out diggers." Though it was Saturday, there were hardly any sales in the afternoon, the weather not permitting much open-air work. In the evening, however, there was an entertainment given by some talented amateurs on behalf of the funds of the English church. The iron room in which it took place was crammed to suffocation with diggers in working dress, who besides hearing some capital songs, both comic and sentimental, recitations, readings, an excellent impromptu stump speech, and a lecture on astronomy by our worthy pastor (I don't think we cared much for the last-named), had the privilege of gazing, modestly and reverentially of course, at the unusual apparition of two charming young ladies in evening dress, and several more in ordinary costume. Sunday again was a pouring wet day, but a temporary lull of wind and rain in the afternoon enabled us to get our tent up, though sleeping in it was out of the question. On Monday it began to clear up. During the week the weather was cold, fine, but windy, with three very sharp frosts and a hailstorm.

On the 10th inst. my partner and I found our fourth diamond, a wretched little splinter of $\frac{1}{4}$ carat. It is somewhat disheartening to work on month after month with no better result than this, while we know of men who, during the same space of time, have made their thousands. To read, for instance, such a list as the following, which I quote from the *Diamond News:* "Some particulars concerning the New Rush at De Beer's.—Whilst at De Beer's at the beginning of this week, we gathered some statistics, which will serve in some measure, though very inadequately, to show the prolific nature of the 'new rush' at that place. The 'kopje' had then been opened twenty days. During that time Mr. Arie Smuts, who purchased a half claim for 50*l.*, had turned out 175 carats, including one stone of 40 carats; Mr. Rhodes, of Natal, 110 carats, including a stone of 14, 16, and 28 carats; Battlesden party, 85 diamonds, including one each of $13\frac{1}{2}$, 10, 8, &c.; Mr. John Frank, 36 diamonds, including one each of 10 and 7 carats; Leppan, 25 diamonds; B. Cawood, 23; Cumming, one of 9; Ruellin, one of $40\frac{1}{2}$; F. Rawstorne, one of 21, and others; Buckley and Fraser, one of 37, and others; Thackwray, one of $8\frac{1}{4}$; a gentleman who does not wish his name published, one of 60, 21, 14, 10; Carey, one of $23\frac{1}{2}$. The latter is said to be one of the most perfect and beautiful diamonds yet found in South Africa."

I myself know of many more instances of great good luck at this wonderful place. What marvel, then, if we poor "outsiders" work on somewhat gloomily at our old claims at Du Toit's Pan! What marvel, too, if we spend a good deal of time in "prospecting," each hoping to discover a "new rush" as rich as that at De Beer's! And truly there is much temptation to do this, for there must be more than one rich kopje in the country; and the fortunate man who discovers fresh diggings has three "prospecting claims" given him for nothing, besides the two to which every digger is entitled according to our rules; and, should diamonds be found, he would at once realise very handsome prices for his spare claims.

Last Monday I went over to a new place about five miles distant. Found the scene very animated—about a thousand claims being already marked out by pick, shovel, or ticketed stick, and the diggers all hard at work, anxious to find out, as soon as possible, whether the spot were diamondiferous or not. I spoke to all of my acquaintances whom I met there, but could not elicit anything very satisfactory. Three or four small diamonds were believed to have been found, and I myself saw a $\frac{1}{2}$ carat picked up on a sorting table, at which there was a tremendous cheering, and nearly all the diggers on the kopje congregated to the spot. Not much liking the appearance of things here, and seeing that I was too late to get a claim, had I been so disposed, I strolled away to another kopje about a mile and a half off. There, creeping about on the ground, I discovered —not diamonds, indeed, but pretty good "indications" in the shape of limestone gravel and bright transparent green stones. Marking one or two likely-looking spots, I returned to the old camp, and worked at our Du Toit's Pan claim all the afternoon. The next morning I set off, with two others and our remaining Kafir—one of the two I hired at Pniel having "bolted," probably with a diamond.

We took provisions and complete mining tools with us. On arriving at my kopje we commenced sinking holes in different parts of it, and found good-looking stuff, but no diamonds. However, in the afternoon a lot of diggers came over from the other "rush," which they said was not worth working. They all liked the look of my kopje, and said "There *must* be diamonds here." Thereupon my friends and I set to work to mark out all the claims to which we were entitled as "prospectors," and the other diggers marked out a couple of claims each.

They all expressed confidence in the place, and a determination to give it a good trial. After seeing thirty or forty claims marked out, and feeling rather proud of having created a "new rush," I walked back with my friends through the scrubby "veldt," where the "knorhaans" were calling, and the red-legged plovers screeching around us, to our big canvas "City of the Pan." I don't know yet how my "new rush" is going to turn out; but I hope to meet to-day some of the men who have been working there. It might turn out a good thing. Several other rushes are reported, one of which, named Albany Kop, is to be surveyed, and claims allotted to-day. Of course the recent astounding finds in the neighbourhood of De Beer's have created quite a mania for "prospecting."

President Brand, of the Free State, has been here all last week, and is probably going to stay a week longer. He seems popular, both with Dutch and English who know him; and many surmise that when these Diamond Fields are annexed to the British colony the ex-President will be made Lieutenant-Governor. But this is mere conjecture, and it appears by no means certain yet which portions of Free State or Transvaal Territory are to be annexed.

The latest novelty at Du Toit's Pan is a fortune-teller, believed in by the Dutch, and even by many of the English diggers. His tent is thronged from morning till night, and he is said to be making from 25*l.* to 30*l.* a day. His charge is five shillings, and his *spécialité* is giving the locality of diamonds. Applicants bring charts of their claims, and he tells them exactly in what part, and at what depth, such and such diamonds will be found. To some, however, the prophet is very discouraging. He has been known to say to a man, "*You* will never find a diamond if you stop here all your life." And the credulous Dutchman has "inspanned" his oxen, and departed, miserable and hopeless, from the busy scenes where he cares not to labour in vain. I have heard the following anecdote of the fortune-teller (he is rather a near neighbour of mine, by the way, and I think I shall consult him). He said to a man, "You will get six diamonds out of that claim within a week." At the week's end the digger came back grumbling. He had found nothing at all. He objurgated the soothsayer. The wise man replied. "Well, six diamonds have come out of that claim, and if you haven't got them, your natives must have pocketed them." Thereupon the digger hastened back to his claim, seized his two Kafirs, took them down to the "trunk" (police station), where they were searched, and six diamonds found upon them! *Si non è vero, è ben trovato;* it is pretty generally believed among the Dutch community.

I am indebted to the *Diamond News* for the following news from the Mathebele country :

A couple of months ago, Lepengkolo, the young king, despatched a band of messengers to all the great Bechouna tribes, officially to inform them, by remitting some elephants' tusks, of the death of his predecessor Mosilikatsi, and of his having taken the reins of chieftainship into his own hands.

Arrived at Shoshong, the Bamangoato chief, Maching, stopped the messengers. Said he, "The serpent has only changed his skin. Do I not know sufficiently of the Mathebele tactics? You are spies! On your peril, I command you to go back! If Lepengkole wants to signalise the commencement of his rule by plundering our cattle, let him come; we are ready for him." The messengers had to turn back. Lepengkole, on being informed of Maching's words, ordered several regiments to take the field, saying, "If my road be blocked up by trees or stumps, my battle axes will cut them down; if by rocks or hills, my crowbars will dig them up!" They have already massacred several Masarva villages of the Bamangoato, and are on their march to Shoshong. We may soon receive bloody accounts.

Monday morning, nine a.m., a fine day, but terribly windy, threatening the stability of the tent in which I am writing. New arrivals of diggers from all parts of the colony and from Europe are very frequent. List of finds at Du Toit's Pan last week not to hand.

Du Toit's Pan, Orange Free State,
Aug. 28, 1871.

I did not think that so soon after despatching my last letter I should have to chronicle a recurrence of that awful weather which entails so much misery on poor diggers. On the evening of the 24th, after a storm of wind and dust all day which had rendered work impossible, and covered everything in our tent with a thick layer of red dust, the gale increased so much that we feared the tent would come down. Fastening after fastening gave way; we were soon almost smothered in dust; then the wind veered round, and rain poured down in torrents. In the morning, after an almost sleepless night, we found ourselves wet through, everything soaked and muddy, and the tent half down. Needless to say that we again had recourse to the friendly shelter of the hotels. But there was no fire in any of them. It was bitterly cold, and, having wet clothes on, we were in a state of "cold shivers" all day. Substantial meals slightly alleviated our misery, and in the evening, dropping into a store, we found two or three friends assembled round a piano, and heard some capital music and singing. I slept that night on a table in the principal hotel, with only one blanket over me, and was *not* comfortable. The weather improved a little the next day, and yesterday being quite fine, we came back to pitch the tent in a fresh place, and so securely that there would be no danger of its coming down in future. Found it had been robbed in our absence of four or five suits of clothes, two rugs, a blanket, a roll of tobacco, a gallon of brandy, and sundry other articles. We questioned our Kafir, but he professed utter ignorance. In the afternoon, however, while our " boy " was absent, fetching water from the dam, a neighbouring digger called me over to the fire-place of some other Kafirs, where he had seen the corner of a blanket sticking out of the ground, and had found several articles of clothing, besides a roll of tobacco and a bottle of brandy, all lightly buried in the loose sand. On searching the neighbourhood we discovered nearly the whole of our missing property similarly concealed. One of the Kafirs said that our " boy " brought the things there. I immediately got two policemen, and had our " boy " arrested as he was returning from the dam. His back will probably be made acquainted with the "cat." He accuses four other Kafirs, whom I believe to be implicated with him. In spite of this and many similar instances, some diggers are still confiding enough to let Kafirs do all kinds of work at their claims without supervision, including sorting. A white man was tried and fined, last week, for buying a diamond from a native. We have now got our tent well pitched, and comfortably arranged inside, ornamented with a bunch of spring flowers on the table.

The lucky men at the "New Rush" are still turning out diamonds in profusion, and several moderate fortunes have been made within the last month. Good finds have been made at Du Toit's Pan too. We stick to our old claim there, and hope that our turn may soon come.

Here is an amusing trait of a Dutchman's childishness. We have a " merry-go-round " here, near the American Bowling Alley. A middle-aged Boer got on one of the wooden horses early one afternoon. He was so delighted that he refused to dismount till late in the evening, having indulged his equestrian tastes to the tune of thirty shillings!

I subjoin a few extracts from the *Diamond News*, which may be of general interest.

A 96-carat diamond has been turned out at De Beer's by Messrs. Beyers and Boulton, a party who lost all their goods and chattels in the flood at Victoria West, on their way to the Diamond Fields. On the same day they also turned out a stone of 15 carats.

A diamond of 72 carats, magnificent as to shape and purity, was turned out at Du Toit's Pan last week by Mr. A. W. Hyde and his companions, from Grahamstown.

The following is the register of temperature for the past week:

	Day. Highest temp.	Night. Lowest temp.
Saturday	83	40
Sunday	85	35
Monday	83	30
Tuesday	92	33
Wednesday	93	28
Thursday	56	28

Résumé of the week's finds at the various camps:

Pniel, 11 diamonds, largest 14½, 88½.
Du Toit's Pan, 67 diamonds, largest 78, two of 72, 64½, 30, 24½, 23, 22½, 19, 17¾.
De Beer's (Old and New Rush), 43 diamonds; two of 96, 76, 29½, 23½, 20, 18½.
Bultfontein, 15 diamonds.
Moonlight Rush, 1 diamond of 10 carats.

I repeat that these returns represent but a very small proportion of the actual finds. I know of many other large diamonds found last week, and I know (and envy) several of the luckiest finders, whose names never appear at all in any of the published lists.

The papers are full of the proceedings consequent on the visit of President Brand and the Executive Council of the Orange Free State. Dinners, "déjeuners à la fourchette," &c., have been given in honour of the worthy President, and addresses, expressive of mutual confidence, have been exchanged between him and the various diggers' committees.

Another very successful musical entertainment has been given on behalf of the English Church Fund, and a grand bazaar is to be held this week in aid of the Dutch Reformed Church.

The weather is lovely to-day, warm as an English July. The wives and daughters of lucky Boers are parading the camp in gorgeous apparel; tired diggers have been hard at work washing shirts all the morning, and now everybody feels fairly entitled to Sunday's rest and cleanliness.

Sept. 3.

Last Monday I went down to the police court to prosecute our Kafir. He pleaded not guilty. I identified all the stolen things, but could not prove his possession of them, or that he had brought them there, so the case was remanded. But I was fortunately able to return in half an hour with three witnesses, an Englishman who found the buried things, a Zulu Kafir and a

Hottentot who saw our " boy " bring the things there, and to whom he gave brandy. Native dialects here became perplexing, as my two black witnesses could speak neither English nor Dutch. At last it was managed as follows: The interpreter of the Court, who understood Zulu, translated the Zulu's evidence, the Zulu translated the Hottentot's evidence to the interpreter in Zulu, and the interpreter retranslated it to the Court in English. Our young scamp was convicted, and sentenced to twenty lashes with the " cat " and a month's hard labour. As soon as the Court closed I saw him tied up to the whipping-post and flogged. The lashes were inflicted very lightly, and he didn't seem to feel them much. Klip Drift is, or was, the place for severe flogging.

In the afternoon I saw a 29-carat diamond, a perfect stone, but rather flat and yellow, found just opposite our claim. In the evening there was a great sale of very " Brummagem " jewellery in the dining room of the principal hotel. High prices were got for a very worthless lot of rubbish. Much rough chaff passed between the auctioneer and his customers. Among the things sold were " silver pen-holders and pencil-cases." There was a slide which worked up and down, but nothing came out. Certainly the buyer might make it a " pencil-case " by inserting in it a stump of ordinary cedar pencil, but I don't see where a pen could go. Some gold (?) watches and chains were also sold, and I heard several 5l. bets made as to whether the articles really were gold or not.

Tuesday seemed a fair commencement of South African spring, a very hot day, lots of flowers springing up over the lately barren " veldt." We found our fifth diamond, a bad-shaped little stone, of about $\frac{3}{4}$ of a carat.

On Thursday evening I saw a man who had begun on Monday to work a quarter of a claim at the New Rush, and had actually found, in the four days, stones which he had sold for 1500l.

On Friday a neighbour of ours, on arriving at his claim, found that his Kafir had got out a 12$\frac{1}{2}$-carat stone that morning, and was keeping it for him in his headkerchief. Whereupon the lucky digger sent all his Kafirs off to get each a glass of Cape Smoke. He himself, with your humble servant and his partner, and several other neighbours, adjourned to a neighbouring refreshment tent, where the landlord immediately set a large musical-box playing, and received orders to " keep on bringing in bottled ale till he was told to stop." We enjoyed the welcome beverage for half an hour, amidst much " diamondiferous" chat, and then all returned to work with renewed vigour and hope.

It was a very hot afternoon. Inventing a new, easy, and graceful position—reclining by the sorting table, I was straightway minded to call it "An improvement on Eve at the fountain; or Afternoon at the Claim." I am not quite sure whether this is a "goak," but some of my neighbours think so.

On Saturday I learnt the sad news that two diggers, one of them a slight acquaintance of mine, a married man, and successful, had been blown up and killed in a well which they were sinking at De Beers, through imprudent blasting, viz., "tamping" with a steel rod, when a copper one was lying handy. The steel rod struck one of the numerous flinty rocks. An explosion immediately ensued, which blew one man's head off, and inflicted such numerous injuries on the other, that he died the next day. Another casualty is reported last week from De Beers' New Rush. A man working a claim there had not been seen at work for eight days, so another man "jumped" the claim, that being the limit for which a claim can be held open without working. He had not worked long when he discovered the body of the original proprietor lying buried under a lot of stuff which had fallen in upon him from a badly constructed tunnel.

On Friday afternoon I witnessed a slight whirlwind in Du Toit's Pan. A tall revolving column of dust moved swiftly through a part of the camp. Sheepskins, hats, papers, were among the things seized by it, and whirled high in the air, the papers and other light articles gyrating right at the top of the column. Yesterday afternoon there was another little one; but the weather is still lovely and summer-like, only rather too hot for hard work, and the time is approaching when many will have to leave the hot, glaring, and dusty "dry-sifting" camps for the various river-side diggings.

There was a fight on Friday afternoon by the dam, between an Englishman, of indifferent character, and a Dutchman. The latter was the conqueror. Both were a good deal knocked about. An element of novelty for the British public is, that in this fight *the police kept the ring.*

Saturday's markets continue very large, and, besides every kind of garden and field produce in season, immense numbers of "buck," spring-bok, blesbok, wildebeest, &c., &c., are being almost daily brought in; but, as some of them have been killed many days' journey from this camp, great caution is necessary in purchasing "buckmeat" this hot weather.

Yesterday morning we found our sixth diamond, a rather pretty little stone of a quarter of a carat. This morning the proprietor of one of the claims adjoining ours showed us a beautiful stone, over 15 carats, which he found yesterday afternoon. Surely we shall get among the big ones soon, as such fine stones are being found all round us.

A great sensation was caused in the neighbourhood of Klip Drift last Tuesday, by the arrest of Mr. Unger, the great diamond merchant, for liabilities, under the Scottish Bankruptcy Act, amounting to 3400*l*. Mr. Unger's house was searched, and he was marched up to the Special Magistrate's Court, escorted by eight policemen. He stated that the debt had already been paid, but lodged a cheque for 4000*l*. as security until the case came off, which it is expected to do to-morrow. The person who had him arrested is named Lowenthal. It is said that he came out from Edinburgh with a power of attorney from the trustee in the Insolvent Estate of Mr. Unger in Scotland.

Klip Drift will now surely cease to be the "metropolis of the Diamond Fields." The principal newspaper of the diggings, the *Diamond News*, has moved all its offices down here, and will be published here in future. The "City of the Pan," daily more flourishing, rejoices greatly thereat. Many large diamonds have been found last week, both here and at De Beer's.

Du Toit's Pan, Orange Free State,
Sept. 10, 1871.

At the risk of making these letters monotonous by mere personal details, I will commence by telling you that I have got a couple of fresh Kafirs at work, who seem very good "boys," and poor "Artemus Ward" would have taken much delight in them, such "amoosing young cusses" are they. At "tiffin time," the first day I had them at work, they commenced improvising pipes after the manner of their people, by moistening the ground, thrusting in a thin stick to make a hole about nine inches long, making a hollow at one end for the tobacco, and applying their mouths to the orifice at the other. Thus, lying on the ground and sucking vigorously, they get huge mouthfuls of smoke, over which they invariably choke and cough, but appear to derive great satisfaction from the exercise; but their glee was pleasant to witness when I presented each of them with a short clay pipe. Moreover, as their costume did not go far beyond the traditional fig leaf in amplitude, and as nights and mornings were rather cold just then, they were further gratified with an old flannel shirt each. They are the two noisiest "boys" on this camp—perpetually shouting, singing, or whistling, but working well and willingly. I feed them on mealie-meal (ground Indian corn), with a little meat once or twice a week; but the public slaughtering place is not very far from this tent, and whenever my "boys" hear of any oxen or sheep going to be slaughtered, they will ask leave, rush off to the scene, and shortly return with huge festoons of the filthiest offal, and so besmeared with blood and dirt that we cannot on those festive occasions allow them to clean our plates and dishes. And the quantity of offal they will gorge at a sitting is perfectly astounding, though it does not incapacitate them from taking their usual huge potful of mealie-meal porridge to fill up gaps with. One of these characters answers to the name of Jacob, the other is called simply "Boy." "Boy" took up a book the other day, and said in Dutch, "Book! Ja! Master must teach Boy to read book." He gives me advice on different matters, and oracular information about the weather, in the most amusing manner. He certainly foretold the storm of Friday night last, and a very pretty storm it was. The usual business; hurricanes, then dust storms, so that you could not see a yard before you for dust, then awfully vivid lightning and deep thunder, then torrents of rain, then more wind, and so on. This time our tent stood it bravely, though the rain came through in places, and we got but little sleep, the tent and everything in it shaking continuously. But yesterday morning it was quite fine again, and, to prove that "it is an ill wind that blows nobody any good," the aforesaid gale had carried off somebody else's white hat and deposited it in our fireplace. I handed it to "Boy" as his perquisite, and this morning gave him a gaudy feather to stick in it, whereupon he grinned exceedingly, said, "Boy is *gentleman* this morning," and departed for his Sunday out, walking with a solemn dignity befitting the wearer of a hat and shirt. Some scoundrels took advantage of the dust storm to attack and rob a digger. They got from him a $13\frac{1}{2}$-carat diamond, several other stones, and some money. The poor fellow's cries for help were heard by the police, but so strong was the wind and so thick the dust that it was long before they could find where he was, and then the robbers had escaped. A man was arrested yesterday on suspicion.

Several other highway and garotte robberies are reported from the neighbourhood of De Beer's, so for the moment revolvers are at a premium, and much worn at night.

I was over at the New Rush, that wonderful Golconda, on Thursday afternoon. It is truly a marvellous place; the diamonds are so numerous there that everyone works his very hardest, and puts on as many niggers as he can get hold of, so at every claim may be seen from six to a dozen men, or even more, all working hard at the different occupations of mining—some descending into deep holes by the aid of rheims or ropes, others hauling up bucketfuls of stuff with a windlass, picking, shovelling, sifting, sorting, while numberless carts and barrows are actively employed all day long in removing the sorted stuff on to the neighbouring veldt. All this, with the white glare of the limestone, the blinding clouds of dust, the yelling and singing of the Kafirs at work, the dull sounds of the pick, the monotonous grating of the stuff and gravel in the sieves, the shouting of mule drivers and cracking of whips, the general "hurrah!" whenever there is a find or a fight, make up a *tout ensemble* which can hardly be imagined from so bare a description as this, but must be seen to be realised.

Soon after I came upon the scene I heard a loud "hurrah," and found that a mule-cart had fallen into a claim. The claim was forty feet deep, but there was a kind of shelf near the top which prevented the cart from falling farther, so that the mules and cart were only just below the surface, and, plenty of diggers volunteering their help, were soon extricated. There was a nigger working at the bottom of the claim. He quite thought the cart was coming down on to him, and his terrified yells afforded much amusement to his sable comrades.

Then I went to see a few friends, and saw that they were nearly all finding a goodly number of diamonds; moreover, many claims were pointed out to me where eighty or ninety stones had been found within a month.

Shortly afterwards a louder "hurrah!" of a different character caused me to rush to a neighbouring claim, where I saw a 91-carat stone, which had just been picked out by a Kafir, who was working for an Englishman and Dutchman in partnership. There was much shouting and congratulation. It was rather a yellow stone, but perfect and without spots. I heard of many more instances of good luck, and soon it was time for me to walk back to Du Toit's Pan and dinner, as the merry bands of native labourers were singing on the way to their tents and cooking fires, and the numerous "traps" of lucky New Rush diggers resident at Du Toit's Pan were galloping gaily past me along the dusty road.

This New Rush is quite the *bête noire* of us poor outsiders And to think that, if we had only known, *we* might have had claims there, and that claims worth 10*l.* to 100*l.* a month ago are now commanding from 500*l.* to 2500*l.*, and good ones hardly to be bought even at that. Well, old Du Toit's Pan is still doing fairly, though; a 115-carat was found here last Thursday, and the following stones are reported in the *Diamond News*, now published here, for the week ending Sept. 8:

Du Toit's Pan, 42 diamonds, largest 60, 57¾, 51, 47, 32, 29, 16 carats.
De Beer's (two camps), 34 diamonds, largest 60, 45, 38, 34½, 32 carats.
Pniel, 21 diamonds, largest 7¾, 6¾, 5¼, 4 carats.
Hebron, 42 diamonds, largest 14⅝, 8½, 7½, 7¼ carats.
Robinson's, 3 diamonds, 2⅛, 2¼, 1 carat.

I must mention, in explanation of the evident paucity of the above returns, that, owing to robberies having been on the increase of late, most of the large finders are naturally unwilling to have their names and finds published. I only give you a *résumé* of numbers and principal weights; but in the *Diamond News* the names of finders are published as well, except on their express request to the contrary. I know of many claim holders at the New Rush who are averaging two or three or more diamonds daily.

The rate of mortality in the camps is rather on the increase. The necessity for speedily providing good hospital accommodation, as the hot season will soon set in, and also for improved sanitary arrangements, is becoming a topic of general discussion, and I believe proper measures will at once be taken for the carrying out of both these objects.

Spring time is coming; flowers are blooming on the veldt, and birds are building their nests. A pair of saucy little fellows, like sparrows, have chosen the tent of a friend of mine as a residence.

Sept. 17.

This has been a week of intense heat. Black men have discarded all clothing; white men would very much like to do the same. Awnings or large umbrellas have been erected over sorting tables, and "new chums" have been asking the portentous question, "If this is only the beginning of spring, what will the middle of summer be like?"

Many very large stones have been found during the week, both here, at De Beer's, and at the New Rush. Old Du Toit's Pan, as usual, bears off the palm for size; a lucky digger, named Humphries, having contributed a diamond of 150 carats to the *Diamond News* gazette of finds. My partner and self have been sinking a deep narrow shaft. We found a little stone in it last Tuesday, which, though only 7-8ths of a carat, encouraged us, as being the first perfect stone we have found. A striking illustration of the great depths at which diamonds may be found has just occurred at the New Rush, where a man, employed in sinking a well, saw at a depth of seventy-six feet something sparkling in the side, which turned out to be an 87-carat diamond. The well-sinking party had not been sifting the stuff which was brought out, but I should imagine after this extraordinary find that they would sift and sort the whole. Two or three "new rushes" are reported at small distances from this camp. I know nothing very positive about them yet, but will endeavour to report next week.

The following advertisement in the *Diamond News* of the 16th inst. refers to the robbery I mentioned in the early part of this letter:

£25 Reward.—The above reward will be given to anyone supplying such information as may lead to the detection and apprehension of the three men (believed all to have been white men) who, on Friday night, the 8th inst., knocked down Mr. J. J. Joubert near the junction of the Dorstfontein and Bultfontein roads, and robbed him of—one diamond weighing 14 carats, one diamond weighing 2½ carats, one diamond weighing 2 carats, six diamonds weighing 5 carats, also one 5*l.* note and a half-sovereign piece.

Here are one or two small items from the same paper, which may be of interest:

A dense cloud of locusts was observed towards the southern horizon, on Sunday last, drawing from east to west.

A 50-carat diamond was found in the stuff thrown out of a sieve at De Beer's the other day, by a little boy. A Dutchman who was near claimed it and took it from him, but the case being brought before the committee, he had to restore it.

Here is my *résumé* of last week's reported finds:

Du Toit's Pan, 55 diamonds, largest 150, 45½, 32½, 20, 18 carats.
Bultfontein, 39 diamonds, largest 7¾ carats.
De Beer's, 33 diamonds, largest 42½, 30¼, 16 carats.
De Beer's New Rush, 47 diamonds, largest 70, 60, 24¼, 23 carats.

Pniel, 23 diamonds, largest 52½, 10 carats.
Hebron, 45 diamonds, largest 10, 8½, 7½, 7 carats.
Robinson's, 5 diamonds, largest, 2¾, 2 carats.
Klip Drift, 1 diamond, 4½ carats.
Moonlight Rush, 1 diamond, 8 carats.

Another outrage on the highway took place this week. A gentleman named Denham, returning on horseback from Du Toit's Pan to his tent at the New Rush, was knocked off his horse, and brutally kicked by three men (probably the same gang who robbed Joubert). Just as he was becoming insensible some people came in sight, and the ruffians decamped without having accomplished the robbery. The injuries Mr. Denham received are, I am happy to say, not serious.

The Bishop of Bloemfontein (Dr. Webb) is here earnestly advocating the erection of a suitable church, and funds are being rapidly subscribed for the purpose. The hospital, too, which will be sorely needed as the heat increases, is also meeting with liberal support.

The want of water is beginning to be much felt at De Beer's and the New Rush. At the latter place a depth of over 90ft. has been reached without finding water. Vigorous efforts, public and private, are being made to obtain a good supply. Meantime, the otherwise lucky diggers at the New Rush have to pay 9d. and 1s. per bucket.

After the great heat last week we had it cooler yesterday. To-day we have much wind, and clouds are gathering, so we must prepare ourselves and tent to bear the brunt of another storm, I suppose.

Du Toit's Pan, Orange Free State,
Sept. 23.

We have just completed another week of hard labour, and still our ill-luck continues, exciting the astonishment and pity of our more fortunate friends.

A fellow-passenger *per Roman* is averaging 30*l*. per day at the New Rush. That place is a perfect Golconda; everyone is full of it. New arrivals from the Colony, meeting friends up here, inquire, "Well, where are you working, old boy?" "Oh! Du Toit's Pan," or "Bultfontein," as the case may be. "Not managed to get a claim at the New Rush?" "No." Then the expression of the querist plainly says, "What a poor shiftless fellow you must be." The consequence is that now there is a perfect mania for "New Rushes;" prospecting parties are out continually, and a report last week (unconfirmed) led to about three thousand claims being marked out at a spot some few miles beyond De Beer's; but I do not hear of any finds. Then, again, a place on the Modder River is said to be turning out well. If true, that would be a pleasant station. Who would not exchange a glaring expanse of limestone dust and gravel, and a barren treeless plain—with drought already beginning to be felt, and serious prospects of pestilence from the wretched sanitary arrangements—for the cool, wooded shores of the Modder, with the home-like rippling of water, and the recreations of fishing and bathing? I am going off to-night or to-morrow morning to a spot on this same Modder, which my *compagnon de voyage* says is only six or seven miles off; but which—having frequently been cruelly deceived in colonial distances—I shrewdly suspect to be about twelve. But what of that? Would not "Sarcelle" cheerfully walk double that distance, even under a South African sun, for the chance of a bit of fishing? Truly, I believe I have not been so long debarred from the indulgence of my favourite sport since I began, at six years old, fishing for minnows, and tumbled into a brook, for which misdemeanour I was forthwith put to bed. My poor old rods, at which I often look so wistfully, suffered most grievously in the long rough waggon journey. There is only one which my skill can make serviceable for to-morrow, and that is a trusty old sea rod, which last year did much execution among whiting, pollack, billet, and codling, off my beloved Yorkshire coast, and since then has killed a fair dish of mullet and Hottentot fish, and even bent with the weight of a big snook in Table Bay. But as usual, the dear topic is leading me into a long digression. It is of diamond digging, not of angling, that I must treat in these papers. But if I do find a river to-morrow, and get any sport, surely the *Field* shall hear of it.

On the 18th, a 16-carat diamond was found not far from my claim, only 9in. deep. A Kafir boy, walking in from De Beer's on the previous day, picked up a $10\frac{1}{4}$-carat in the road close to a heap of refuse stuff from the rough sieve of an old Dutchman. A neighbour, who saw the boy pick it up, took him down to the magistrate. The stone was finally awarded to the Dutchman close to whose heap it was picked up.

Half of the claim in which the 124-carat stone was found was sold by auction on the 18th, and fetched only 8*l*.

On the 19th the skeleton of a Bushman was found 4ft. deep in a claim at Du Toit's Pan. The feet, strange to say, were discovered in another claim several yards distant. These relics are supposed to have lain there for upwards of a century—not a pleasant thing to find when looking for "sparklers." On the next day, a large fragment of an ant-hill was found at a considerable depth in another claim.

We had heavy rains on the night of the 21st, and pretty strong wind, but our tent stood it bravely. It rained all the morning of the 22nd, and no work could be done. Nature is getting animated—too much so for comfort. Our tent swarms with the most ferocious flies; fleas annoy us now and then; and to-day we are invaded by black ants, and they don't seem to mind hot water.

Partridges, knorhaans, &c., are, I fancy, beginning to pair. Their calls may be heard very near the camp. But now to rummage over fishing tackle—a pleasing task, which will call up numberless half-sweet, half-bitter *souvenirs* of bygone ramblings with rod and fly book; of fair Yorkshire, Derwent, Rye, and Driffield; of pleasant Derwent, Wye, and classic Dove in Derbyshire; of lordly streams in Kent, the garden of England, well stocked with lusty trout; of my old favourite, the winding Lézarde in *la belle Normandie* (I hope the Prussians did not net it); of the dashing, cascading "Gaves" among Pyrenean ravines; of blue lakes amid eternal snow peaks. Enough; I must put the reins to my imagination, and reconcile myself to the fact that I am at Du Toit's Pan! And here is the *Diamond News* before me, from whose list of finds I make my usual *résumé*:

Du Toit's Pan, 33 diamonds, largest 84, 59¼, 20, 17¾, 10¼, 10⅛ carats.
De Beer's New Rush, 258 diamonds, largest 44½, 24, 19, 16¾ carats.
Old De Beer's, 44 diamonds, largest 15½, 11¼, 8 carats.
Bultfontein, 21 diamonds, largest 11½, 10½, 10 carats.

I also extract from the published lists the following particulars of good luck, nothing very extraordinary for the New Rush. One gentleman has found in three weeks *eighty-five* diamonds, but there are not many large ones amongst them, the aggregate weight only amounting to 104 carats.

Du Toit's Pan and the neighbouring camps are busy with church and hospital schemes, and subscriptions and money are forthcoming in abundance for all these good purposes. The ball I mentioned in my previous paper came off on Thursday last, and was a grand success. Above 150 persons were present, of whom quite one-half were ladies. The costumes were as *ravissant* as could be desired. The gentlemen, too, were nearly all in evening dress, and an uninformed spectator would scarcely have believed that he was looking on an assemblage of diggers. The spacious area of Parker's new Masonic hotel afforded a broad floor for the dancers. A good band was in attendance, and the supper was really first-rate—far beyond my anticipations of the highest culinary art in Du Toit's Pan. One trivial detail slightly marred the *tout ensemble* of the tastefully laid out supper table. Our candlesticks were all simply empty bottles, and the labels had not been removed. *Voilà tout.*

Friday, Sept. 29.

I am obliged to close this letter to-day, because I am starting with a party for a three days' shooting and fishing excursion to the Modder River. I am preparing an account of my first expedition to that river. and hope to forward it to you by next mail.

On the afternoon of Tuesday, I, having walked a distance of thirty miles the previous night, was resting in my tent, when I heard two shots fired not far off. I took no especial notice of the incident. as there are plenty of plovers about, and I mistook it for the report of a fowling-piece. But I afterwards ascertained that a young man had dragged an elderly one out into the "veldt," and there fired two shots at him, the first of which was said by a Kafir who was near to have passed over his head, while the second entered just below his eye, completely destroying that organ, and lodging in the back of the head. The man was still living yesterday, but no hopes are entertained of his recovery. The aggressor is very cool and unconcerned. and when charged before the magistrates with attempted murder pleaded that it was an accident. There is a very strong feeling against him among the diggers. and although it appears that there is insanity in his family. I think if the victim should die there will be much clamour for his execution. I have heard it rumoured that he recognised the old man as the person who had robbed him of some diamonds ; many others believe he wanted to rob the old man. and credible persons say he had previously threatened to shoot him.

During the week we have had three thunderstorms, in one of which the lightning was painfully vivid, while the instantaneous and deafening explosions of the thunder were louder and more startling than I have ever heard before. The hot weather is fairly setting in now, and with it frequent storms and heavy rains, also plagues innumerable in the shape of flies, fleas, ants, &c.

Fine diamonds are now being frequently found at the New Rush by parties who break up with sledge-hammers the stones carted off from claims. In one instance a man was walking behind a cart loaded with such stones. One fell out, the cart wheel went over it, broke it, and a 21-carat diamond came out. Finds at the New Rush claims continue to be magnificent. Many diggers are returning to the colony or to England, some only temporarily. Mr. Arie Smuts, the owner of one of the best claims, who is supposed to have made something like 20,000*l*. in three months, has sold his claim piecemeal—100*l*. or 150*l*., I believe, per six square feet.

We have had no luck yet. Perhaps it will come all at once.

London, *Jan.* 16.

On the 4th October, the day after my return from the second excursion to the Modder River, my partner and I went over to the famous De Beer's New Rush, *alias* Colesberg Kopje, to work half a claim there in a good position on half shares. Our said half, being covered with a great heap of refuse stuff, was not at present workable, so we hired a cart with a couple of mules, and were busy all day carting off stuff, and depositing it in the allotted space outside the claims. There was a strong wind blowing; as usual, the whole camp was enveloped in clouds of stifling, penetrating white and red dust; the heat was excessive, and it was very thirsty work. The enormous profits made by hotels and canteens, and the increase of drunkenness, are not to be wondered at, considering the hardships of summer work at the dry diggings. I tried the effect, during the day, of two or three long drinks of ginger beer, but found my thirst so little allayed thereby, that I was tempted to accuse our canteen keepers of putting salt into all the liquids they supply to the thirsty diggers. Towards sundown we walked wearily back to our tent at Du Toit's Pan, and cooked a rough, hasty dinner. Our boys' wages were due, and I paid them; then they declared their intention of leaving our service. The work at the New Rush was too hard for them, they said. In vain I harangued them in my best Low Dutch, explaining to them that it was a grand place, that there were " plenty diamonds," and that we should make them a small present for each diamond found. One was decided to leave, the other hesitating, and the next morning neither of them made his appearance. This was a great nuisance, as we intended immediately removing tent and everything to the New Rush, and working hard at our claim there, and in the commencing summer it would be hard lines for a white man to do anything but the sorting.

We heard on Oct. 5 of a 105-carat stone found two days previously at Old De Beer's. Walked over to the New Rush, got the remainder of the old stuff carted off. chose a suitable place for pitching our tent, hired a mule-cart, drove back to Du Toit's Pan, three miles distant, and removed tent and all our property in two journeys, arriving with the last load in the dark, so would not pitch the tent that night, but lay down in our blankets on the grass among our boxes, cooking utensils, and general miscellanea. It was a very hot night, but we were tired and slept soundly. In the morning we set to work, after a light breakfast at a friend's tent, to pitch our own and arrange our Penates. I felt terribly weak and ill, and as soon as the work was done felt fairly compelled to lie down, and fell into a strange, feverish sleep.

From the 5th October to the 5th November I find a total blank in my diary, for during that time I was prostrated by low fever, being delirious several nights and parts of days; dysentery and very severe diarrhœa came on before the fever left me. I got hardly any rest or proper food, and lay in profound misery on my straw mattress, sweltering in heat, tormented by legions of green and black flies, which I now and then had energy enough to flick away from my face with a wildebeest's tail as they came swiftly on me with a hideously loud buzzing, making most pertinacious attacks on the corners of my eyes, my nose, and mouth. It was so hot that I could not bear any covering over my face. Sometimes, too, I was without water. With very few exceptions, which I shall ever gratefully remember, almost everyone was too much engrossed in the incessant, eager, hurrying work of the Rush to think for a moment of a poor fever-stricken wretch. Had it not been for the great kindness of two good Samaritans, fellow passengers from England *per Roman*, I should have fared badly indeed. I hope that G. and W. may see these lines, and read in them the expression of my heartfelt gratitude. But I have dwelt long enough on this theme.

After making several attempts to fight against the effects of the combined fever and diarrhœa, and crawling feebly about on a stick, hardly recognised by many of my associates—such a lank, hollow-eyed skeleton was I—I at length determined to remove to the riverside at Pneil till I recovered a little of the strength I felt I could never regain in the pestilential air of the New Rush, with its filth and bad water. And from Pneil I thought I would return for a brief space to Old England, where I knew the experience gained on the diggings would enable me to make money in several ways, and to organise several lucrative speculations before again proceeding to the Fields. One of the friends before referred to drove me over from the New Rush to Pniel in a spring cart drawn by two mules and two horses. The roads are terribly rough within five or six miles of Pniel, and though the cart was a most comfortable one, I suffered agonies from the jolting, for I had lost nearly all my flesh, and discovered bones of whose very existence I was previously ignorant. But I began already to feel that I was homeward-bound.

At six p.m., I was safely deposited at Jardine's most comfortable hotel at Pniel, where I received every kindness, had medical attendance, and enjoyed excellent food, to which I was soon able to do full justice. During my illness my partner, having succeeded in getting four Kafirs at the advanced wages of eight shillings per week and food, found several small diamonds in the New Rush claim, and he is in confident hopes of very large finds when they get down a little deeper. It is truly a wonderful place. I will give you a brief account of it in a separate paper.

Previous to my leaving the camp we sold our old Du Toit's Pan claim for 16*l*. 10*s*. Wanting to lighten my luggage as much as possible, as the passenger-cart only allows 40lb. of baggage, I gave my gun, revolver, and many other articles to an auctioneer at the New Rush, and he got very good prices for them. I heard of many more cases of sickness—one death— in a very short time, from the same diseases which had attacked me, and felt happy to be away from the camp. It is a great place for making money, that is certain ; but, under the present abominably defective sanitary arrangements, unhealthy during the hot season. I had to stay ten days at Pniel, as, though the comfortable waggons of the Inland Transport Company start thence weekly for Cape Town, they are generally very full at this time of year with lucky diggers going home to the Cape to spend Christmas with their families. It must be delightful for a digger who resides at the Cape to reach his home, family, and friends, in eight or nine days, or even less, from the Diamond Fields. All the seats are engaged long in advance, and it was only by the accident, fortunate for me, of an invalid staying at Jardine's feeling too ill to proceed, that I got the chance of a seat in the waggon leaving Pniel on the 13th November. I found that the old diggings at Pniel and Klip Drift were nearly deserted, scarcely fifty claims being worked on both sides of the river, and the little towns presenting a striking contrast to the New Rush in everything—in their quietude and appearance of peaceful stagnation; in the large, dark boulders and bright gravel of which the claims were composed, instead of the red sand, glowing white limestone, and crumbling green trap of the New Rush; and, most refreshingly, in the broad stream of the Vaal, with its rocky, trout-suggesting rapids, its deep pools, its bright green islets, and the grand shade-giving trees which fringed its banks.

Pniel and Klip Drift are by no means "worked out" yet, a stone of $34\tfrac{1}{2}$ carats was found during my stay there, besides several smaller ones, and the "river-stones" are generally of very good quality. Three diggers from the New Rush, arriving at Pniel on the Saturday afternoon during my stay, and of course hastening at once to the river to bathe, found a nice little diamond on the surface, on their way down to the waterside.

And now I am in Old England again, and have almost regained my strength. Though I have been one of the unlucky ones, I cannot but speak well of the Diamond Fields, where I have seen so many fortunes realised in a marvellously short time.

The daily yields of nearly all the claims at the wonderful New Rush, or "Colesberg Kopje," are large and certain, but claims there cost from 1000*l.* to 4000*l.* each, and are regarded as safe investments. There are, however, plenty of good claims to be had cheap at Du Toit's Pan, Old De Beer's, and Bultfontein, and I heard before I left of a great "new rush," four miles from the Colesberg Kopje.

I believe firmly that thorough prospecting will soon reveal the existence of innumerable rich diggings. The new gold discoveries in the Transvaal, about four hundred miles from the centre of the Diamond Fields, promise to be very rich, and are already attracting many colonial fortune seekers.

I am very far from regretting my first visit to the South African Diamond Fields, and hope ere long to be "outward bound" again.

PART V.
THE GOLD FIELDS.

CHAPTER I.

THE TATIN.

The Tatin Gold Fields were discovered, I think, in 1869, are situated far in the interior, about 800 miles above the Diamond Fields. From what I have heard, there seems to be no alluvial gold there, and consequently no surface digging. The gold there is in quartz-reefs, and the auriferous quartz is being worked by an English company, who have taken up, at great expense, the heavy machinery necessary for quartz-crushing, amalgamating, &c. The quartz is said to be now yielding very fairly; but I think that, independently of the very long, trying, and expensive journey, there is very little actual inducement for any private digger with small capital to visit the Tatin Gold Fields.

CHAPTER II.

THE TRANSVAAL, OR LEYDENBURG, NEWLY-DISCOVERED GOLD FIELDS.

DURING the month of September, 1871, considerable excitement was created on the Diamond Fields and in other parts of the colony by the news that gold, both alluvial and in quartz-reefs, in apparently good paying quantities, had been discovered in the territory of the Transvaal Republic, and notably near Marabas Stad, 160 miles from Pretoria, the capital of the Republic.

A gentleman named Button, a resident in the district, was appointed Gold Commissioner for the Transvaal Republic, and he and other gentlemen immediately set to work to energetically and carefully explore the auriferous region.

On the 25th September, Mr. Button writes as follows to the Government Secretary at Pretoria :—

Marabas Stad, 25th September, 1871.

SIR,—I have the honour to enclose a small sample of alluvial gold, which I regret is all I can send at present. My two friends, with the twenty Kafirs, have not yet arrived; and, owing to the unsettled state of the country, no native labour can be procured here. I intend leaving tomorrow for Leydenburg to make arrangements that will enable me to work the deposit efficiently. Will you please oblige by exhibiting the gold to the honourable members of the Volksraad, and explain my position. The sample, small as it is, will prove that the metal does exist in the alluvial state, and the deposit from which it was taken is payable beyond doubt.

Your obedient servant,
(Signed)   EDWARD BUTTON,
Gold Commissioner.

This letter was received with great satisfaction by the members of the Volksraad (Legislative Council) and the public present. The sample of alluvial gold was forwarded from Pretoria by waggon to Natal, to be sent on to the Consul-General of the Transvaal Republic in England, together with a box full of gold-quartz specimens. Large quantities of the auriferous quartz, and small samples of the alluvial gold were also forwarded about this time to the Commercial Chambers of Durban and Cape Town, to be exhibited before being sent on to England. Three different parties, consisting of Messrs. McFie, Gray, Leathern, Brooks, and Webber, at once started for the new Eldorado; and many other persons, both on the Diamond Fields and in Natal, prepared to leave for Marabas Stad. Mr. Leathern, soon after his arrival there, wrote a letter, of which the following extract was published in the *Natal Mercury* of 25th November.—

My reason for writing to you now is to tell you the news, which you very likely have heard before this, that a new Gold Field has been discovered in the Transvaal, on the road to Zoutpansberg, near a place called Marabas Staadt, 160 miles from Pretoria. I returned from the Diamond Fields and heard of this discovery, but did not believe it, thinking it to be a dodge of some land speculators to sell their land. I and two others went with a cart and horses, determined to try if there was gold there, and in payable quantities, which I found to confirm the description I had heard of it. I went to the farm purchased by Mr. E. Button, late of Natal, where I washed the soil and found alluvial gold, twenty-four grains in three hours—fine nuggetty gold. I also went about on several quartz-reefs, and found lots of gold in the quartz—the out-crops—so that I calculated that the quartz underground must be very rich indeed. I have brought the alluvial with me; also some quartz, and a small bag of the wash in which the gold is found. The only drawback I can see in the affair is the shortness of water, but that can be managed by making reservoirs or dams. The rainy season is coming, and there will be lots of facilities for making the dams. There is one place where the water can be led out about three miles, round a hill and back. I was thinking of bringing the specimens to the Chamber of Commerce. The large nugget must be returned, as I have promised it. The people are going mad with excitement about the gold.

In a letter dated Pretoria, 11th October, to a friend at the Diamond Fields, Mr. Leathern says:—

Send up as many people as you can. There is plenty of gold—alluvial as well as quartz—and they need not be afraid.

This is about all that was known about these new Fields when I left the Diamond Diggings, but the excitement there was already intense, and a great many parties were leaving for Marabas Stad and neighbourhood. Many of them will, I fear, regret this over-haste and imprudence, as I believe, though neither Mr. Button nor Mr. Leathern say anything about it, that the climate up there is far more unhealthy than that of the Diamond Fields, and fever terribly prevalent there during the hot season, which was just setting in. But "auri sacra fames" will make a man face anything.

We have only heard hitherto of the auspicious results of a little prospecting, but we may now soon expect news of what some of the working parties have done, and almost everyone seems confident of the success of the Transvaal Gold Fields.

Advertisements like the following were frequently to be seen in the *Diamond News* in November:—

GOLD, GOLD, GOLD.
A CERTAINTY.
TRANSVAAL REPUBLIC.

THE undersigned has for Sale, Farms in the Waterberg and Leydenberg districts.

For further particulars, apply to

FRANK COWELL, Auctioneer, &c., De Beer's.

CHAPTER III.

ROUTES TO THE GOLD FIELDS.

THESE new Fields can be reached either from Natal or the Diamond Fields, according as the digger wishes to go direct after the new gold, or to work some time at the Diamond Fields first. I believe the distance from Pniel is about 400 miles. At present, of course, bullock waggons are the only available means of conveyance for general passengers and goods. Private parties can, however, purchase carts, horses, or mules for the journey, and if the fields turn out well, quick-travelling transport companies will soon be started. Already some of our enterprising store-keepers of the Diamond Fields have laid in a good stock of all gold-diggers' tools and necessaries, while many waggons were advertised to start from the Diamond to the Gold Diggings. With regard to the route from Natal, Mr. Leathern says:

> The best road for people to go by is either through Newcastle, then along the post road to the Vaal River, Stander's Drift; from that to Heidelberg; thence to Pretoria; then to Neilstrom; then to Makapan's Poort; then to Marabas Stad; and then to Button's farm; or another road people can go by is by Harrismith to the Sand Drift, then to Heidelberg, and thence to Pretoria. The road is pretty good, barring a few mud holes, which the President has promised to have filled up. The only really bad place is about thirty miles from the Fields, and that is not so very bad. Twenty Kafirs in about three days would make it good. There is lots of wood, water, and grass along the road.

I would not at present advise any one to take out tools, &c. from England, at any rate until we have some more certain news of the successful working of these fields, as everything can be bought comparatively cheaply at Natal, or on the Diamond Fields. That there *is* gold, not only here but in many other parts of the neighbouring interior, appears certain, from the frequency with which gold has been found in the possession of natives, and the quartz and auriferous indications noticed by interior hunters and traders. In fact, a great many, even of the more accessible parts of South Africa, which promises now to turn out one of the richest mineral countries in the world, are well worthy of careful exploration by practical mineralogists.

Printed by HORACE COX, 346, Strand, W.C.

www.ingramcontent.com/pod-product-compliance
Lightning Source LLC
Chambersburg PA
CBHW031731230426
43669CB00007B/314